ABHA IN AI AI

FOUNDED ON FEAR

Letterfrack Industrial School,
War and Exile

Peter Tyrrell

Edited and Introduced by
DIARMUID WHELAN
University College, Cork

Foreword by
PATRICK GALVIN

IRISH ACADEMIC PRESS
DUBLIN · PORTLAND, OR

First published in 2006 by
IRISH ACADEMIC PRESS
44, Northumberland Road, Dublin 4, Ireland

and in the United States of America by
IRISH ACADEMIC PRESS
c/o ISBS, Suite 300, 920 NE 58th Avenue
Portland, Oregon 97213-3644

© 2006 Introduction by Diarmuid Whelan

WEBSITE: www.iap.ie

British Library Cataloguing in Publication Data
An entry can be found on request

ISBN 0 7165 3402 9 (cloth)
ISBN 978 0 7165 3402 0
ISBN 0 7165 3403 7 (paper)
ISBN 978 0 7165 3403 7

Library of Congress Cataloging-in-Publication Data
An entry can be found on request

Typeset by FiSH Books, Enfield, Middx.
Printed by MPG Books Ltd., Bodmin, Cornwall.

Contents

Foreword

Peter Tyrrell's long night of the soul is recounted in a very detailed manner in the following document. For many months he painstakingly revisited the dark corners of his early life in a Catholic Boys' Home in order to bring to our collective attention the state of a nation: a nation governed by fear and ignorance. He did this to try and influence the course of history. The misfortune was that the nation was not ready for his story when he told it. Indeed the jury is still out on whether it is currently ready to take responsibility for its institutionalized kidnapping of the soul, and relentless brutalizing of the mind and body, in its state funded religious institutions.

As you read through the account of Peter Tyrrell's life you will see reflected in it an Ireland that we are all familiar with, some of us more so than others. You will also recognize that Peter's life and dramatic death were not in vain. His soul speaks to us through his written word, with his many observations on the human condition both in 'neutral' Ireland and the rest of war torn Europe. The unseen tragedy is that in spite of our position in the literary world, Peter's writings lay amongst a Senator's papers until their worth was recognized by the editor of this book.

Peter's life might well have been saved by recognizing him as the author of a literary creation. As an editor I recognize in his work the delight in being able to compose and express in an orderly, dispassionate way, the reality he lived through. As an artist I see his mind seeking redemption in order to deal with his reality. He sees kindness in the guards, who definitively help truncate his familial bond. He sees saintliness in Brother Kelly, who breaks forever his trust in God and in himself. He revels in the camaraderie of army officers, who know that he is human fodder. He lauds the kindliness and efficiency of nurses and doctors at the German prisoner of war camp, who all know that they have been beaten by the triumph of collective good.

As this document stands I trust it will provide important additional source information for many academic disciplines. Having spent three years in a reform school in the middle of Ireland from the age of 12 to 15, I can validate that the needless and relentless physical brutality meted out to innocent children was a fact. It was not a series of isolated incidents, as many of those who have a special affiliation with God and the religious orders would try to tell you. It was institutionalized savagery, brutality, neglect, abuse and hypocrisy. How people who considered themselves to have had Jesus Christ as their role model, could have continuously and collectively, acted in this way defies any level of logic or rationale. I can also tell you that in reform school there were no holidays and no periods of remission from the systematic brutality, abuse, mental cruelty, exploitation and denigration of the young.

Peter Tyrrell wrote this account in 1959. He burnt himself to death several years later in dramatic fashion. As he recognized himself, once he had to make any contact with his past it reopened the horror. Had he not sought to redress the system he might still have lived. When he was encouraged to write his account of his time in Letterfrack, he had to relive the trauma which was so immense that his written recollection, sanguine as it was, offered no therapy. When he then found that there was no audience for it, he was rejected on two counts, one as the victim and the other as the artist or the teller of the tale. Paradoxically his account of life in the British army, where he travelled extensively and witnessed much of the tragedy of war, seemed therapeutic. Surrounded by death, destruction and horrors of enormous proportions he managed to develop as a person, take on some responsibility, explore the universe and deal with his irrational fears. In recounting this period of his life he also created a document that, with little guidance, could have been a stand alone literary text.

In 1957 in my first volume of poetry 'Heart of Grace' I recounted the horror of my own experiences as a child in a reform school in early twentieth-century Ireland. I was believed by my editor and my publisher. I found little recognition from my Irish literary peers but that mattered little. It has taken fifty years of rewriting that horror in verse, prose, drama and latterly and most effectively in cinemascope, to be believed in my own country. While the film 'Song For a Raggy Boy', based on my book, could also appear to have been based on 'Founded on Fear' it remains a sanitized version of what really did happen. No words or visuals can convey that reality. The publication of Peter Tyrrell's book adds strength to the collective voice and fulfils his aspirations to help change forever the way we educate our youth and liberate those souls silently trapped in enforced denial.

I commend Peter Tyrrell for his bravery and determination. I commend him for his duty to detail in bringing to life for us an Ireland some of us need to forget and others need to take responsibility for. I commend him for his observations on war which should instil in us a determination that such atrocities will never happen again. Most importantly for Peter and his kin, I commend his editor Diarmuid Whelan and his publisher for faithfully bringing Peter Tyrrell's work to the attention of an audience long denied him.

Patrick Galvin
July 2006

List of Illustrations

With the exception of Picture 1 and Picture 9, which are printed with the kind permission of Mary Schofield and Mary McCourt, all visual material is from the Sheehy Skeffington collection in the National Library of Ireland.

Acknowledgements

There are two ladies without whom Tyrrell's manuscript would never have made it into book form. Charlotte Holland is the godmother of all UCC historians, but especially in this case by typing up Tyrrell's entire text she made easy what seemed to many men impossible. I was fortunate enough to find Lisa Hyde and have her as editor for this collaboration. I sincerely doubt the preparation of books is always as urgent, pleasant and professional as this one has been, but this has certainly been my experience. If only Peter's path had crossed yours.

I have been lucky enough to have been able to call on the friendship of Frank Daly, Alex Daly, Ciarán Madden and Lana Fitzsimons, who have commented on the text and proof-read it in part or whole.

I am grateful to the National Library of Ireland, and in particular to the Manuscripts department, where I spent a truly fruitful year as part of the NLI archival studentship scheme. I'm grateful to Aonghus Ó hAonghusa and Gerry Lyne for permission to use the text, but I'd like to record my thanks to all my colleagues in the NLI, especially Jenny Doyle, Ciara McDonnell, Katy Lumsden, Elizabeth Kirwan, Paul Moran, Peter Kenny, Pat Sweeney, Tom Desmond and Bridget Clesham. I hope people will feel that my treatment of Tyrrell and the industrial school is fair-minded, and to the extent that it is, I owe a great deal to Professor Joe Lee's guidance and tuition, without which I would never have been able to even approach a document like Peter's. Professor Eunan O' Halpin, Deirdre McMahon and Hiram Morgan helped me get into the inner sanctum of the National Library and have not only made this book possible, but by providing me with this unique opportunity, have considerably enriched my historical perspective. Michael Kennedy has not only commented on the text all along the way, but gave it the strongest possible recommendation to Irish Academic Press. Professor Dermot Keogh provided me with a base and the academic setting and support. On a personal and professional level I owe him an immense debt.

Owen's sons and daughter Micheline, Francis and Alan Sheehy Skeffington didn't hesitate for one second when it came to allowing their father's papers to be published. I'd like to thank Dr Patrick

Galvin for his heartfelt Foreword and a special thank you to his partner Mary Johnston, who proof-read Peter's text entirely, and is a model of intelligent compassion, warmth and spirit.

I owe a great debt to Peter's two nieces, Mary McCourt and Mary Schofield, who provided me with photos and background detail. It took great courage on their and their family's part to have such a harsh light shone on their grandparent's circumstances and the education of one of their father's. It can't have been easy to deal with so graphic and unbidden a ghost, but without their support Peter's story would never have been told. My sincere thanks.

Finally I'd like to acknowledge my friends, family and especially the young lady who chose to spend her days with me. You have enlivened and made bright my time with this. Looking back, none of this would have been possible without my father Pat Whelan. For giving me all the chances Peter never had, I am forever your grateful son.

Diarmuid Whelan
August 2006

Introduction

'My story, which is true, should be published in my own name.'

'I am looking forward to re-writing the story.
But should anything happen, i.e. an accident, or death (my death)
I hope it will still be possible to publish the story based on my manuscript.'

'The thing is that it will one day be printed.'

The text you are about to read is a troubled and strange document, one that gives a rare view into a still controversial part of our recent past. In a way it is like a deposition to history both of a young boy and a man who is now long dead. Although committed to paper in the late 1950s, it has taken nearly half a century to make its way before us.

The story behind this document, Peter Tyrrell's text, begins with the discovery of a charred corpse in Hampstead Heath on 26 April 1967. This body was so badly burnt that it was impossible to identify. The only clue to its identity was a torn postcard found next to the body with the words 'Skeffington' and 'Dublin'. In June of the following year, Senator Owen Sheehy Skeffington received a letter from The London Metropolitan Police. It stated:

> I am directed by the Commissioner to return as requested the letter from Peter Tyrrell, which you kindly forwarded to assist enquiries, together with a Photostat copy of the pieces of postcard found near the body. As positive identification of the body has not been established the original pieces of the card will be retained. Your assistance in this matter is appreciated.[1]

That was the last that Owen Sheehy Skeffington heard of Peter Tyrrell. Within two years Skeffington himself died of heart failure. With his death the story of Peter Tyrrell and his search for justice arising from his days in Letterfrack were almost lost forever. In a biography of Skeffington entitled *Skeff*, his wife Andrée gave a clearer idea of the connection between Tyrrell and her late husband.

Arising out of his campaign against corporal punishment in schools, Owen got a letter from Peter Tyrrell, an Irishman living in London. He had been committed to Letterfrack Industrial School in 1924 when he was eight years old, because of his parents' poverty. The cruelty and severe beatings he had witnessed and suffered during his time there had haunted him all his life. 'I was always terrified of going to sleep at night because of the bad dreams of being beaten', he wrote. Owen encouraged him to write down his experiences, and promised to do what he could to get them published.

Owen was soon to get many pages of manuscript in instalments, and later met Peter Tyrrell, who subsequently contributed to the *Tuairim* report on Industrial Schools, published in 1966. Eventually some of his memories, edited by Joy Rudd, were published in *Hibernia*. When years later this unhappy man burnt himself to death on Hampstead Heath, it took the British police a year to establish his identity. They did this by tracing the unburned corner of a postcard in his pocket addressed to Owen.[2]

This is the fullest account of Tyrrell's life that we have. Several other small snatches of his life have surfaced since his death. A recent account of one industrial school, *Children of the Poor Clare's* suggests that a 'year after the publication of the *Tuairim* pamphlet he committed suicide by setting himself alight on London's Hampstead Heath'.[3] Another snippet from Tyrrell's life can be gleaned from Mary Raftery and Eoin O'Sullivan, who produced and wrote the *States of Fear* documentary. Their subsequent book, *Suffer the Little Children*, adds to our knowledge of Tyrrell by relating that he served in the British Army in the Second World War and was a Prisoner of War in Germany. They recount that Tyrrell portrayed the Nazi POW camp favourably in contrast with the Christian Brothers' Industrial school regime, declaring that his time with the Germans was 'like a tea party' compared with Letterfrack. Later still, many of these details are reassembled in a column by Mary Raftery in *The Irish Times* and another by Paddy Doyle, author of *The God Squad*, one of the earlier accounts of life in an Industrial School.

These glimpses of Tyrrell's life, bequeathed to history through a barely connected vine, all concentrate on the same essentials. He was born into a life of poverty, was an inmate in Letterfrack by the age of 8, and was deeply traumatized and abused by that institution. He spent the Second World War with the British Army at the 'tea party' of a German POW camp. The remainder of his life was spent as an emigrant in Great Britain where he was loosely involved in a campaign to remove corporal punishment and reform Irish industrial schools until his untimely death by gruesome suicide when he burned himself alive on Hampstead Heath in 1967. To join all these incidents together was the torn postcard to Skeffington to give the clue.

It turns out, however, that a great deal more than this remained. After a period of nearly 40 years 'many pages of manuscript in instalments' as well as a wealth of correspondence between Tyrrell and Skeffington were discovered. They had been lying with the rest of Senator Sheehy Skeffington's uncatalogued private papers, first in the attic of his family home and more recently in storage in the National Library of Ireland. Even though these papers came to light in an era when the claims made by Tyrrell have won widespread credence, they are astonishing for their capacity to recreate the entire atmosphere of the system which Tyrrell was unfortunate enough to have lived through and brave enough to have written about.

These papers tell us that Tyrrell was born in the same year as the Easter Rising, 1916, a parallel that may lead some minds to view Tyrrell as an emblem of the human wastage of the independent Irish regime. But there really is no place for political overtones at the beginning of a narrative that is based on clutches of vivid and immediate memories of a young boy's life before Letterfrack.[4] His first eight years were spent on his family's small farm near Cappagh, Ahascragh, Co. Galway, where he was born into a life of poverty. He tells us that although his father James Tyrrell was well thought of in the community, in his own household he was slow to carry out work, improvements or the basics of farming. What little land they had was poorly managed. The family home was a one room 'barn' without windows. It was a great strain to feed the family of ten children and they were often short of food. As a consequence, their mother, who in Ireland's sharp social gradations came from a 'better' background, had to go borrowing (or according to an earlier account which Tyrrell wanted to amend – she went begging). And it was this offence that would have brought their situation to the notice of the civic guards. A cursory visit to the Tyrrell house led the authorities to petition the courts to commit over half of one family. Six of the children were put 'into care' in January 1924, taking the 8-year-old Peter along with his older brothers, Joe, Paddy and Jack. His two younger brothers Martin and Larry were 'sent to the nuns in Kilkenny' as they were too young to go to Letterfrack.

The following ten chapters deal with his experience of St Joseph's

Industrial School near the small isolated village of Letterfrack. Tyrrell's account begins with an almost hallucinatory passage describing the kindness of the civic guards and the serenity of the Christian Brother who accompanied them from Ballinasloe through the beautiful countryside, before they are introduced to an almost nightmarish scene of an emaciated and wan troop of young boys being chased feverishly by a Brother with a stick.

> Now all at once a Christian Brother comes running out, he is chasing the young children with a very long stick and beating them on the backs of the legs. We can now hear the screams of the little boys, some of them are only six years old. We are now frightened and struck with horror.[5]

This was Letterfrack and it got no better.

With the exception of the first day when there was apparently a rule that a new boy was never disciplined, an entire new world of emotional trauma and physical pain opens up to Tyrrell. Even though his family were used to appalling living conditions, he complains bitterly, perhaps unfairly in some cases, about the hardships of Letterfrack. There was an alarming monotony in the plainness of the diet and the smallness of the portions. They were always cold, as their undernourished bodies could not provide enough warmth in the large unheated rooms of the school. Although they washed themselves regularly, their bed linen was rarely changed. Their own personal clothes were removed upon arrival (quite sensibly to remove social stigma and gradations) but again their uniforms were infrequently laundered. As a result lice were rampant: 'During my early schooldays we used to take off our shirts and shake them over the fire and then listen to hear the lice crack. It was like a fireworks in miniature.'[6]

A clear indication of the harshness of the regime (an inadequate diet and excessive cold) was the prevalence of chilblains. To an extent some effort was made to ameliorate this when the school doctor prescribed a daily dose of cod liver oil. Equally disturbing is the indication that little or no effort was made about oral hygiene. Some of the descriptions of rotten breath and bleeding gums leave a lasting impression.

> Con Murphy...has always been my chum...his health has failed terribly, he works beside me in the tailors shop, his mouth and gums are diseased, and by pressing his gums he can bring puss and blood from them.[7]

Like many a similar set up in boarding schools, the days quickly merged into one another with the unflinching routine of each day the same as that past.

> the boys would have risen at 6:40... When the boys had washed and dressed they would have gone down and the disciplinarian would have taken them then up to the church. At 7:10 they would have had morning prayers with the disciplinarian, guiding them and leading them. That was another role of the disciplinarian to guide them in prayer. Then there would have been mass at 7:30 followed by break-fast... They would have then embarked on what's known as charges or chores where the boys cleaned and tidied the dormitories under supervision. Then the dormitories were locked and out of bounds for the rest of the day. There was sweeping and dusting of the dining room, chapel, sacristy and so on. These would be the sort of things that happened. Then there was an inspection of the boys by the Resident Manager at 9:00 prior to them going to school. Then the Brothers would have thought [sic] in school from 9:00 or 9:15 until 2:00 with a break for a light collation at 11:15 ... Then in the afternoons they would have taken some of the younger boys for knitting classes or seen that they did knitting classes and the older boys went to trades. There was a tea break and then the brothers took them for games, band practice, music. Then they supervised the recreation at 5:45 and then at 6:15 they taught religion for half an hour. They had night prayers before supper... That was followed by recreation and then the boys would have gone to bed in or around 8:30. The night watchman would have arrived in or around 10:00.[8]

In Tyrrell's account there seemed to have been little attempt to break the monotony of the days, with recreation or extra activities. Only towards the end of his days in Letterfrack is there any mention of school plays or bands or other pastimes that schools adopted to provide the bare minimum stimulus for young boys. However, by this stage the view of the teenage Tyrrell is utterly cynical. In his mind they are merely money generating schemes to bail out the faltering finances of the school, which were imperilled by the activities of one Brother in particular, who embezzled funds in order to fund his lifestyle of finely tailored clothes, drinking, a new car and almost incredibly – a girlfriend. The warped effects on the children can be seen when the superior and the parish priest forbid him from seeing his 'girlfriend':

> When Fahy stopped going with the girl he started taking boys to his room at night to commit improper offences. Such offences were often committed quite openly in the dormitory at night and many boys talked about it next day.[9]

However, bar one or two instances the phenomenon of sexual abuse does not feature in the text. It can, however, be inferred from certain silences or elisions such as a Brother disappearing into a closed room at a particular time with a particular boy. Only in the first letter to Sheehy Skeffington and in some other letters does he make an explicit accusation of sexual abuse. In addition to saying that 'three of the Christian Brothers were sadists', Tyrrell added 'and one was a pervert'.[10] Graphic as Tyrrell's account is, in relation to sexual abuse it is to an extent sanitized. Some of the incidents that happened to him were not mentioned in the story that he sought to publish. An earlier letter of his to the Christian Brothers is more explicit:

> On several occasions after a meal I was taken into the pantry, which was at the end of the refectory...He would lock the door and make me undress and then...was made sit on a stool and would be put over his knee and flogged severely.[11]

Nonetheless, although sexual abuse cannot be dismissed, neither as the cause of Tyrrell's trouble, nor as a phenomenon of Industrial Schools, on the evidence of Tyrrell's writings it seems to have been isolated to one or perhaps two individuals and a handful of occasions. What was both widespread and endemic was physical abuse. It is the portrayal of the prevalence and severity of this that is the true condemnation of Letterfrack in this era. It is shocking that it was carried out by a handful of Brothers who were entrusted with the care of these boys from the age of 6 up. It is hard to believe that such a regime of calculated and persistent abuse of boys with, for example, straps cut from a rubber tyre or horsewhips, could have gone unnoticed. And if it was noticed, then it is a searing indictment of the standards of care that it was tolerated, whatever the circumstances or mitigating factors.

Certain episodes, particularly of the abuse, remain in the mind long after. One of them is the ritualistic flogging of naked boys as they entered or left the showers. A particular form of cruelty seems to have been the practice of forcing them into showers that were too hot, by the fear of being beaten or actually being beaten. Those who were last or merely tardy were consciously beaten. Then when the showers became cold or freezing and the boys would attempt to avoid the jets of water, they would again be lashed at.

The same Brother initiated a reign of terror in the refectory by introducing a no talking rule that was punished with immediate and amazing severity. This Brother would ritualistically punish his charges – the 'monitors' he selected – for crumbs on the floor, for dirty fork tines and a myriad of other 'offences'.

> When Brother Vale was beating a boy during a meal, I often tried to count the number of blows being struck, but always lost count after seven or eight. There was a better chance of keeping count, by looking away from where the beating was taking place, and concentrate on the sound of the rubber as it struck the child's head and back. Another way was to count the number of screams, as some children – but not all, would scream in terror after each blow. Big Kenny was not beaten again after he had passed a motion of the bowels during a severe beating during breakfast one morning.[12]

It was the 'torture' inflicted by this Brother in particular that seems to have made the entire Letterfrack experience an eight-year nightmare that never really ended for Tyrrell. Without this particular Brother, Tyrrell's time in Letterfrack would undoubtedly have gone better. The awfulness of his time does to an extent revolve around the barbarity of one particular individual. So to an extent there is a certain element of subjectivity to it. Tyrrell was unfortunate that Brother Vale was the disciplinarian for most of his time there. He was also unfortunate that Vale was removed from Letterfrack and entered a 'mental home' only after Tyrrell had left. Another subjective element is that the emotional effect of this abuse is hard to gauge in that it seems to vary from person to person. A latter day account, *Fear of the Collar*, makes the point quite well when it shows how one boy would cry and scream when hit. After the Brother had let him be, he would casually chuckle to an aghast onlooker that his screams were only to make his tormentor go away. Whether he was pretending to be brave or not, it indicates that punishment affected boys in different ways. Some could bear it while others could not.[13] Clearly, it terrorized Tyrrell. Being hit, the fear of being hit, the awful anticipation of being hit, the fear of living under the oppressively watchful eye of Vale seemed to terrorize more than the action itself. It is purgatorial to read, and leaves us hoping the end of Tyrrell's time in Letterfrack would somehow come quicker.

All these occasions of abuse could legalistically in some perverse way be understood as 'discipline'.[14] What cannot be explained away is the cruelty inflicted in the classroom for what the Department of Education explicitly proscribed, that is, punishment for 'mere failure at lessons'. Some of the saddest passages in Tyrrell's account relate to instances of boys being repeatedly abused simply because they did not know an answer. We now know that this was widespread and by no means confined to Letterfrack. Indeed it was largely due to Sheehy Skeffington's complaints over the persistence and excesses of corporal punishment in 1950s Ireland that led Tyrrell to contact Skeffington. What Tyrrell's account does demonstrate is the effect these corrections had on students over an eight-year period. Boys with stammers were beaten to make them speak normally. Boys with poor memories – 'a lazy mind'[15] – were beaten to make them remember. The unsurprising effect is that their faculties were impaired and their conditions made worse. In certain cases they ended up as cultured imbeciles. The lack of care, ignorance and abject cruelty involved in these cases – inflicted on them by individuals who had received training in the education of young boys and who themselves were educated – is hard to fathom. A different era, with different standards some might say. Perhaps, but the Brother who allowed the defenceless and ill boy known as 'Caleba' to be brutalized by other boys is a moral perversion that would shame any society.

The net of guilt spreads even wider. Although it may in some cases be laid at the feet of certain individuals, and though we are happy to point at the religious orders, it is clear that it is not exclusively the fault of both. Tyrrell's text shows the extent to which the goings on of Letterfrack were well known in the community, and in some cases were carried out by laypersons. One of the most damning aspects of this account is the way the lay teachers and the instructors, the tradesmen, labourers and caretakers are all woven into the society of the industrial school. It was of course a major part of the community and a sizeable portion of the local economy, but it is surprising to a latter day eye that so many were employed there. What one imagines as a remote, almost cloistered order really was nothing of the kind. The sad thing is that those who knew of the brutality were either complicit or were barely able to utter it themselves. As in the sympathetic case of Annie Aspel who acknowledged what was going on to the young Tyrrell but could not bring herself to mention it, it is almost as though a silent hand were covering her mouth. The 'good' laypeople of Letterfrack, that is, those who did not brutalize the children, feared the Brothers themselves who in this case were their moral guardians and, no minor detail, their employers. The others, who worked there and also knew, were themselves not a little intoxicated with their own tiny measure of power, and abused it accordingly. The one lesson that Skeffington would have us draw from Tyrrell's account is that all levels of society are complicit. The individual, the community and the nation bowed to authoritarianism and did not have the moral courage to stand up to the abuse of authority.

This is the merit of *Founded on Fear*. It allows us make sense of the industrial school mess. It enables us see the phenomenon realistically. It provides us with actual examples that resonate and linger in our minds. As well as the gruesome passages teeming with the monotony of destruction, there are occasional snatches of relief, and even joy. It is hard not to feel the young Tyrrell's elation and excitement at Christmas, even if this is tempered with the knowledge that the good food is only for the day, or that the Brothers metamorphosis from oppressors into playful fellow celebrants of Christmas lasts equally as long. There is a similar, almost strange sense of liberation when we hear that the Brothers have departed for a six-week holiday, or that the boys' annual day out to the nearby Tully strand will not be cancelled, and that this event, with its almost sublime quality, will actually go ahead. It is also a relief to hear that the parents are still alive and, despite their obvious poverty, send them letters, a cake, or clothes and money. It's hard also not to feel Tyrrell's bitterness towards his father for landing him in Letterfrack, or to understand why he hardens his heart toward his beloved mother. After eight years in Letterfrack the brevity of his letter to her is the most eloquent testimony: 'My dear mother, Just a line hoping to find you well, as this letter leaves me at present, Peter.'[16]

It also allows us to see the havoc that was wreaked. This is very clear from the portion of Tyrrell's memoir that deals with his time after Letterfrack. After he was released he returned to the family home and worked as a tailor in Ballinasloe for over two years. Here we can see how pronounced the psychological effects on the young Tyrrell were. There was no release or deliverance. He had been scarred and it would haunt him. This manifested itself in a number of ways. He could not deal with any responsibility or stress. He sweated profusely in the most normal conditions. He was sullen and uncommunicative, avoiding conversation with all of his family except his mother. This was in contrast to one of his other brothers from Letterfrack, who became aggressive and could fly into rages at the drop of a hat. His relations with women were crippled. Even though they found him sympathetic and attractive, he was inhibited and crushingly nervous in their company. He felt no self worth and could not imagine that any girl would want an industrial schoolboy. This was part of the terrible social stigma that affected ex-inmates. He felt as though he belonged on the lowest rung of society. As a consequence he avoided as much of society as he could, walking the long way home through fields rather than come under the eyes of his neighbours. Because of this social suffocation he could not adjust to normal life. It was more because of this than economic necessity that he left for London. The bewilderment and insecurity he felt there – with no address to go to, no clue where to stay, no idea what to do with himself – resulted in him accepting the suggestion that he should join the British Army, which he did in 1935.

He was posted to Scotland, with the King's Own Scottish Borders regiment. Despite many trials he adapted very successfully to army life and served in Malta and Palestine, and for most of the war in India, and even the Himalayas. He overcame many of his fears, received further education in the Army, and was twice promoted. He fell in love in India with a beautiful young girl, Angela Dennison. From his letters to Owen Sheehy Skeffington, he gives a good portrait of her. 'She was seventeen when I first met her. She was sitting on the floor of her house eating curry and rice from a very big green leaf. She looked lovely and beautiful and perfectly natural...She was polite and well-mannered, but I liked her best when she first told me to go to hell saying "Go to hell Paddy, you bloody pig". She called me Paddy, pronounced "Paddee".' They had a relationship in India in the middle of the war, and it is clear that she and her family were keen for him to propose to her, but he was unable to not only because of his tenuous position in the Army, but also because it seems that he was both too nervous and too lacking in self-esteem to be able to go through with it.

> I was not well, and I would have to face this awful fact. I was being driven in opposite directions by an equally powerful force. I wanted to marry her more than anything in the world but was afraid that I would not be good enough, or that I would let her down. This was my mental conflict.[18]

Just how fond of her he was can be gauged by his agreeing to go to a dance with her. He was literally terrorized by the prospect of this for weeks. Eventually he went, but only after steadying himself with drink, and was delighted when it had to be abandoned due to an air raid. The effect of Letterfrack on his life, even in this period when he was beginning to free himself from his past is clear from the cruelties he inflicted upon others; people he did not wish to hurt, but nonetheless did:

> But when I was worried or depressed I took it out on the Indians. This went on for two years... That night I began to identify myself with the Christian Brother. I found myself behaving in almost the same manner as Brother Vale. It was then that I began to think of sadism as a terrible and contagious disease. I remembered in previous years I used to think for days and days how best to hurt somebody I didn't like. I bought Angela my girlfriend an expensive watch and a few weeks later I went to her house and asked for the watch back. I was in love with this girl, yet I deliberately hurt her. A few hours later when I had fully realised what I had done I remembered that look on her face as she handed me back the watch.[19]

Sadly, because of incidents like this and because he was not able to take the final step, their relationship ended.

After the Allied invasion into France he was redeployed to the Western Front in 1944. His company landed in Holland. Over the following few months they fought their way through to near the German border, where he was wounded and captured. He details his four months in Stalag XIB Fallingbostel and describes it as a 'heaven on earth' compared with Letterfrack. Tyrrell was undoubtedly impressed with his treatment by the Germans. There was a civility and togetherness in the POW camp and military hospital that was at odds with his memory of school. Because he was well treated by the Germans he was reluctant to believe stories of Nazi extermination and preferred to blame it on disease rather than mass murder, and even goes so far as to say that had a gas chamber been offered to him when he had been in Letterfrack, he would happily have chosen it. It could also be noted that he failed to perceive the obvious parallel between the German treatment of the Russian prisoners with Ireland's treatment of its industrial schoolchildren. Western prisoners were treated humanely, while Russians were abused and starved by the Germans. It was something which perhaps should have sprung to mind when he saw the similarities himself: 'Most young children suffered from chilblains. The backs of the hands were red and swollen and a mass of watery sores. I noticed this amongst some of the Russian Prisoners of Stalag Eleven B.'[20] It has to be said that whatever his subjective feelings about the two regimes, his comparison of the food allowances is startling.

> The bread ration is two thin slices a day, two potatoes, a portion of sausage meat, a table spoonful of sugar, and on alternate days we get a portion of honey or jam. There is now no salt. We get black coffee twice daily and the sauerkraut which the doctor has advised us against eating. The bread ration is half what we got at Letterfrack. The potato ration is about the same. The sugar is slightly more in prison than at Letterfrack. The butter or margarine is about the same. At Letterfrack we got fish or rice or rhubarb on Friday, which we don't get in prison. Here in prison there is a cheese ration once a week or sometimes twice. So taking the food ration all round we were slightly better off at school in Ireland. But there is more variety in prison. But older prisoners from different camps say that it is the smallest ration they have seen. Don't forget we are living in a country which has been fighting a bitter war for six years. She has been fighting three of the most powerful nations on earth. Life here in Stalag 11B Fallingbostel during the last months of the war is hard and unpleasant. Yet it is a Heaven on earth in comparison to my life at school.[21]

That a grown man could feel better cared for in a Nazi POW camp right at the end of the war with Germany on its knees, than as a young man in peacetime Ireland speaks for itself.

The war experience seems to have given him a great deal of confidence in himself and shown him that he could overcome his fears. He returned to England in late 1945 a different man with a good job in the Ministry of Supplies. In many respects this was the crucial period of his life.

> This job lasted almost two years and I must say I was beginning to really enjoy life. I had learned to mix and enjoy people's company instead of being the odd man out. I was no longer afraid of people. I had learned to cast aside that terrible inferiority complex. I didn't blush or tremble when I met

superiors. I didn't jump out of my skin when my name was called ... Yes I had beaten most of my fears. I learned to cycle, I learned to drive a car, but failed in the test, which didn't worry me because I feel I could pass another time. I learned to swim, and done a lot of mountaineering whilst in the Himalayas. So there was a good deal to be thankful for. I was afraid of going in the boxing ring, not so much of being hurt as being laughed at. I did eventually put my name down and entered the ring at the depot Berrick on Tweed. But my opponent had such long arms I couldn't get near him.[22]

His war experiences show fully the downward slide that accompanied his rejoining the Irish emigrants in London. Unfortunately, after the war his job disappeared and he found himself unemployed. At this crucial juncture two things happened. Firstly, he returned to tailoring. His newly won status and confidence disappeared and he found himself travelling for work again. At the same time he met one of his friends from school. This seems to have been the catalyst for his preoccupation with his experience in Letterfrack.

As we were being introduced, Thornton recognized me immediately, and before I had a chance to speak 'O Yes, I know Peter, we met in Ballinrobe' said Thornton, and as he did so gave me a wink. There was no mention of Letterfrack (I have never been to Ballinrobe). When Thornton and I were alone for a few seconds, he said very quickly 'Don't say anything about Letterfrack, if ever you want to speak about the school, always call it the SHIP.' It is the most awful disgrace in the world to be identified as a boy from the Christian Brothers.[23]

His reintroduction into an exclusively Irish community seems to have played a major part in a recrudescence of anger.

I should mention that before meeting Thornton, I had almost forgotten Letterfrack. I was inclined to be over confident, I was becoming a snob, almost too self centred, a hero, I was gambling heavy and winning about ten pounds a week. I spent a lot of money on clothes and would hardly go out without first pressing my trousers. I was a proper swank, always showing off. But after meeting Thornton, I gambled heavily and lost, I began to drink more. I travelled to London and met other lads from Christian Brothers Schools who told me stories even worse than Letterfrack.[24]

Although noticeably different in many respects to his compatriots – they jokingly referred to him as 'the professor' because he carried a pen and paper and might write a few notes in the pub – and even though he seemed to drink less than they, after a few years 'observing' the Irish in Britain he fell into their cycle – a daily routine of work and the pub. He also seems to have lost his bearings, so to speak, and ended up travelling around most of the major cities trying to find work – Leeds, Liverpool, Birmingham, Bristol, Glasgow, Newcastle, but always returning to London.

This part of his narrative is an equally necessary part of his story simply because as so many of the ex-inmates of Irish reformatories and industrial schools emigrated, it is integral to the industrial school experience. The aspects of exile that he did deal with were handled almost obliquely, but it is nonetheless a very revealing portrait. As with the rest of his writing he matter of factly relates the daily life of the uprooted unmarried Irishman in London: the mindless grazing every evening in the pubs, the exigencies, intrusions and complications of communal living are all told without embellishment.

> Many Irishmen in Britain live five or six in one room without even a place to hang up their coat. Many live in places like the Salvation Army Hostel or the Church Army...where they sleep in huge dorms. They have no home life or comfort. Many go straight from work into the public house and from there to bed. As I have said before they have no ambition, no purpose in life, no personal pride, no thought of progress, no sense of continuity. They live for today only. Their education was to prepare them for the next life; the soul is saved at the expense of the body. We are taught in school that to be exalted we must first of all suffer a great deal. The more we suffer the greater will be our reward in Heaven. We are reminded very often that this world is a Vale of Tears.[25]

Tyrrell came across a great number of ex-inmates and encouraged many of them to recount their experiences. His efforts met with mixed results. Some people were willing to talk about their experiences but refused to take it any further. Others, including his brother and his friend Tom Thornton, were highly defensive on the subject. As he said himself, this line of questioning had to be handled very carefully; asking the wrong Irishman about his background was 'dynamite'.[26] From a few descriptions that he related, he had experience of some of these explosions.

> Recently I was having a chat with some Irish men in a pub who were talking about our problems at home. I said the only way to end partition is for all Irish people abroad to return home and build up our country and therefore create a healthy economy and at the same time prove to our brothers in the North that we are a civilized community. At present there is no evidence that we are. One of the chaps had to be held by his pals until I left the pub, because he wanted to fight me.[27]

This is a minor theme running through the latter part of his account – the reactions of the Irish in Britain to any criticism of Ireland, the Christian Brothers, priests or the Irish government. In retrospect, some might agree with Tyrrell when he stated that he failed 'to understand why thousands of Irish people express a hatred of England and the English in view of the fact that the Irish spend the greater part of their lives in England eating out of the hands of English people'.[28] And while he understood the historical reasons for this, it was baffling to him that so many of these poorly treated Irish people continued to swear blind loyalty to the institutions, leaders and country that spat them out.

Tyrrell felt no such allegiance. While he never saw himself as an economic emigrant, he did feel that he had been very badly treated. Increasingly he became acerbic in his denunciations of the industrial schools and the Christian Brothers, but also denominational education, priests and religion itself. The problems of Ireland, in his opinion, were directly traceable to this. What sets him apart from the crowd, apart from his outspokenness, is that he also rejected a blind nationalism. While he was concerned about improving the Irish nation, he saw no role for the IRA in this. A large part of his rejection of the IRA seems to be down to the sea change in British attitudes to the Irish after the IRA bombing campaign of 1939. To Tyrrell's sensitive and nervous soul the hostility he encountered when he returned after the war was particularly unwelcome.

> I went to London where I heard wages were much higher than in the Midlands, and found great changes since 1935. In spite of the bombing, and the great shortage of houses, the population had increased by several millions. I spent a day in

the east end, and found that whole streets had disappeared. Later I went to north London to find digs but was shocked and amazed to learn that the Irish were most unpopular. Most landladies simply shut the door in my face when they learned I was Irish. One landlady was more friendly and advised me to go to the Irish quarter. I said 'I didn't know that there was such a place'. 'Oh yes', she answered, 'Camden Town is where most Irish people live. There they can get drunk and fight as much as they like. We always had Irish lads here until they started going about with bombs in their pockets, just before the war.' 'I am sorry', she added, 'I don't wish to offend you, but your lads are too big a risk.' Every word cut into me like a knife.[29]

To have rejected the twin salves of Irish abstraction – God and guns – was no mean feat. Naturally he paid a price for it, and on more than one occasion he was threatened, assaulted and even pulled down off a soapbox in Hyde Park for denouncing the ills of Ireland. As he said himself, the irony of this was that he was only quoting a priest.[30] Other things he said were clearly too uncomfortable.

Before leaving London I made a habit of visiting the Irish public houses in the East End (Whitechapel) where almost all the customers are Irish, and I must confess that the behaviour of many of the men was a disgrace to any community. I was severely beaten up for telling them what I thought. I told them we were known abroad as irresponsible liars and drunkards. That the Catholic religion had kept us the most unhappy and the most backward race in Europe. Evidence of our ignorance and backwardness lies in the fact that only a fraction of our people can earn a living at home, and also due to the fact that there were hundreds going about with guns in their pockets. We were a nation of gangsters. I told them there were thousands of overfed priests living on the backs of the people. These parasites must be made to do some useful work. The priest is Ireland's greatest enemy. He is doing untold harm.[31]

It was through the Irish Centre in London that he was advised to contact Owen Sheehy Skeffington, who at the time, 1958, was gaining notoriety for his stance on corporal punishment. Skeffington was the son of Frank and Hanna Sheehy Skeffington. Frank was murdered in Easter Week 1916 after he characteristically attempted to prevent looting in the streets. He was among other things, a socialist, a suffragist, a pacifist and an anti-vivisectionist. His wife Hanna was the well-known feminist, who was on Sinn Féin's executive council, and who broke with de Valera when he took the oath. Their son Owen imbibed many of his parent's characteristics, most notably his father's socialism and pacifism. Like his parents he was highly outspoken and a seemingly lone voice against many aspects of Irish society. He was censored on several occasions and his papers are testament to the extent of personal abuse he sustained for his beliefs. Like his father he was also a committed educationalist and it was in this sphere that he began his criticisms of the brutal ethos of much of Irish education. From his position as Senator (1954–70) he was a consistent opponent of several Ministers for Education, most notably Richard Mulcahy, who refused to believe or investigate the charges of abuse and punishment that Skeffington had documented.

And this is how he came to Tyrrell's attention in London. Skeffington saw that Tyrrell's accusations about Letterfrack in his first letter to him had 'the ring of unvarnished truth about it'. Skeffington invited him to his home and encouraged Tyrrell to write an account of his time in Letterfrack. Over the next five months Tyrrell put together a 70,000 word manuscript that is the text of this book. They communicated until 1967, and Tyrrell's half of the correspondence is all that remains. After completing his manuscript, he wrote a great deal more of what he called 'additional notes', which amounted to extra narrative, some of which has been incorporated into this introduction. Much of the material was repetition, or thoughts on a variety of subjects that might not necessarily demand our attention. But from these letters we can see that Tyrrell relied on Skeffington's original idea which was to write 'a booklet' to outline the conditions of Letterfrack and the industrial schoolboy's situation, an aim he more than achieved. It certainly wasn't easy for him, and it took both a huge effort and a heavy toll: 'I was very tired and done very little this weekend. I rushed through the last year as I got sick of it, and became very depressed. There are many things I can't remember, and there are things which are too terrible to put in writing, which I can remember.' Along the way Skeffington sent him material relating to the debate back in Ireland on corporal punishment and some national school incidents.

> Thanks for the newspaper cuttings which I am returning. I can see that people are getting worried. Am sending a few pages and will write again on Saturday... The present chapter 'I join the Regular Army – chapter 13' is going to be too long, so I will

have to make it into two chapters, making 15 in all. This is really a life story, which I was not prepared for.

However, the feeling that he was out of his depth and a little at sea continued. He was writing very much in isolation, although he did run it by some of his family, like his 'brother Joe... [who] was the first to leave Letterfrack. He has verified everything I have written in the early chapters.' Understandably, he felt the 'necessity for a little moral support, as most people have advised me against what I am doing. Most say it would do more good to forget about everything. But I am determined to carry on in spite of the fact that my brother is a priest and my sister is a nun in the States.'[32]

What is perhaps most compelling from the retrospect of nearly fifty years after he began his account is the sense of urgency he felt when he first sat down to write it. He was convinced that his text would genuinely make a difference, and that it would lead to some positive changes in the industrial school regime. By the beginning of the 1960s Tyrrell knew that it was going to take longer:

> Thanks for your card. Am glad you have made some progress. I know it will take a long time – another two years perhaps. The thing is that it will one day be printed. Anything written which you don't like may be crossed out, as it will save time later. I am keeping fairly well thanks. It's difficult to be well when one isn't happy. All good wishes, Peter.[33]

By the mid 1960s there seemed to have been a tacit understanding between them that it could not be published in its current form, most likely because there was too much supplementary material that was written after the first 14 chapters. Tyrrell to an extent became exasperated at the idea of re-writing it all, as expressed in a letter to Skeffington dated 25 March 1964:

> I regret that in spite of all we have said, I may not be able to rewrite the 'booklet' when it is arranged. It has caused me considerable worry for several years, all day and every day, and in recent weeks it has been worse. I fear that unless I get the whole thing off my mind completely, my health might fail.
>
>   As I see it the real purpose of the 'booklet' would be to provide the necessary documentary proof, before I launch a campaign in this country. What I am planning

is public demonstrations, which I feel is the most effective method. This would be done, with or without police permission. I have already given full details of what is happening in the schools to the police in Leeds and London. I think that the threat of public demonstrations will bring about the necessary changes. I am a member of the 'Secular Society' and they will probably help. The work of arranging the manuscript would be enormous, and if you couldn't do it last year, how can it be done this year? The cause of the delay is all my fault. I led you astray completely when writing the 'notes' which should have stopped three years ago. I was not thinking of a booklet but a full length story. For the purpose of a booklet, enough material was written in five months and completed four years ago. Much of what is written in the postscript notes could be omitted. I am returning your receipt which I don't need. If you agree to drop the whole thing, you may keep the money for your work over there.[34] You may keep or destroy all my material.[35]

After receiving this letter, Skeffington immediately replied and suggested that Tyrrell write a small article, which he would pass on to Joy Rudd, an ex-student of Skeffington's who was in London and already known to Tyrrell. She was able to place this article in *Hibernia* magazine and in the interim Skeffington agreed to try to edit the text as best as he could.[36] After this the frequency of letters drops off dramatically, with just a few letters between then and 1967. A reason for this is that Tyrrell, through Joy Rudd, got involved with the *Tuairim* group in London. This organization was founded in 1954 'in order to bring together members of the Post-Treaty generation and to provide a platform for young people with new ideas... who are able to give constructive views on Irish problems'.[37] It published pamphlets on a range of issues including partition and unification, the United Nations, Ireland and Europe, proportional representation, planning for economic development and Irish education. It's members included a host of Irish political and judicial luminaries such as Donal Barrington, Ronan Keane, Miriam Hederman O'Brien, Garrett FitzGerald and David Thornley to name just a few. The pamphlet which Tyrrell contributed to directly was the thirteenth of the *Tuairim* studies, and it was entitled *Some of Our Children: a report on the residential care of the deprived child in*

Ireland by London branch study group. It was published in 1966 and Tyrrell was named as one of the contributors to the work of the group. His early associations with the group were entirely positive as a letter to Skeffington in November 1964 relates:

> A meeting of *Tuairim* was held at the Irish Centre last night. The subject of the discussion – 'Irish Industrial Schools'. Joy Rudd and others gave the history of such schools, during the last hundred year. I told them about Letterfrack. The meeting was a great success...Our aim now must be for secular schools. Education should be in the hands of educated people who have been trained for that work.[38]

Unfortunately, it seems that they refused to incorporate his experiences, or to even mention any abuse greater than the routine and excessive corporal punishment.[39] Even though some members clearly believed in his testimony, either for fear of legal implications of unproven allegations, or simply because they genuinely believed that the punishments of 1964 were less severe and frequent than 1934, they refused to incorporate any of his testimony.[40] In the end a mild rebuke was inserted into the text of the pamphlet.

If nothing else this incident illustrates just how difficult it was to get a hearing for abuse claims. When even sympathetic and progressive characters like Rudd and Sheehy Skeffington found it impossible, for reasons of legality or credibility, to publish his experiences, it should remind us how different an era the early to mid 1960s in Ireland were. A parallel from the year before Tyrrell died – 1966 – is instructive. In that year Skeffington made the firing of John McGahern a cause célèbre. It was easier to bring into the public arena a current case of a gross abuse of authority, which by virtue of McGahern's dismissal was an indisputable fact. It could also be said that this particular case was the culmination of thirty-five years of opposition to censorship. In the Tyrrell case, his writings were an almost isolated example. It would take a whole catalogue of abuses, the testimony of many individuals, and the removal of the church's own credibility before anything similar was possible in terms of child abuse in Ireland.

While it might have been expected that the Christian Brothers would stonewall him and contemptuously dismiss his complaints and allegations, it was possibly the disappointment of seeing his experiences set to one side by reform minded people that could have led to his despair. The one thing which we should bear in mind before we jump to a conclusion about Tyrrell and *Tuairim* is that suicide was something that had been on his mind for many years, all the way back to Letterfrack. In letters he wrote over the years Tyrrell had hinted at taking just such an action. In one series of supplementary notes to his text, he explicitly talks about walking out into the countryside where he would commit suicide out of sight of anyone.

> In the summer of 1939 I made up my mind that life was not worth living. I wanted to die. My death must appear to be from natural causes or an accident. My plan was to stop eating for several days, and then wander into the jungle... When I seen John Kelly dead [a fellow inmate in Letterfrack], I no longer feared death, because he looked so much better dead than alive, he looked happy and perfectly relaxed, his face was no longer drawn in pain, as I had so often seen before, the lines had gone from under his eyes, he seemed as though about to smile. From then onwards I thought of death as a reward for having lived, something to be desired, a prize for having accomplished an ambition.[42]

Tyrrell suffered from depression and it is likely that he was manic depressive.[43] The strain of what he was trying to achieve was crushing. The urgency of what had become a quest, even a mission, changed his entire demeanour: 'I am often reminded by my old friends that I have changed, I was a much nicer person years ago. I was agreeable and friendly. Today I am silent and when I speak it is to find fault and complain. In the old days I was afraid to complain or comment. I was afraid to disagree, I knew people were wrong and yet said "Yes that's right" when the answer ought to have been "no".[44] Some thirty years after he first looked upon death as a release, he chose the route of anonymous suicide, albeit in the way of the anti-Vietnam protestors who burned themselves alive around the same time.[45]

Finally, is the text realistic? The simple answer is that individuals must judge for themselves, but in my opinion it is a very fair and keenly observed portrayal. Tyrrell's claims have been borne out by time, and none of the details have been refuted by counter-evidence from the Christian Brothers at the Commission to Inquire into Child Abuse module which dealt specifically with Letterfrack on 16 June 2005. Having interviewed the respondent for the Christian Brothers on that day, Br. David Gibson, I can confirm that the named individuals, specifically those accused of abuse by Tyrrell, were all present in Letterfrack at that time, and all were removed from Letterfrack subsequently. While Tyrrell admits to some exaggeration when discussing Letterfrack with Skeffington, he seems to have been scrupulous when it came to actually writing down the events. 'A few things which I told you (when we met) in Dublin were exaggerated, and I therefore did not write about them.'[46]

Similarly, when he claimed that he had approached the Christian Brothers and had written to them and other authorities over the years he was being absolutely factual.[47]

> My brother visited Letterfrack in July 1955... I met him a month later and he told me that Letterfrack was just the same. He had spoken to about twenty children who complained of daily beatings. The pets received better treatment just as they did thirty years ago. The Christian Brothers were just as cruel and as savage as ever. Drastic action was now necessary. Instead of writing letters to the Ministers responsible and the Clergy – which were never acknowledged, I must think of some method of bringing the hateful bullies to their senses. I went to the Christian Brothers at Marino and warned them that I was about to start a great campaign against the torture of children in Catholic schools all over Ireland. I have heard awful reports from other schools especially the Deaf and Dumb school at Dublin, and the convents. I got no satisfaction from the Brothers at Marino so I went to the clergy, who warned me against interfering with the Christian Brothers schools, saying you are playing with fire, the Brothers are well able to look after themselves.[48]

In June 2005 it became known that Tyrrell had in fact written and visited the Christian Brothers as early as August 1953. Having received no acknowledgement Tyrrell visited the Christian Brothers. The Brother who met him that day subsequently wrote to the order's solicitor to inform him that Tyrrell might contact him in the future:

> I took it that he was working on the blackmail ticket and after listening to him gave him your name and address as our solicitor. I know you will know how to deal with him if he approaches.[49]

As the representative of the order acknowledged some 50 years later, it was 'a totally inadequate response'.[50]

Other incidents mentioned by Tyrrell complicate our picture of Letterfrack: it was not all abuse by the Brothers upon the children. One example of a more widespread brutality and authoritarianism was the beating of a young lay teacher by an older Brother. Tyrrell also related how new Brothers were encouraged, to the point of instruction, to carry out corporal punishment. Other more complex issues like bullying and abuse of inmates by other inmates are all presented in his account. Part of the tragedy of his time in Letterfrack is that we can see from Tyrrell's own life story how those who themselves were bullied could turn around and become an oppressor. It is something which he is honest about and to which he admits he fell prey to. His remarkably even-handed account signals that ultimately abuse is a human phenomenon. As he pointed out himself, there was good and bad in Letterfrack. He reminds us that although it was set in idyllic circumstances, Letterfrack was impaired by a lack of money. Yet, our sympathy on this point is tempered when we see how the finances were divided unevenly and how one Brother in particular spent the school's resources on himself. But Tyrrell also spends a surprising amount of space extolling the virtues of various individuals, who were 'good or kind'. From his very first letter to the Christian Brothers in 1953 he made it clear that many did their best in the circumstances, and he has no hesitation in referring to one Brother as 'a saint'.[51]

More generally, there are a whole series of examples from Tyrrell's account that bear out what he was saying. From a historical point of view the detail is faithful, as the way the world heavyweight fight between Jack Dempsey and Gene Tunney, or the great storm that practically wiped out an entire fishing fleet up the coast in Mayo, appear seamlessly in the narrative. Perhaps one of the most convincing examples is a simple aside that he knew one New Zealander amongst a group of POW escapees who were killed toward the end of the war. This particular incident was made into the Steve McQueen film *The Great Escape* years after Tyrrell's death. And one of the people killed after recapture was indeed a New Zealander called Christiansen, the very same man whom Tyrrell recalled knowing.

In the end, the final stamp of veracity is to be found in Tyrrell's narrative 'style'. As Skeffington noted from the first letter, it has 'the ring of truth, unadorned'. It is free of embellishment and is told at the level he lived it. Beginning with the almost childlike recollection of cutting the horns of their family goat, the remaining years in Letterfrack are related by someone who we would guess is little more than a teenager. His hurt and fears are transmitted unpolished and raw onto the page. Likewise, his account of his time 'under fire' in the army recreates the immediacy, the confusion, and the fear. Perhaps this was because of the speed he wrote it at. No sooner were his twenty or thirty pages written than he posted them off to Skeffington. Remarkably, for a man who professed to have only the most basic writing skills, he managed to make it appear almost seamless: there was barely a correction in the four hundred or so pages of manuscript. Bar four or five passages scribbled out, the text runs like a long letter written in one sitting. But it wasn't. There were over twenty separate envelopes sent, each with their postmarks to indicate just when they arrived, and each with their package of narrative literally stitched together with needle and thread by a 'tailor to trade'. He assembled it so quickly, so urgently and so simply, that he wrote as though he were reliving it. It all comes across in a frightened, unstoppable, defenceless and uncomprehending way: the way he experienced it.

Diarmuid Whelan
July 2006

NOTES

1. London Metropolitan Police to Owen Sheehy Skeffington, June 1968. Sheehy Skeffington Papers NLI MS 40,543/12.
2. Andrée Sheehy Skeffington, *Skeff: A Life of Owen Sheehy Skeffington* (Dublin, Lilliput, 1991), pp. 190–1.
3. Mavis Arnold and Heather Laskey, *Children of the Poor Clare's: The Story of an Irish Orphanage* (Belfast, Appletree, 1985).
4. As a further challenge to the mainstream 1916 narrative, the elements of Tyrrell's account arise from the three main lacunae of modern Irish history: those who went to industrial schools, those who joined the British Army, and those who emigrated.
5. See below p. 13.
6. Tyrrell to Sheehy Skeffington, MS 40,543/3.
7. See below p. 81.
8. Testimony of Br. David Gibson to *Commission to Inquire into Child Abuse*, 16 June 2005. p. 46. http://www.childabusecommission.ie/public_hearings/diary. htm Accessed 8 August 2005.
9. Tyrrell to Sheehy Skeffington MS, 40,543/1
10. Tyrrell to Sheehy Skeffington, 22 July 1958. MS 40,543/1.
11. Tyrrell to Chistian Brothers 16 Aug. 1953, *Commission to Inquire into Child Abuse* transcript (16/06/05), p.120.
12. MS 40,545/12.

13. 'To boys who don't mind it, corporal punishment does no good; to those who do mind it, it does harm – not physical harm, mental harm; and to some who have never received it the sight of it being inflicted on others can do harm, particularly to young children.' Owen Sheehy Skeffington, 'Some Debating Arguments Against Corporal Punishment in Schools. 24/2/57' OSS Papers NLI. MS 40,542/15.

14. *Rules and Regulations for the Certified Industrial Schools in Saorstat Éireann.* 'Discipline: The manager shall be authorised to punish the children detained in the school in case of misconduct. All serious misconduct, and the punishments inflicted for it, shall be entered in a book to be kept for that purpose, which shall be laid before the inspector before he visits. The manager must, however, remember that the more closely the school is modelled on a principle of judicious family government, the more salutary will be its discipline, and the more effective its moral influences on the children.' Sec. 13 (Punishments) reads: 'Punishments shall consist of: (a) Forfeiture of rewards and privileges, or degradation from rank, previously attained by good behaviour. (b) Moderate childish punishment with the hand. (c) Chastisement with the cane, strap or birch. Referring to (c) personal chastisement may be inflicted by the Manager, or in his presence, by an Officer specially authorized by him, and in no case may it be inflicted upon girls over 15 years of age. In the case of girls under 15, it shall not be inflicted except in cases of urgent necessity, each of which must be at once fully reported to the Inspector. Caning on the hand is forbidden. No punishment not mentioned above shall be inflicted.' The inspection books listing the punishments in Letterfrack have disappeared. *Commission to Inquire into Child Abuse*, http://www.childabusecommission.ie/public_hearings/diary.htm. Accessed 8 August 2005. 'Evidence of Br. David Gibson before Mr. Justice Sean Ryan', 16th June 2005. 'There are no Punishment books', p.114.

15. 'Brother Dooley told us that this boy had a lazy mind and it was hoped that the beating would make him think like normal children.' See below p.13.

16. MS 40,545 /2. When he returned from Letterfrack the first thing his mother said was 'I thought there was something wrong, you have written only three times in the last two years. How could you forget me?'

17. MS 40,455/8.

18. See below p.135.

19. MS 40,455/8.

20. MS 40,545/6.

21. See below p. 157.

22. See below p. 161.

23. See below p. 163.

24. MS 40,545/1.

25. MS 40,543/11.

26. 'I have spent the last few years asking people why they have emigrated, and if and when they desire to return. But such questions are dynamite. Most Irish men and women consider it an insult to be asked a personal question like 'Why did you leave home?' 'Will you ever return?' Most of those people are deeply religious and patriotic.' MS 40,545/8.

27. Ibid.

28. Ibid.

29. See below p. 163.

30. 'When I quoted the priest in Hyde Park recently, they (the Irish) pulled me off the platform.' P. Tyrrell to OSS 16 Oct. 1965. MS 40,543/11.
31. See below p. 170.
32. MS 40,543/8.
33. MS 40,543/7.
34. Skeffington sent him back a cheque for the money Tyrrell sent him. MS 40,545/15.
35. MS 40,543/11.
36. 'Early days in Letterfrack: Memories of an Industrial School by Peter Tyrrell'. *Hibernia*, June 1964.
37. Quoted from original prospectus of the group.
38. Tyrrell to Skeffington 7 Nov. 1964. MS 40,543/12. In another letter Tyrrell refers to Rudd as 'sincere and conscientious'.
39. The only direct reference to Tyrrell's testimony in the Report is the following: 'We have received accounts from a number of ex-pupils of boys' schools alleging excessive corporal punishment in the past . . . The belief that beating was good for boys appears to have been widespread in Ireland in the past but is probably less prevalent today. 'They reported on conditions in Letterfrack that 'We were particularly impressed by the appearance of the boys. They seemed to be well cared for and were neatly dressed in bright, casual clothes, coloured and floral shirts, blazers and sports jackets. They were cheerful and talkative and, except that some of them had very small physiques, had not the appearance of being deprived or depressed.' *Some of Our Children: A Report on the Residental Care of the Deprived Child in Ireland by a London Branch Study Group* (Tuairim, 1966), p.22.
40. 'We have, however, heard from a number of sources stories of recent punishments which we consider to be either unsuitable or excessive. In the absence of any verification that the alleged punishments actually took place or took place in the form described, they must be treated as hypothetical.' *Some of Our Children.* p.39. A belief that testimony was insufficient is the crux of the issue, both in Tyrrell's case and in the industrial school abuse phenomenon more generally.
41. One of the main reasons for McGahern's dismissal was that he did not marry in a church. But it was also to do with the content of his novel *The Dark*, which dealt with themes only too familiar to Tyrrell.
42. MS 40,545/8.
43. 'I have always suffered from long periods of Depression, after which I would become extremely happy for no apparent reason.' 'During the Summer of 1943 I was admitted to the British Military Hospital (47 B.M.H) suffering from nervous trouble (mental depression) although my state of health had greatly improved.'
44. MS 40,545/2.
45. In November, 1965, Norman Morrison, a Quaker from Baltimore, followed the example of the Buddhist monk, Thich Quang Due, and publicly burnt himself to death outside the office of Robert McNamara the US Secretary of Defence. Soon after two other pacifists, Roger La Porte and Alice Herz, also immolated themselves in protest against the war.
46. MS 40,543/2.
47. As well as his letters to the Christian Brothers, Tyrrell claims to have written to

Seán Lemass and John Charles MacQuaid. I have not been able to locate these letters but there are copies of letters he wrote to the Archbishop of Westminster (March 1958) and the *News of the World* (April 1958). MS 40,543/1. See plate section.

48. MS 40,545/13.
49. Letter from Christian Brothers 27 March 1957 to Maxwell Weldon (solicitors for CBs), *Commission to Inquire into Child Abuse*, 16 June 2005.
50. Testimony of Br. David Gibson, *Commission to Inquire into Child Abuse*, 16 June 2005.
51. Brother Kelly. MS 40,545/11.

Note on the Text

What follows has been entirely transcribed from manuscripts posted by Peter Tyrrell to Owen Sheehy Skeffington over a five month period. From November 1958 his story arrived in individual envelopes, which in most cases were literally stitched together. Each page was numbered and with few exceptions they are all in sequential order. One or two pages are missing from the original manuscripts and probably never entered into Skeffington's possession.

There were several difficulties in transcribing Tyrrell's text. The main one was that he seemed to confuse commas and full stops, with the result that some sentences went on too long and others were ungrammatical or syntactically challenging. I have corrected this while trying, as faithfully as possible, to retain his style. It might not be a perfect writing style, but it is one that is particular to him: it is conversational, it blurs tenses, and it inhabits the past more than the present, but all to good effect. Another tic of his writing was to give capitals to every second word, which perhaps reflects his authoritarian education. The occasional grammatical infelicities are retained simply to allow the reader to hear his voice. Misspellings have been corrected on the highly subjective grounds that Tyrrell was a proud man; while a few of them give an idea of what his accent was like (Senator was occasionally spelt 'Sinator'), others like 'cartmendor' (carpenter) are too wide of the mark to be intelligible.

Foreword

It is with deep regret I find it necessary to tell my story, which I know will cause great pain and suffering to thousands of good and kind people in Ireland.

Many of my readers I feel sure will ask the question, why I have waited so long? The answer is, because I had hoped to bring about improvements of conditions in Catholic homes for young children by other means.

For a number of years I have been writing to responsible Ministers in the government, and the Catholic Church, as well as to the Christian Brothers and their solicitors in Ireland. But not only have I failed to bring to an end the criminal brutality, which in many cases reaches a degree of torture, but I have failed to get a single reply to any of my letters.

If Letterfrack was an isolated case, or if any responsible person could prove to me that children are not being savagely ill-treated in Catholic homes, I would gladly throw away my pen. But I am certain beyond any shadow of doubt, that the appalling happenings, which I am about to tell you, are still going on to this day. Beating of children in almost all Catholic schools is the general practice. Education and training in Catholic schools is founded on fear, the fear of corporal punishment, and the fear of *hell*.

Each day of my life I try to fight fears, most of which are imaginary. In a few cases I have been successful, but very often I find a method of escape. Many times in my life I felt it my duty to hurt others, as I had been. The Irish are amongst the world's most backward peoples. We are also most unhappy. The child who is beaten by someone bigger and stronger than himself, will very often grow up bitter and full of hatred of society. He will want to get his own back. He may one day hit back. *I warn society against the child who has been hurt.*

Peter Tyrrell
February 1959

1
Background

It was raining that night in the summer of the year 1921. We didn't have to look out to see what the weather was like, because there were holes in the roof. It was a felt roof, but a storm had blown part of the felt away several years before.

We had a visitor that night, a distant relation of the family, a man called Costello. He hadn't said very much yet, but we all knew what he wanted, he usually spent about three hours in the house and gave Dad a pipe of tobacco before asking Dad to give him a hand on the farm for a day or two, this could mean anything up to two weeks. Of course Dad would never refuse anyone. He loved to do favours for people, for which there was never any payment. He could do almost any kind of property repairs, new doors, windows, floors or even a new roof, yet he would do nothing at home. The last time Mr Costello was here, it was almost a year ago, Dad had promised to repair the roof the first fine day, but everybody laughed when the roof was mentioned, it had now become a good joke. Dad became very angry and threatened to put us to bed, but we knew he couldn't do that, because six of us slept on the kitchen floor on an old mattress, and we could not go to bed until Mr Costello had gone home. There was only one other room in the house, where Mother and Dad and my other two brothers slept. There were no windows in the house and the floor was cobble stone because it was intended to be a stable, but Mother once said we moved in when the old house fell down, the gable end of the old dwelling is still standing. It's raining much heavier now and Mr Costello has moved over to the corner to a more dry place, as there was a rain drop going down his back. Dad was now talking about his future plans, he had just got up from his stool and marked the place on the wall where he was going to make two windows, but Mother reminded him that he had marked the windows ten years ago. She also reminded him that he had not cut any turf for three years, that no crops had been sown for two years and the last time potatoes were sown they were allowed to rot in the ground before being dug up. I was sitting with my young brother under the table, it was fairly dry there and besides there wasn't much room, with my sister and six brothers, all in a tiny kitchen. I could see my father's face now, it was very red, he was furious. No one had ever spoken to him like that before. He went over and placed his fist on Mother's nose, he threatened to leave her, he then said he would throw her out. Dad was well liked by everyone in the village, the neighbours all spoke well of him and he was most obliging and was always ready and willing to give a hand. If there was a sick horse or cow in the neighbourhood Dad was always there, his advice was second to none.

A neighbour once said that James Tyrell knew more than the doctor, the lawyer and the schoolteacher all put together. Yet in spite of all this, Dad at home was a lazy and irresponsible husband and father. Dad was now back to his old form. The argument with Mother was over and forgotten about. He was now telling Mr Costello a story, yes he loved to tell stories, and could keep an audience well entertained all night. Dad was not a liar as there was always an element of truth in everything he said.

It's now after one o'clock in the morning. We had no clock in the house, but Mr Costello told us the time, the rain is now easing off and everyone is getting restless. Mother usually makes tea when a friend or neighbour calls. But there is no sugar and only just enough bread for the breakfast. I heard Mother say early in the day that 'all the two pounds (£2) which uncle John had sent us from the States was gone'. Dad's reply was that 'God is good'.

Mr Costello is now getting ready to go and Dad says 'what's your hurry' which is considered good manners amongst country folk. The visitor has now gone, and Mother is getting the bed ready on the floor. We all kneel down to say the rosary. Yes Dad is very religious. He prays and asks God to send us food for to-morrow. We have four acres of good land which has not been tilled for years and yet Dad prays every day and asks Almighty God to provide for us. There is no turf for the fire, although we have more than twelve acres of first class bog. We could supply the whole village with turf, but we haven't even any for ourselves: instead we must search through the woods for sticks and fallen branches. On our way back from the woods, we pick crab apples, blackberries and nuts. We go through the neighbours' fields to hunt for potatoes and turnips, cabbages, or anything which will keep us alive for one more day. It's now late autumn, Mother said the other day that it would soon be winter. I am not yet six years old but I can remember last winter.

Mother used to go out begging and borrowing from the kind neighbours. One day she came home with 10 shillings, and my sister Norah and five brothers all ran across the fields to the village in their bare feet to buy food. They bought four big loaves, two stone of flour, butter, a pot of jam and two lbs of bacon. They were so hungry that they had eaten a whole loaf on the way back. Whilst they were away my eldest brother and I went to get sticks for the fire. Mother fried a whole pound of bacon on the big pan, and we all stood around the table dipping our bread in the fat. (We did not use plates, but soaked our bread in the frying pan). A few weeks after Dad got a job breaking stones for the new road. He got 12/– a week. One day shortly after, a lady came to see my Mother who was still in bed. We were all told to go to the wood and play and not to return before dark.

When we got home we're informed by the lady that God had sent us a baby brother. My eldest brother Mick now was employed as an apprentice butcher for a few shillings a week. His employer was most kind and always gave him a parcel of meat to take home on Saturday night. We managed all right for the winter, by this time I had started going to school at Ahascragh, and the teacher Mrs Kennedy gave us lunch each day which she brought from her own home.

Dad lost his job in the spring and we couldn't go to school, because we had no clothes. I missed the school very much and the lunch which the teacher gave us was very nice indeed. She also gave us a sweet every day. We were always asking Mother to let us go back to school and we were told that very soon we would be getting a parcel of clothes from the States.

About October 1923 another boy was born and Mother became very ill, from which she never fully recovered. She was confined to bed for several months. When she did get up she could get about only with great difficulty. Mother now became very fat, her hands and joints swelled up. She suffered terribly from rheumatism. Although she was only about thirty-eight, Mother was now an old woman. She cried with pain all the time.

The parcel of clothing did arrive, but it was too late. An inspector for child welfare came to inform my parents that we would be all taken away and confined to a Catholic home where we should be given a good education and taught a trade, that is all the children under fourteen years. We went to school again a few days later. We all had new clothes. Joe had a light grey suit, Paddy had a blue serge, but I can't remember what colours the others were. I got a jersey and pants. My sister Norah was now going out to work for a draper in Ballinasloe called J. Smith, and later for the sergeant of the guards. My second eldest brother James, was also working for Lord Crofton, who lived in a mansion in the wood about two miles away. I remember one day when the school was closed taking James his dinner, it was half a griddle cake with butter and a pint bottle of tea.

He gave me several apples, which were very big and sweet. I had never seen a real apple before, as the crab or wild apples were small and sour and very hard. The apples my brother gave me were better by far than those we stole from Nolan's garden when they set the dogs after us. I heard that crab apples were dangerous to eat. I stayed with my brother until he finished his meal and then walked back with him to where he worked in a ten-acre turnip field. I asked him for a turnip to take home, and he told me to ask the foreman, who gave me a whole armful. It was now beginning to get dark and I had never been so far away from home before. I still had a mile to walk when I reached the wood wall, and about three hundred yards was thick undergrowth. If I had come back the way I came that is to follow the path, there would have been no difficulty. I stopped at the wood wall, it was now quite dark, I would have to pass 'Nolan's corner' or the place where uncle Peter saw the ghost. I wish Dad had not told us that story, he was always frightening us about banshees and devils and bogymen. I went into the wood now but ran out again after about twenty yards. I followed the wall around until I reached the path. This path took me straight to our own far acre field a distance of only a hundred yards away. By this method I was able to by pass the haunted corner.

When I arrived home I discovered that it was Saturday and Mick had brought home a sheep's head, which Mother cooked with the turnips. I was happy to have been able to get them, as Mick was very fond of boiled turnips. It was good to see everybody standing around the table, enjoying a meal, and I felt proud that I should have been able to contribute. Dad was now getting ready to go out, he always went visiting when the chimney wasn't drawing correctly. When the wind came from the north the kitchen was always full of smoke. The smoke made me cough and gave me sore eyes. Mother advised me to sit on the floor. This was a good idea, because smoke has a tendency to climb. James was now home and having his supper. I was hoping he would ask Mick to go with him to set the snares, they often set snares on Saturday night, to catch rabbits. For several weeks now they caught nothing. Mick said the rabbits in our district were too clever and he mentioned going to Clonbrock which was several miles away, in which case I would not be able to go, as they would go on bicycles. There was no mention of setting snares, they were going to a dance at the cross roads.

When they had left I noticed Mother was crying. She always cried when there was no food, but we had enough to last two days. Mick had brought home a stone of flour and tea and sugar. Joe had bought a few stones of potatoes with the money he made from collecting bottles, jam jars and rabbit skins. Mother looked at me and said, 'they are coming to bring ye away on Monday'. It had been completely forgotten about, at least no one ever mentioned it. I was hoping, said Mother, that we could be all together at Christmas. We have been promised a goose. I had a letter from Mr Costello saying he was thankful for the work Dad had done, and would bring the goose on Christmas Eve. Last Christmas was the worst ever. We had nothing except the can of flour which Mother borrowed from Mrs Cosgrove. Mother went early next morning and asked the Parish Priest if we could be allowed to remain at home for Christmas. The P.P. promised to do his best. On the following Monday a Civic Guard called and said that we would not be taken away for another month. The time now seemed to fly, the days came and went like minutes. The goose did arrive on Christmas Eve. We got £3 from the States. My Mother, Jack and I went to the village, with the donkey and cart. We bought more groceries than I had ever seen before, in addition to a double supply of tea, sugar, bread, flower, butter and jam. We also bought cutlery. We got cups and saucers and nine mugs. Jack reminded Mother that as we would be leaving home soon, we didn't need so many mugs. That made Mother cry which spoiled every-thing. On the way home we met many friends, including Mrs. Linard, Mrs. White and Kate Tulley. Mrs Linard invited Jack and I to call before we left home.

When we turned off the main road to go down the boreen, the cart wheels got stuck in the mud, it was always bad this time of the year, and we had to get off the cart and lift it bodily out of some of the deep holes. We were an hour late getting home. When Mother mentioned the condition of the boreen to Dad he promised to repair it immediately after the New Year. He then went on to explain in detail to the two neighbours the way in which he planned to carry out the repairs. First of all the boreen would have to be cleaned, all the mud would be shovelled away, and then the holes filled with small stones from the quarry. As the boreen was two hundred yards long, about twenty tons of course sand was needed. Dad knew where he could buy coarse sand at one shilling and six pence a ton.

I am sure Dad really intended to carry out the work. I think he believed what he said, but he just couldn't tackle anything at home. I have seen a concrete floor he made for Beck White, a new door for James Spellman and a wooden gate for the Dillons. He cured Nolan's cow when she broke a leg. When Mitchell's' horse fell into a bog hole the whole village turned out to give a hand, but after many unsuccessful attempts, my father who was asleep by the fire, when told about the trouble didn't even wait to put on his coat. He done the job in one hour, the horse was in perfect health when released. It was common knowledge that Dad was the best judge of cattle or horses in the district. Only a few months ago Paddy Linard asked Dad to go to town with him, as he wanted to buy two young pigs.

The kitchen was now full of smoke, it was difficult to recognise anyone. We were sitting on small stools which James and Paddy had made by simply getting a very straight branch of a tree and cutting it into short blocks about nine inches long. Paddy Linard told Mother it was dangerous to sit on the damp floor, and it would spoil our new clothes. We were now having tea with plenty of bread and jam. Mother said we could have as much sugar as we wanted, it was good to drink tea from a new mug with a handle. The other day I burned my fingers when holding the jam-jar of tea. The following day was Christmas. We were up earlier than usual because it was fine and warm. I liked fine weather because I could wander through the fields. Jack and I would go to Tulley's to see the foal and the lambs, old Pat Tully never set the dog after us, as did the Carty's.

Mother said she would cook the dinner outside to-day because she was sick of that dark smoky hole. Mick said he would knock a big hole in the wall after Christmas, right next to where Dad usually sits, so that he would have to do something about the windows. When we arrived home, dinner was ready to serve. I found it difficult to use the knife and fork for the first time, so I just ate with my fingers. The goose was boiled with onions, and the soup, which was served in mugs, was delicious. It was by far the best meal we ever had, and I can never remember eating so much. After dinner, Dad prayed out loud and thanked God for everything he had sent us. He asked God to be merciful and kind to his children in their new Catholic home.

Early one morning about two weeks later a loud knock came to the door. It was the Civic Guards. They waited outside, until we had breakfast. I remember well, my Mother washing my face with the dishrag, and telling me not to be lonely. She was saying between sobs that we were going to nice Christian people, she promised to write often and would send us a homemade cake with raisins and currants. She would be able to come and see us perhaps in a year, if God wills it. We were now ready to go, that is six of us. My two eldest brothers and sister as well as the baby remained at home. We were now going up the boreen. I could hear the screams of Mother and Dad. Something dreadful had now happened. Mother was running to try and catch up with us when she stumbled and fell to the ground. Mother had been bad on her legs since baby was born. She was now being assisted to her feet by a kindly policeman. We had now reached the police car, which was an old Ford. It was parked on the main road as the boreen was too narrow. The distance to Ballinasloe was four and a half miles. We sat on the policemen's knees.

We were served with tea on arrival at the barracks, and then Joe was sent across the road to buy sweets. I wondered why everyone had cried because to me, it was all so exciting, something quite new, an adventure. We were now having great fun, the guards were marching us up and down the barracks. I wondered then why people should be afraid of the police. I thought they were so good and kind. Dinner was now being served by a kindly middle-aged lady.

After dinner we were given more sweets, and a lady now arrived to take us to Galway. It was the same person who first came to our house several months before. We were now all lined up in the barracks, the guards and the cook were saying goodbye. Four, that is Joe, Paddy, Jack and I went to the station, Larry and Martin were too young to go to the Christian Brothers, so they remained in the barracks overnight, and were taken to the nuns convent at Kilkenny the following day. The journey to Galway was not unpleasant. I remember Joe who was then thirteen years old, asking the lady who was our escort, how she could write a letter with the rocking of the train.

My thoughts now went back to what my Mother had said to me one evening when we were alone. She talked about her own home life in Roscommon before the match was made. This seemed very strange to me, because I could not think of her being anywhere else. I had imagined her to have been always in the village of Cappagh with Dad. Mother told me how when she was about twenty-four years old, her father brought her to the October fair at Ballinasloe and in the presence of a man called a matchmaker an agreement was reached to the effect that she would marry a man called James Tyrell on a certain date. Mother explained to me what it was like, coming to Cappagh, after leaving a good home. Her house was of two stories and whitewashed. She had twenty acres of good land, in front of the house was a beautiful garden, with apple trees, there was a spring well less than a hundred yards from her back door. In Cappagh we had to travel over a mile for water.

I no longer felt any love for my Father. I never spoke to him again unless it was necessary. From then onwards I thought of him as the man who hurt Mother, the man who brought my Mother from a beautiful home to a filthy stable. I thought of Dad as an irresponsible person, who ruined Mother's life and changed her from a beautiful girl into a crippled old woman.

The train had now reached Galway station and we were taken in charge by a Christian Brother called Dooley.

2

First Year at School

We are now on our way to Clifden by train. Brother Dooley is talking to Joe, he is friendly and asking a lot of questions about our home and parents, have we ever been to school? What standards were we in, our age, etc. I notice his hands, they are blue, he is probably cold. Every time I look at Brother Dooley he seems to be looking at me, so I just look away or look on the floor. He now takes off his hat and places it on the seat, he is very bald, I never seen anyone without a single hair on his head before. Brother Dooley now speaks to Jack and I. He said he is happy because we are so young there will be plenty of time for us to go to school, and learn a trade. It's a pity he said, that Joe can only spend a year at school. He would then go to the bakers shop.

He told us that we may find everything strange for a week or two, we would have to live with very many other lads just like ourselves. We would attend Mass every morning at seven o'clock. Paddy now said we usually went to eleven o'clock mass at home, and added that if we go to seven o'clock we would have to get up in the middle of the night. At this, Brother Dooley laughed. It was good to see him laugh. He was much too sad looking. Perhaps, you went to bed late at home said he. Joe answered we couldn't go to be until the neighbours left the kitchen, because we slept on the kitchen floor. Brother Dooley asked what time the neighbours left. Paddy answered and said we didn't have a clock.

The train was now slowing down. We had reached Clifden. The place looked strange, at home, the fields were flat but here the land was hilly and there wasn't much grass. There was a nice man now taking us to a waiting car, it was the same kind of car in which we had travelled to the police station. It must have been late now, but it wasn't too dark as we travelled along the road we seemed to climb hills all the time and then down the other side. There were mountains all round us, and we could see beautiful streams and waterfalls.

When I seen the water I felt dry. I asked brother Dooley if I could have a drink from the waterfall, and he said we would be at Letterfrack in half an hour. It seemed ages before we arrived at the school. We had to stop once because there were goats on the road

11

which reminded me of our own goat at home. I then remembered the time several years before when the goat attacked my young brother. We decided to cut her horns off, we caught her and took her into the kitchen. We all stood around holding the goat while my Mother started cutting the first horn with the saw. What happened now made Mother scream, she cut too near the head and the horn started to bleed. We were all now afraid, and Mother said her prayers.

The motorcar was now stopped as we had reached the monastery where the Christian Brothers lived. We had tea in the master's room, and then were taken to the infirmary and given a bath by the nurse. We slept in the infirmary that night and had our breakfast next morning there. There were too big boys ill in bed, one was called John Cane, a shoe maker, and 'scykey'. I think 'scykey' was a nick name, and he was suffering from an injured leg.

Brother Dooley had now arrived and said he would give us a change of clothing. My brothers asked to be allowed to keep their own suits which were quite new. Brother Dooley informed us that it was against the school rules, for any boy to keep his own suit, so we had to give up our nice American clothes. We were given suits which we did not like, they were made from very tough material like a blanket.

We were now taken down a hill towards the school, on our right was the monastery, and next to the monastery, several men were engaged in cutting down trees, where the new chapel was to be built. We continued down, on our left was the glasshouse. Brother Dooley explained that fruit and vegetables grew there all the year round. I was very interested in the green tomatoes which I thought were apples. Sixty yards further we came to the new building, where the Electric power house and laundry were, upstairs was the very young children's dormitory. We now climbed about a dozen steps. This was the terrace. On the left was the water pump, on the right was the bakehouse, next door was the tailors shop, next the shoemakers, the carpenters, the black-smiths, the mechanics shop. Next was the room where articles were made from plywood and were cut out with a fret saw machine. Next door was the darning and knitting room and the last room was the office where the superior and the office Brother worked. We will turn about to go back down again, on our right is the gymnasium and next-door is the wheelwright's shop. Another twenty yards now and we are back on the terrace, there is a gate at each end, and steps going down to the yard where the children carry out physical training drill and games. As we stand on the terrace, we can see a hundred and sixty boys, some of them are playing handball, others are playing 'tig', but the majority are just standing about some leaning against the wall.

Now all at once a Christian Brother comes running out, he is chasing the young children with a very long stick and beating them on the backs of the legs. We can now hear the screams of the little boys some of them are only six years old. We are now frightened and struck with horror. We looked at Brother Dooley, he explained that the children get lazy and they just stand about or lean against the wall.

We are now taken down the steps to the yard or playground. I am now very lonely and frightened. Most of the children are terribly pale, and their faces are drawn and haggard. They are not like the children at home in Ahascragh school. They were always happy and smiling. The children of Letterfrack are like old men, most of their eyes are sunk in their heads and are red from crying. Their cheek-bones are sticking out. Joe now said, look at their hands. There was a boy of about my age (eight) the backs of his hands were terribly swollen, they were just a red mass of raw flesh. Brother Dooley explained that it was chilblains, which were caused by the cold, and not taking sufficient exercise.

We were reminded that we may be the same unless we played and ran about. We now came to a boy of nine years, he was leaning against the wall, they called him 'caleba' he was holding his hands loosely in front of the body, he was apparently asleep. There was another boy, beating him with a stick, to try and keep him awake. A boy now came running past us, he was about ten years old. He had very fair hair and was wearing glasses as he was almost blind, he was being chased by the same Christian Brother we seen earlier, beating the children. We were told his name was Brother Walsh, he was hitting the fair haired boy across the back and the legs with a heavy stick. Brother Dooley told us that this boy had a lazy mind and it was hoped that the beating would make him think like normal children.

Brother Walsh now blew his whistle, and we all lined up, in what was called divisions. I was put with the second youngest division or number thirteen table in the Refectory (Dining Room). We were now marched off to school. Jack and I were put in the infants, as we had not been to school very much at home. Paddy was in second standard and Joe in third. Brother Walsh was in charge of our school, that is infants, first and second standards. Mr McAntaggart, the band-master, taught the infants, Brother Walsh the first and second.

The infants had no desks, but would stand around the blackboard, we were given a slate and slate pencil. It was the custom not to punish children the first day. McAntaggart was himself an ex-industrial school inmate from Artane. He did not beat the children very severely but slapped them on the hands with the drumstick, after every subject, or in the case of sums, after each sum, if the answer was incorrect. I had not been very long in the school probably a few weeks when Brother Kelly came into the classrooms, and told McAntaggart that in future the infants should use the bandroom as there was a fire there (Brother Kelly was then the office Brother).

After school we had lunch at about one o'clock, lunch consisted of a bowl of soup and two potatoes, the following day, we had a small slice of meat, two potatoes and a spoonful of peas or cabbage. Some days we also got half a slice of bread. After lunch unless we were detailed for washing up, we had half an hours recreation. At two o'clock boys went to their respective workshops or farms, the very young children would be under Mr Griffin, or work in the darning and knitting room. Mr Griffin taught us to tease the hair or fibre which went into the mattresses. This fibre came to us in ropes and had to be loosened up bit by bit with the fingers. This work was normally done in the Gymnasium, when the hair fibre was well teased it was then put into sacks and delivered to the tailor's shop, where mattresses were made.

Boys left the workshop at five o'clock for one hour recreation, and school again from six until seven. We then had supper, which consisted of a mug of cocoa (unsweetened) and one and a half slices of bread and margarine. After supper we played for half an hour and then went to the schoolroom to say the Rosary. We were in bed by eight thirty. The following morning, we were called at six am. We went to the washroom where soap and water was provided. After having washed we were lined up to be inspected. Those who did not wash their head, face, neck and arms correctly, were beaten on the hands by Brother Walsh, who was in charge of St. Michael's Dormitory. We then got dressed and paraded down stairs in the school, to say our morning prayers, before going to the chapel to Mass. After Mass we were marched to the yard, and sometimes would do drill. At other times, we were allowed to play until eight o'clock, when we would have breakfast of cocoa and one and a half slices of brown or white bread.

On Sunday we got tea with sugar. Sunday was a day devoted almost entirely to religious education or prayers, except for two hours in the afternoon, when we went to the football field to play football. As there was no school in the normal sense, on Sundays, we were not beaten as much as on weekdays, except by Brother Walsh who would sneak out of his room which was at the end of St.

Michaels Dormitory. He would listen, or look through the key hole, and anyone who was talking or out of bed was taken away, and beaten naked. About ten or fifteen boys were picked out each Sunday, at about 6.30 am. The reason why some of the children were awake was because we normally got up at 6 am during the week. Brother Walsh normally used a leather strap, but on Sunday he preferred a stick and heavy cane.

During my first eighteen months, or two years at school, there had been three different people in charge of the kitchen and the refectory. Mr Hogan, Mr. Ackle and Brother O'Rourke. Hogan and Ackle had been inmates of Letterfrack. Mr Hogan was a thorough gentleman. I heard it said that he had been a soldier in the British Army. Ackle always carried an ash plant and often flogged the very young children during meal times. Brother O'Rourke was very good and kind, and would give extra food when requested, he had ginger hair and was young, about twenty five.

We are now about six months at school and it's summer time, additional desks are provided at the back of the school. We have up until now been in the band room, but are now back again with Brother Walsh. As I sit at my desk, I see my brother Paddy and others being savagely beaten on the back, the head and face. They are now doing mental arithmetic, as they are asked a question, they must answer immediately, or be beaten. At first the lads used to leave their desk and line up to be slapped, but now they are beaten at their desk to save time. The lesson is over, we are dismissed, and I run to speak to Paddy and ask him if the strap hurt very much. He just laughs and says it was nothing, but I can see that his right eye is swollen and almost closed.

It's now the month of June, and everyone is talking about the holidays. The first four Brothers will be going away for six weeks very soon, the three in charge of the classrooms and dormitories, and the office Brother usually leave together. The boys are also on holiday at this time, which means that the classrooms close down for lessons, and the boys are at play during the school period, but go to the workshops in the usual way. Every one looks forward to this time of year. It is the time that the pets get beaten up, by the other lads. The pets are the Christian Brothers favourites, almost all Brothers have at least one pet. The pets are with the Brothers at most times except when they are going about looking for information. They are expected to spy on other children and carry stories to their masters. When the boys notice a pet nearby, the word 'nix' was passed round, and everyone was now on their guard. But the pets were useful in some ways, if we wanted something, say for example a new pair of braces, or a change of boots, we could buy the pet over for a penny or a few sweets, he would then speak to the Brother concerned, this method was usually successful and we got what we wanted.

During the holiday period we were not beaten except by the superior Brother Keegan. He used to come down to the yard everyday about ten o'clock, he carried a long heavy stick. Brother Keegan was a big man and he usually wore leggings. I never seen him beat the very young children, but he would often take two or three lads away and beat them with their pants off. On one occasion I noticed two boys, after such a beating, their legs were cut and bleeding. There never was any reason given for this beating, but I heard that it was the result of information carried by the pets.

I myself can't remember been beaten in this manner, but I have been beaten on other occasions by Keegan. He would come around sometimes on a Saturday morning when we were not at school lessons, and would blow his whistle, we would fall in, in the usual manner and he would examine the head and hands, he would then make us take off our jersey and shirt and examine them for body lice. Children who had lice in their hair or clothing would be 'skinned' which was the word for being beaten with the pants off. Keegan in spite of all this was a very religious man, his brother was a priest and came to the school on two occasions.

Keegan was just as strict with the Brothers as with the children, he *never* allowed late nights, nor did he allow the Brothers to have girlfriends. Brother Rairdon was in charge of the farm for seventy years, he never came near the yard. He was very severe with the boys under him. 'Bulldog', one of the boys on the farm, told me that Rairdon was in the habit of making the boys kneel down before beating them on the back and legs with a blackthorn stick which he always carried.

Brother Scully was the farm Brother after Rairdon, he was very good to the children. I remember him taking us to Diamond Hill about a mile east of the school one Sunday. He gave us bread and jam and then told us stories. He then sang us a song the words were, 'work boys, work', and he continued, 'as long as you've enough to buy a meal, you'll be happy, bye and bye, you'll be happy, bye and bye, if you only put your shoulder to the wheel.' He then gave us a pinch of snuff which made us sneeze. Next day we got a parcel from home and a letter from Mother with a half crown in it. We couldn't agree on how much we were to get each so we went to Mr Griffin for advice.

Mr Griffin was a schoolteacher at Letterfrack for more than forty years, he was present in the yard every day, and was good to the children, he would read and write their letters for them. When the Brothers were on holiday, Mr Griffin often took us for a walk to the sea front about a mile away. We could go in the sea or not, as we desired. We would then all sit around and he would tell us stories. He once told us about when he and another teacher came to Letterfrack in the year 1882. They were then paid eight shillings a week, and his friend left to join the army, because he wouldn't get another shilling. Life is good during the holidays. We can pick blackberries in the football field. We can play in the school room when it's raining, or we can leave the yard without being beaten. Yesterday I went to the kitchen and asked Mr Logan for a crust and he gave me a big piece of bread and sweet tea.

Cunningham a big boy in infants can make a rag ball to bounce just like a rubber ball. He has lots of cloth, which he got from the tailors shop, he gets a small piece of cloth and sews it together folding it up as small as possible, and continues to sew until it is perfectly round, he has an old inner tube of a bicycle which he cuts into very narrow strips. This thin rubber is now wound round the rag ball and is kept very tight. It is wound in many different directions and then fastened securely. It is then covered with another piece of material and again sewn until it is perfectly round. He also made spin-tops which were as good as any from the shop. The Letterfrack boys made their own toys. Cunningham was eleven years old and still in infants, he never learned to read or write.

The holidays are now almost over the Brothers will be back in another week. The children no longer smile, very few of them play, they just stand around in small groups, they just whisper to each other, they are afraid to be overheard. That frightened look has returned to their faces. The next few days are spent polishing and cleaning the dormitory. Every boy sweeps under his own bed, it is then polished. The wash basins are cleaned thoroughly and the taps are cleaned with brasso everyday. Our boots must be repaired before next week. There will be an inspection on Monday. It's now Sunday. We go to Mass in silence. After breakfast we go to the football field. Our last day of freedom for another year. We have lunch. Mr Hogan is in charge and he is responsible for the cooking, he is a good cook and he gives extra potatoes and cabbage if asked for. Brother O'Rourke has been in charge until recently, some say he is ill in hospital, others say he has gone away to another school. Mr Hogan comes to the school quite often. There was a story that he is going to marry the nurse. After lunch Brother Keegan, the superior, comes to the yard, he always carries that big stick. He doesn't often beat the lads, but we are afraid of him.

He brings his dog Spot, a cocker spaniel and Mr Griffin has his little dog Toby a ginger crossbreed. Keegan now lifts Spot and throws him at Toby and they start to fight. Keegan often does this because his dog always wins. Keegan's dog Spot now has little Toby by the throat, and is shaking him. Brother Keegan is now clapping his hands and laughing loudly. One of the older boys now lifts Spot off the ground by catching him by the hind legs. Spot now looses his grip, Toby is now badly hurt and some of the boys are crying, because Mr Griffin lets them play with Toby. Mr Griffin now carries his dog away to the glasshouse where it is warm.

Brother Keegan now takes us to the football field for an hour. There are two footballs for the whole school, so that the majority, either watch the game, or play Cowboys and Indians. We return for tea. After tea Brother Kelly reads a letter, from a man who has left the school more than ten years before (Brother Kelly the office Brother has been on holiday and just returned). This man writes of conditions in Letterfrack from 1910 until 1916 during which time he was an inmate of the school. This man writes saying that escapes were so common, that both gates were kept locked day and night and a monitor kept watch on the terrace all the time. Escapes were attempted in spite of the fact that when caught children were *skinned* every day until they were removed to a reform school for several years. Brother Kelly never beats the children himself, nor does he know they are being beaten on the head and face.

The following morning Monday, we report back to school after six weeks. Brother Dooley in charge of 5th and 6th standards, Brother Byrne 4th and 3rd, and Brother Walsh, infants, first and second. Our school is in silence. As Walsh walks in we jump to our feet. The entrance to our school is at the rear, and it is an offence for any one to glance round when the door opens, two boys are called up and warned but not beaten, Walsh never carries the strap the first day, every one knows this

We don't do very much at lessons. We say our prayers, and Mr Moran teaches us Irish. He is a native of Letterfrack. Brother Walsh then takes over, and asks questions about what happened during the time he was away.

We are now reminded of the coming exams that we must work hard in the future, and that backward children will be severely beaten. We must not speak or whisper or look around during classes.

We must not speak in the Dormitory our beds must be kept clean and tidy. All beds must be kept in line, every boy is held responsible for the floor under his bed, it must be swept every day and kept polished. We must use insect powder on our clothes in order to kill the vermin.

Pants and jerseys would be inspected every night before going to bed. Any boys found to have lice on their clothes would be beaten. Every night we would spend fifteen minutes picking lice from our clothes and bedding. In future all boys must ask permission before going on to the terrace for a drink of water, as the pump is on the terrace. The same day at school Mr McAntagart has now left, and a new band master Dan Kelly has replaced him. Mr Kelly is a very small man, he is now teaching the infants, he also uses the drumstick to beat us, but he only slaps us on the hands. We stand around the blackboard for sums, and get slapped as usual when the answer is not correct. I and most of the infants now look round as Brother Walsh beats the boys in first standard. He stands at the back of each one as he is asked a question, and beats them on the back if he does not answer as soon as the question is put. Walsh now rushes down and shouts at Mr Kelly for allowing us to look round, he then lined us up against the wall and slaps each one three times. Mr Moran now takes charge of first standard and Walsh goes back to his own class, second. He starts off by giving everyone two slaps because someone was talking, and no one will say who it is.

He then starts off with catechism. No one is able to answer the questions quick enough, so they are ordered to lay their hands on the desk palm downward, and are beaten on the backs of the hands. Brother Walsh then says everyone is asleep so he orders every one to stand up for the remainder of the morning.

My brother Jack and I are in infants. Jack and I always manage to be together, and Cunningham the boy of eleven is on my other side. He is very backward and is beaten several times during every lesson. We are now preparing for an exam which is to be in a month or so. After the exam, most of the boys are promoted to a higher class. Jack and I now go to first. Cunningham remains with infants. My other brother Paddy goes to another school next door under Mr Griffin. I am very happy now because Paddy has left second-class. It was painful to see him being beaten every day. Paddy was always good at school when we were at home.

My older brother Joe now has finished with school except for one hour in the evening from 6 pm until 7 pm. I see Paddy every day now after school and he is getting on very well. He likes Mr Griffin who is an old man and every one says he is the best teacher in the school.

When Brother Dooley, who is in charge of the senior boys, is unable to do a sum he sends for Mr Griffin. Mr Moran who is our teacher in First is very nice, he never slaps us unless Walsh tells him to do so. Mr Moran leaves us for an hour each day because he has to teach Irish in the other school. Walsh now takes over our class while second class is learning a subject from their books. Walsh stands behind each boy whilst he asks a question. He beats everyone at the end of half an hour. We now get another letter and a cake from Mother this is the 3rd since we left home. Everyone at home is well, Dad has got a contract to supply stone for the mental Hospital at Ballinasloe at 2 shillings and six pence a ton. Mother says Dad has put in the two windows in the old house and he will soon make a concrete floor.

It's Sunday and after Mass we have drill in the yard, Brother Dooley takes charge. We are all lined up, the boots are inspected, and many boys are beaten for worn boots. We are now taught exercises, bending the arms, forward sideways upwards and downwards, we are taught to bend the body to the left and right, keeping the hands on the hips. Then we do full knees bend, and touching the toes with the fingers, keeping the knees and legs perfectly straight. We are taught how to turn to the left the right and about. We now do marching in single file, in twos and fours.

Brother Dooley beats the senior boys on the back and the legs with a walking stick. He beats John Cane so severely that he leaves the ranks and runs screaming out of the yard, he goes to the lavatory and refuses to leave. He is now being beaten for a long time, four boys are ordered to carry him to the infirmary. He is bleeding from the mouth and nose. John Cane is sixteen and due to leave the school very soon. We are now marching around the square, and Brother Dooley rushes through the ranks and hits big Scally with the stick on the back, for being out of step. We are now dismissed. That evening we are given a lecture lasting an hour, we then say the Rosary. Brother Dooley asks us all to pray for him as he is suffering from rheumatism. The next morning, I am awake early. Brother Walsh has just returned from the chapel, and he is taking six or seven lads away for being awake. It's now about 6 am. I can hear the children screaming. He has taken them to the washroom and flogged them with a stick. It is a crime to be awake before we are called.

During the months that follow life does not alter very much, boys come and go at the rate of about two a month. We now have a new boy called John Coyne, he has been sent to the school because his father has murdered his mother, and his father is in prison. There is a very young lad he is only three and a half. His Mother has just died. He is the youngest boy ever to arrive at Letterfrack. Most of the Brothers come every day to see this little lad, and they make a fuss of him. He is not beaten for several months. It's now dark very early in the evenings, it's almost winter. All the lads are looking forward to the time when they get apples and nuts. We will get an apple and a handful of nuts. Big Tom baker told me that nobody gets beaten that day, unless they leave the yard or do something very bad. Tom Baker is over fifteen. Tom also said that we will be allowed to talk at meals that day, just like Christmas, or Easter. Last Easter we got a letter from home and a cake. For breakfast we got a boiled egg and a slice of currant cake.

3
The Second Year

My brothers now play with lads of their own age and I have made friends with Con Murphy, Tommy Gordon and Martin Mullins. We are all in the same class.

We play together with a rag ball, which Cunningham has made. This ball is really wonderful. It will bounce straight up. Other lads have tried making a rag ball but they are not round enough, so they bounce to one side. I often wonder why Cunningham is unable to learn at school because he is so good at making toys, the other day Tony Hewitt gave him a cotton reel he got from the tailors shop and he made a lovely spinning top by cutting the wide rim off with a piece of glass and then pointing one end. He then pushed a piece of wood through the centre and then got a coffin nail, which he hammered into the narrow end. Cunningham will make a toy for anyone for a half slice of bread. Last week he made a car with four wheels, and two seats from a piece of wood and cotton reels. He promised to make me a boat for Christmas because I help him with the sums.

I am now in first standard and he is in infants so he can't copy off me, but he has a small piece of chalk and we go to the lavatory, and do the sums on the floor. He is now beginning to understand simple addition and yesterday he got two sums correct, and he was only beaten once. Tommy Gordon has promised to teach him the alphabet. It will be wonderful when Cunningham learns to read and write, his ears are cut and bleeding from being beaten. Brother Walsh now spends a half hour a day with first and infants when his own class are learning Irish. Walsh now beats everyone on the head and ears with the strap. Dick Hunt is called cauliflower ears, because they are very badly swollen and festered, they were almost healed last month, but now they look awful.

It's now Sunday morning and about twelve of us are lined up to be beaten in the washroom at the end of St. Michael's dormitory. We are ordered to take off our pants. Walsh now goes away to his room and returns with a stick. It's a new stick, which he cut a few days ago. I am at the very end and I have to see all the others flogged before me. The Murtaugh boy is now being beaten and he is screaming loudly it's frightening to hear this almost daily. It's my turn next, after about six blows I manage to run away, down the stairs and into the bathroom. Walsh now follows me down, he is now hitting me on the head and face and back, as I put up my right hand to ward off a blow he hits me a heavy blow on the arm. My arm is broken. I spend two weeks in the infirmary. A Doctor called Lavelle is now in Letterfrack. Old Dr John who lived on the hill is now dead. Lavelle comes to the school once a month. Walsh now comes to tell me to say I fell down the stairs. There is only one other boy in the infirmary, Caleba. He is suffering from sleeping sickness. The nurse has now left Letterfrack, and Brother Byrne visits us every morning and evening. The food is sent from the main kitchen and the cocoa is cold by the time we get it.

We are now alone in the infirmary, Caleba and I. The nurse used to sleep in a room at the end, but she has now gone away. Mr Hogan has also left, and Mr Hayden the baker told my brother Joe that they have got married and are living in England. She walked with a slight limp and some say she had a cork leg.

It's very lonely in the infirmary with the wood all round us. Caleba is very ill and has eaten nothing for two days. He is always asking for water, and I have to get out of bed and climb up on a chair to switch out the light. I hate going into the bathroom for the water because there is no light there.

Dr Lavelle came to see us again the next day. He spends a long time with Caleba. Brother Keegan and he come to my bed. He asked me how I had fallen down the stairs, and I said that the stairs were slippy because they were polished every day. He then found marks on my head, ears and back. He looked at my hands. He then took the bed clothes off my bed to examine my feet and legs. The backs of the legs still had marks of the stick. He then left with the superior. The Doctor again came in the late evening to see Caleba.

That night I had to get water only once. When I awoke next morning I went to see Caleba. He was very quiet, so I got back into bed and must have fallen asleep again. The breakfast of bread and cocoa had now arrived, and Brothers Dooley, Kelly and Keegan had arrived. They told me that Caleba was dead. There was no school that day, so the boys were allowed to come and kneel by the bed of the corpse to pray. The body was now laid out in the room next to the road. After the funeral I remained in the infirmary for a week, alone every night. I was terribly frightened and would have run out if the door was unlocked. I was now allowed up and could go and have my meals in the refectory, before the others, because Brother Byrne explained, my arm might get hurt again, when the boys rushed in for their food.

A new nurse had now arrived. She was tall and thin, she was very good to me and often made tea in the infirmary kitchen. She would sit on my bed knitting for several hours each day. When I was well enough to return to school she said I would be leaving the next day. The thought of returning to school and the dormitory made me ill. I was allowed to remain another two days. On the afternoon of the last day the nurse took me for a walk through the farm, which was only a hundred yards away. I liked the farm, there were lots of hens and chickens and geese as well as turkeys. Tommy Mannion who lived near Letterfrack worked on the farm. He told us there were more than a hundred birds in the wire netting enclosure. There were also a dozen tame rabbits and a baby fox, which was found on Diamond Hill. We now stood and watched the water pond, and again walked on through the farm. We continued towards Diamond Hill. We now sat on the grass and she asked me if I was looking forward to returning to school, and was surprised when I answered no. On our way back we passed a field where the bull and many cows were. When we arrived back at the infirmary the nurse went to the monastery where she had her supper, and I went to the refectory. I was late and the boys were already seated. I went to the kitchen and got a mug of cocoa, and a slice of bread and dripping. I liked dripping.

I sat at my own table beside Martin Mullins. He told me that Brother Walsh would soon be leaving and another Brother would be in charge of us. That was good news and now I was no longer afraid. When I returned to the infirmary the nurse was waiting. The dressing was now taken off my arm and I had a bath and to bed. When the nurse sat on the end of my bed after making tea, I asked her if she had any brothers or sisters. She said she had a sister in the States. Her Mother and Father had died recently. Next morning the nurse and I went to Mass and I joined the boys. I had missed many lessons and now I was told by Mr Moran that I would have to catch up with the other lads, or else stay in first class for another year. I didn't want that, so I decided to ask Martin Mullins to help me with the lessons and sums during playtime. During the next few weeks, life was a little better in the school. We were not beaten so much on the head or the face, only on the front and backs of the hands.

We tried to keep our clothing clean of vermin, but it was impossible. Whenever lice were found Walsh always flogged us. He still kept on beating boys on Sunday Mornings. It's now well over a month since I have had my pants taken off. The two Down's brothers, the two Finnegans, Tommy Berry, John Coyne, Murtaugh, the Feericks from Castlebar, the two Giblins, the McLoughlins from

Leitrim, John Bowen and a new boy from Galway, Tommy Ward, Haywood, all of these boys and many others I have seen flogged on Sunday at six thirty a.m.

Most of the children in St. Michael's dormitory wet the bed so there is a night man who goes around. He lives a mile from Letterfrack, near the haunted house in the wood. When he finds a bed wet he puts the child across his bed and beats him with a strap. The night man now gets sacked for stealing clothing. He also steals coal and potatoes. The new night man is much better to the children. The boys who wet the bed have a towel fastened to the head of the bed, and they are called periodically. The reason for the towel is to indicate who should be called. The new man is a very good Irish speaker, and he is able to help us with our Irish lessons. He comes to the dormitories about nine o'clock. Last night he sat on the end of my bed, and told me that he remembered when Mr Griffin first came to Letterfrack, well over forty years ago. He remembers playing football against Griffin in Cleggan in the year 1899. Brother Walsh now leaves the school. He takes second class for the last time. He beats no one on his last day. The new Brother has arrived. His name is Conway and he is very young. Everyone stands up as Brother Walsh leaves the school. He says good-bye and there is not an answer, the children stand motionless and with bowed heads.

It's now on the day we get apples and nuts. We all parade in the yard and bags of apples and nuts are brought from the office. We each get an apple and two handfuls of nuts. There are four main feast days, Christmas, Easter and Tully strand day – when we go to the seaside for a day – and Halloween. Our teacher Mr Moran is now very ill. He has been confined to bed for several weeks. Dr Lavelle sees him everyday, but he is getting weaker, and we are asked to pray for him. The following week he died aged thirty three. All the boys are allowed to visit Mr Moran's house. Mr Moran's father is the school blacksmith and Miss Moran is his sister. She is in charge of the knitting and the darning room. We are now without a teacher in first standard, so Brother Kelly the office Brother spends an hour a day with us and the superior takes us on catechism, as we will shortly have an examination when the priest visits the school in three weeks. Brother Kelly now leaves the school and is replaced by Brother Murphy. Everyone is sorry to lose Brother Kelly, because he has been good and kind to everyone. He never refused to give us a stamp when we were writing home. Catechism is now the only subject we are taught for the next few weeks, and the superior is in charge of us each day. He does not beat us very often, only just a slap on the hand.

As there is no one in charge of the cooking so Mr Hayden the baker gives a hand, and the new officer Brother Murphy also helps. All the Brothers now take charge of the meals in turn.

We heard the other day that there would be a new man coming shortly to take charge of the refectory and kitchen. They say he has been in a deaf and dumb school for seven years. The priest has now arrived and we all have to wash ourselves carefully and comb our hair. Brother Keegan has brought down two big white combs, which he bought in the village. The catechism exam is very simple and most of us pass, those who are backward are given another chance.

It is now almost Christmas, and we have a mission which lasts a week. Every year at this time a missioner visits the school and he says Mass each morning, and gives a sermon every evening, which lasts an hour. This is to prepare us for the feast of Christmas. At the end of the mission everyone makes a confession. On Christmas Eve we do little or no work except to decorate the school and the refectory with Holly and we make chains of ivy.

Christmas day is a big occasion and there are few restrictions. After Mass we have breakfast without having to parade and be marched to the refectory. In addition to the usual, bread and margarine we have corn (?) loaf and extra tea if required. During the day we can talk anywhere without permission, and we may leave the yard or go into the Village to the shops. About half the lads get a parcel or letter at Christmas. We get a cake and half a crown. With the money we go to the village and spend it all on sweets and chocolate. It is the practice to share everything with the children, who have no parents or those who do not hear from home.

Dinner is very good. We have roast meat, gravy and peas, followed by Christmas pudding. Very few are able to eat the pudding, so it is kept for the next day. For the evening meal there is cake, bread and jam and tea as required. After Christmas discipline is greatly relaxed. We attend the workshops or other duties, such as darning, knitting and cleaning and polishing the dormitories, but we do not attend school for a week. The Christmas spirit lasts until the New Year.

We are now back at school, and all the Decorations have been taken down, and life is back to normal. We have not yet got a regular teacher. Brother Keegan teaches us now everyday and the new Brother spends a little time with our class in the evening. Brother Keegan now enters the school and finds the boys in second standard talking, so he calls Brother Conway and tells him that he must exercise more control. He should also use the strap when necessary. He now uses the strap for the first time, but I notice that he holds the strap only about six inches over the hand, whereas Walsh always lifted it high over his shoulder. It's now very cold weather and the older lads are sliding on the ice in the yard. They always throw buckets of water on the yard at night time so that there is ice in the morning.

Dr Lavelle now sees all the children and he orders all those under ten years to go to the infirmary for cod liver oil daily. I now attend the darning class each day after school, and Miss Moran tells me to sit beside big Giblin and he will show me how to darn socks. I like the darning room because there is a fire in it. Some of the boys are being taught how to use the knitting machine, and others are learning hand knitting. It is in this room that all the stocks, socks, and jerseys are made. Miss Moran is a good teacher and the boys learn quickly. Brother Keegan sometimes comes, and one day I heard him telling Miss Moran to beat the children and he gave her a stick, which she took and threw in the fire. She said she knew her business and if he was not satisfied he could get someone else. I was in the darning room for six months. I heard Miss Moran tell the bandmaster that her age was twenty-five, and she thought twenty-five was very old.

Brother Dooley has now left the school, and he is replaced by Brother Fahy from Artane School Dublin. He is a native of Claremorris, Co. Mayo. As Brother Fahy is in charge of the senior boys I don't see him except on Sundays when he takes drill parade. We also get a new teacher called Seán McLoughlin, a native of Connemara. He teaches Irish. I heard him tell Mr Griffin he had been educated at Clifden. He intended to continue his studies, and would get a better job later on. The bandmaster Dan Kelly has also left and John Hickey takes his place. Hickey takes charge of our class in the evenings and also infants, and he is very cross with the young children and punches them in the face. He holds them by the right ear with his left hand and hits them in the face with the other. Hickey is five feet two inches and he has fair hair which is brushed straight back. I am told that Brother Fahy and Hickey are very friendly. Some say that Hickey was a pet of Fahy's many years before at Artane school. Every year there is a concert or a play, and every day now the band is having rehearsals for a play, which is due to be shown next month.

Brother Byrne is training a lot of boys who are also taking part in the play. After being shown at Letterfrack, they tour many towns in Galway and County Mayo. All the children who go on tour return with presents of some kind. On Sunday afternoons Fahy organises boxing matches between the boys. He has bought two pair of boxing Gloves. The first two to fight are 'Bullock' Fanning and Dick Whittington. Although there is a difference of two years in their ages,

Fanning is fifteen and Whittington is thirteen. And now he pairs off Tommy Ward with Joe Kelly aged fourteen who is two years older than his partner. The older boy wins in each fight. When Fahy does not like a boy, he orders him to fight a bigger and older one. It will be summer again in another month and we are preparing for our annual examination in sums, reading, writing etc. After which we shall have six weeks holidays, if we pass the exam, we will advance to a higher standard.

Brother Keegan said yesterday that we would definitely go to Tully strand this year. We did not go last year, owing to the bad weather, and when the weather improved, the lorry had broken down. But Tom Baker told my brother Joe, that that was often the excuse in previous years, and the real reason why there was no outing last year was because there wasn't enough money in the bank.

4

School Layout and Sanitation

Letterfrack in the present year 1925 is a comparatively new school, as I stand on the terrace, and face westwards. The yard or playground is just below. Straight in front is half the main building and on the left the other half, or at right angles to the first. On my right front is a wall on the ball alley, which runs from east to west. It is about ten feet height with wire netting on top. This wall connects the main building to the terrace. At the back of the wall are the toilets near the terrace end. At the back of the wall at the other end is a room where the boots, polish and brushes are kept. The toilets and boot room are entered from the yard. On the extreme right of the first half of the main building is the band room. Next door is the school for infants first and second classes, and the next room is for third and fourth standards. The next is called the library where fifth and sixth standards work.

The entrance to the library is also the entrance to the refectory and kitchens, in other words there is a small hall or porch inside the main entrance. And on the right is the door leading to the library on the left to the refectory. In the centre or between the two doors is the stairs leading to the dormitories, underneath the stairs is a tiny room where the sweets are kept or the 'shop'. At the top of the stairs on the left are the wash basins for boys in St. Patrick's dormitory, At the far end of St. Patrick's dormitory there are four rooms, where the Christian Brother, the band Master, Mr Griffin and the baker sleep. At the top of the stairs again on the right, the door leading to St. Michael's dormitory (there is a toilet at the top of the stairs). We are now in St. Michael's dormitory on the right and just inside the door is the mechanics bedroom.

There are six rows of beds or seventy two beds in all, in each dormitory. At the other end of the dormitory is the Christian Brother's room straight through and to the left is the stairs leading down to the bathroom the yard can be reached by this way. At the top of the stairs again, the door to the left leads to the washbasins there is a toilet in this room. At the other end of the washrooms, is the entrance to the new building, where the very young children sleep. The new building has been erected at the back of the second half of the main building.

St. Michael's upstairs, and the refectory down below is in the second half. The first and second half of the school are connected, and not detached, as I may have led you to believe. The main kitchen is at the far end of the refectory and leading to the new building (downstairs) where we find the laundry which is well equipped with modern washing and drying machines. Next door is the motors or engines for supplying electric light etc. The Main school building was built in the shape of the letter L, which made up half of the square. The other half was the terrace and the ball alley.

Most of the workshops are on the terrace. We now face eastwards, or away from the school, from right to left. The bakers, tailors, shoemakers, carpenters, mechanics and next is the room where fret saw work is done (plywood is cut by machine and small articles are made). The blacksmith is between the carpenters and mechanics. Next door is the darning and knitting room, and last is the main office where the superior, and the office Brother work. The wheelwright shop is situated at the west end of the gymnasium behind the ball alley. If we go along the terrace just past the main office, turn right, the chapel is sixty yards along on the left.

A new chapel is being built a hundred yards to the right. Fifty yards from the new chapel is the monastery. Where the Christian Brothers live. The infirmary is about eighty yards east of the monastery. We can now see the farmyard. In the farmyard is the slaughterhouse. The school land consists of about a hundred acres of fair and a hundred acres of poor land. There are about five local men employed on the farm, including Festy and Tommy Mannion, John Cusack carries out all the property repairs. There is a tradesman employed in each of the workshops, to teach the children a trade and also to make work for the use of the school, such as furniture, clothing, boots, pullovers, socks, and shirts etc. Mattresses, sheets and pillowcases are also produced.

As well as making for their own use the workshops carry on a lively trade with the local farmers and fishermen. Letterfrack School is to a great extent self supporting, in as much as that most requirements are produced from within. The school has its own powerhouse. The water falls, which comes from the hills and through the wood, drive the dynamo which supplies electricity. Letterfrack is less than a mile from the sea and as the wind blows in from the Atlantic, it carries salt water which, when it hits the hills, turns into rain, hence the heavy rainfall on the west coast. We are almost surrounded by hills amongst which are the Twelve Pins (or Bens). The land in Connemara is very poor and there is only a few inches of soil. The poor quality of the land is due to the salt in the air. The vegetation is very poor, and animal life suffers from this poverty. The cattle sheep and horses are a lot smaller here than anywhere else in the country. The Connemara pony is a very tiny and most beautiful animal. The mountain goats are fairly plentiful in the hilly country of Connemara. I have not yet seen any snow here, and Con Murphy told me that he has seen very little snow in these parts, he has been here for three years. Yet it must be very cold as most of the children get chilblains in the Winter, and I have seen several with frostbitten ears.

There is a quay about a mile and a half from the school. It is here the ship is tied up every summer, when a shipload of coal is brought from Scotland. We have a wonderful time unloading the coal, which is carried to the school in an old Ford lorry. Last year the superior borrowed another lorry. And it took three days to unload all the coal. As this is during the summer holidays, we all get a chance to see the ship. Before the ship was due to leave last summer, Mr Griffin took us to see her sail home. Mr Griffin said goodbye to a man who was an inmate of our school twenty years ago. Mr Griffin said he could not remember him, but the man remembered Mr Griffin and gave him a tin of tobacco. He promised to be back again with the next load of coal.

It's Saturday night and everybody has a bath. Brother Byrne is in charge tonight. We get undressed in the dormitory, and go to the bathroom about twenty at a time. It's good when Brother Byrne is in charge because he never carries a stick or strap, and he allows us to talk in the bathroom. When we return to the dormitory we get a change of shirts and socks. Sheets and pillowslips are changed every two weeks. After being washed shirts and bed linen are sent to the tailors for repair, socks go to the darning room. On Saturday night jackets and pants are examined. If they are badly torn, they are changed. Repaired clothing is sent from the tailors shop every Saturday to the dormitories. I am now put to work in the laundry, and if the weather is fine I hang out the washed clothing on a line and on bushes at the back of the kitchen, but I don't like this work because there are too many rats, where I have to hang the clothes. I told Annie Aspel about the rats and she laughed, saying they won't eat you because they are well fed. Much better fed than you boys. She told me that all the garbage, bones, fish loads, potato peelings, and all the waste are thrown out there. So she came out and showed me how to chase away the rats. She told me to throw stones at them and they would go away.

Annie Aspel is in charge of the laundry. She lives outside the school. She said that some years ago all the waste from the kitchen was taken and thrown over the drain about a hundred yards away from the laundry, near the football field. She remembered making a complaint to the superior several years before about the rats and his answer was that the rats were God's creatures, and they were sent for the benefit of mankind. He went on to explain that everything, and every animal and every insect had a purpose in life. Annie said her age was forty-eight and told me she had never been married.

She had seen thousand of lads coming and going, and couldn't understand why so many parents brought children into the world, and didn't look after them. She thought it sinful for children to be taken away from their parents at six or seven years. It was high time she said that they opened schools for parents. Annie Aspel then came closer to me and spoke in what was almost a whisper, saying my dear boy I have not been here with my eyes shut. I know what is going on. I don't have to ask questions. I can see in your face, what I have been seeing in the faces of hundreds of children for many years. No one will ever take the place of your own Mother.

The whistle blew and I went away for dinner. Brother Murphy was in charge of the refectory, and he said we could 'talk away'. We were now called to silence for a few minutes, and told that brother Vale would shortly be coming to take charge of the cooking. He would arrive after the summer holidays. A small boy at our table now put up his hand and Brother Murphy came over to see what was the matter. The boy complained that Matt Feerick had thrown a potato peel at him. Matt now jumped to his feet and shouted to the boy who complained 'you bloody sweep', at this Brother Murphy laughed loudly. Next day we are all given new caps by Brother Keegan. They are grey and blue. I have never worn a cap before, so when I go to Mass I forget to take it off.

5
Third Year

The summer examinations are now on, and all pass except Murtagh and Stapleton, so after the holidays I will be in second class with my brother Jack. We have had a fairly good time since Brother Conway came. He is very young for a teacher and he plays handball with the boys. Next week we start our holidays, and I hear that Brother Keegan has bought four new footballs, so it's going to be much better holidays than last year. Instead of just looking at other lads playing, we will be able to have our own game. As there are about a hundred and seventy boys in the school, we will not have a football every day, but about two or three times a week. Brother Keegan has now placed a monitor in charge of the young boys, one for infants and one for first class.

We had a monitor when I first came to the school, but he was a big bully and he kept most of the food for himself, so Tommy Gordon reported him and he was skinned by Keegan and sent to his own table. Scally was his name and he would wait in the lavatory and flog the boys who did not give him what he wanted. Scally had a strap just like the one Walsh had. He got it made in the shoemakers shop, it was two pieces of sole leather sewn together. He is the only one of the old bullies left, the others have gone out of the school. There were another two, one called Ackle and Moore who used to cut the children's hair. Ackle had been away to several jobs but had to be sent back to the school because he was no good. Ackle said he preferred being in Letterfrack, because he could always get his own way. He was always a pet and paid his way by carrying stories. He was most selfish and cruel to the younger children.

It's now the first week of the holidays, and four of the brothers have gone away, Fahy, Byrne, Conway and Brother Murphy the office Brother. The weather is wet so after I finish in the laundry I join the other lads in the gymnasium, where we usually go. Brother Keegan is there and he is showing the older boys how to climb the rope ladders, which are attached to the roof but hang loose at the other end. The ladders are climbed by using the hands only and the body should be kept as straight as possible. There is a billiard table also in the gym, but only the masters and the Brothers play.

There is a physical training instructor now in the school. He teaches drill and exercises by numbers. He is also teaching a class in the band room a new play, which will be acted after the holidays, before going on a tour to try and get money for the school. The play is called H.M.S. Pinafore. We have some very good singers amongst the boys, Joe Cavanagh, George Gordon and young Hunt. Tommy Gordon is coming on very well at the piano and Matty Feerick is a fairly good step dancer, although they are still very young. We now have a very good band, it's said to be the second best in the country. Hickey the new bandmaster is very good at his job, but terribly cruel to the band boys. They practice every day in the yard, and Hickey stops the band every few minutes and kicks two or three of the lads from behind. He also hits them on the head with a drumstick. There is a lot of talk about a new lorry coming to the school, and we would have it in time for 'Tully strand'. We still have the old Ford and it's all tied together with rope and bits of string, but it still goes, and never gets stuck on the road.

There is a now a new wheelwright carpenter called John Cumming who has only one ear. They say he got the other ear shot off in 1921 during the trouble. The weather is now much better and we are able to play football daily, and the manager said yesterday, that we would be able to go to Tully strand next week if the new Lorry arrived. So every day we ask Joe Carmody, who is the mechanic if there is any news of the lorry, and he said it would arrive in a few days. The Lorry has now arrived and it's called a 'Guy'. As it's holiday time we can all go to the garage and have a look at it. It's very much bigger than the Ford.

The date is now fixed for the seaside. We will go next Tuesday, provided the weather is fine, and the Manager Keegan does not have to go away on business. Tuesday comes round, the weather is good we are all waiting and excited in the yard after breakfast. The word goes round that Brother Keegan is gone to the village but would return in an hour. It's now 9:30 a.m. Eleven o'clock comes but no news. A shout goes up that brother Keegan has been seen, he is on his way down. As he comes down the steps he blows his whistle. We all fall in, and there is complete silence. Brother Keegan is very sorry but he has to go to Clifden to bring back a new boy.

He promised we would go to Tully strand the next day Wednesday. But the next day some thing else happened. 'John Fagan' was taken away to a mental home. That was the boy who used to be beaten on the head by Brother Walsh in order to make him think like other boys. Dr Lavelle said that he was insane. Big Tom Baker said that

'Fagan was alright, he had the sense to run and lock himself in the Lavatory whenever he seen Brother Walsh coming.' He wasn't beaten so much since Walsh left. Except that big Scally used to chase and beat him on the legs with the strap.

We were now promised that we should have the trip on the first fine day. The cakes which had been baked for the original outing, had to be eaten on Sunday as they were already stale. My brother Joe who worked in the bakehouse told me that they were baking new cakes and currant loafs, so that we did actually go to Tully strand about ten days after the day originally planned. It was a warm and beautiful day we were all on the beach in less than two hours. We were taken in the old Ford lorry and the Guy. The Ford was driven by Joe Carmody and the Guy by Brother Keegan. Mr Griffin also went with us. The older boys played football, or went swimming, and the youngsters played games or paddled about in the shallow water. In the late afternoon, bread and jam and cakes were given out. Races were then organised, as well as jumping, and the long jump for which there were prizes of sweets and chocolate.

At about 5:30 in the evening the men were all tired out, and the first parties were already getting ready to return. Brother Scully had us all gathered around. We were all sitting cross-legged on the sand listening to a song. Brother Scully was a good singer and never refused to give us a song. George Gordon also sang as well as Joe Cavanagh. The first two loads had already gone back to the school. And now big Downs gave us the 'Minstrel boy' and Brother Scully finished the day with his old favourite, 'work boys, work and be contented'. After which we all started to march back towards the school, and as we met the lorries, we climbed on as our turns came. Many of the older lads marched the full three miles back to the school. After a late supper, we all went off to bed, without saying the Rosary.

The holidays quickly came to an end, and we are once again back at school. Brother Conway allows us to pick our own seats at the desk and when we are all settled nicely next to our pals, he decided with a smile on his face to change us all around. Brother Conway although he is young and very quiet, is wide awake to all the tricks. He is a good teacher, although he appears to take it all as a joke. If he sees that a boy is nervous when it is his turn to read a lesson or do a sum on the board, he quickly passes him by and calls on him later, when more at ease. Conway is a good Irish speaker although he is not allowed to teach Irish, because he does not come from Connacht, and we are taught only the Connacht dialect.

My brother Joe is now due to leave school as he is almost sixteen. He has been at his trade now every day for over a year, and has not attended school in the mornings, only one hour from six to seven in the evenings. Boys leaving school are usually given a suit and a pair of shoes, which are made to measure by the lads in the workshops. A shirt and socks are also supplied, which are made in the school. I know I shall not miss Joe very much because we have not seen much of each other, due to the difference in our ages.

The new brother has now arrived to take charge of cooking and the refectory. We are all whispering to each other, the first morning at breakfast that Brother Vale takes charge. It's always exciting when a new brother arrives. Everyone is asking himself the same question: is he quiet? Or is he cross? All eyes are now on Brother Vale as we take our breakfast in silence. I have heard that Brother Vale has just spent seven years in a deaf and dumb school near Dublin. He wears dark glasses, so we can't see his eyes. He speaks very little as he signals for us to sit down, stand up etc. His age is about the same as Walsh or Fahy. Annie Aspel in charge of the Laundry said his age is about forty five, or as she puts it, the age when they all go strange.

Nothing very much happens for almost a week, it was on Sunday, when we are usually allowed to talk at meals. After been given permission, we were about half way through our breakfast when the boys on number three table began to speak. Like a flash Brother Vale rushed to the table and beat everyone across the back and the head with something which was neither a stick nor a strap. We couldn't see him carry any weapon. He struck everyone about six blows at terrific speed. The screams and shouts were most frightening. The boys on number three table were about thirteen years old. A few minutes after we were given permission to talk my brother Joe discovered what it was that the boys were beaten with. It was an eighteen inch long piece of rubber, and had been cut from a solid rubber tyre. Vale now pushed the rubber up under the shoulder of his Jacket so that the impression was plainly visible from the outside. Nobody else was beaten during the meal, but when breakfast was finished, Vale went around and examined the floor under each person. Any one who had allowed crumbs of bread to fall on the floor, were ordered to get down and pick them up, as they did this they were beaten with the rubber.

I had not yet been detailed to 'serve'. That means, that two from each table remain behind and do the washing up and cleaning etc., they also served the food for the next meal. This work was normally done by boys over twelve years of age and as I was just over eleven I should be free for almost another year. My brother Jack and Cunningham were on serve during this week, but they were told to-day that they would have to carry on for another three weeks. Jack was beaten for having dirty forks. After the knives and forks have been washed and dried they are shown for inspection.

We are allowed to talk at dinner, but not in the evenings. Times have now changed for the worse. Life was more pleasant after Walsh had gone away. We got a break from the stick and the strap. Already the children's faces were beginning to light up, and they were much more happy than before, but now all that fear has returned. Paddy told me he gets slapped during every lesson, but he is not worried because he thinks he will be out of the school in another year. He is now working in the mechanics shop, and he is learning very quickly. He said the mechanic is a great tradesman. Jack is now working permanently in the kitchen. Each day he collects the meat from the slaughterhouse, and the other rations from the store. He goes to the bakehouse for the bread.

A rehearsal for the new play is to take place to-morrow night. And we will all be admitted. I understand that it is a full dress rehearsal and the costumes have all been made in the tailor shop. Martin Connelly said he has been working on the suits and decorations for two weeks. I have never seen a play before, and I am really looking forward to seeing it. The new P.T. instructor and Mick Hayden are taking part, and Mr Cumming. Brother Byrne has been teaching everyone their respective parts. I am told there is also singing and dancing. The band boys have all a new blue suit, and new stockings with fancy tops. If the rehearsal is a success the play will tour the main towns of Galway and Mayo, going to a different place every Sunday. Con Murphy a chum of mine is in the band. He plays a cornet, and he has promised to bring me back something. He said they may get apples, oranges, or sweets.

Con Murphy said he comes from near Dublin. He was only seven years old when he came to Letterfrack in 1923. He does not remember his parents and has never received a letter. Tommy Gordon plays a clarinet and he also plays the piano. The band Master thinks Gordon is very intelligent and should have a great future. His brother George has now left the school. He was able to conduct the band at the age of fourteen. Their parents come from Belfast. The Gordons are well liked by everyone in the school, partly because they are the only lads from the north, and also because their manners are better than most boys from the country. Tommy Gordon's mother visited him last year, and she stayed in the infirmary with the nurse. Very few parents or relations visit the school. There is Tom Thornton who has one leg. His father comes to the local cattle fair every year. He is a very big man from near Westport.

The only other boy who receives a visitor is Roche. His Mother comes to see him every year. I think she also comes from Westport. The last time she came he would not see her, because she came wearing a black shawl and she carried a basket of fruit. The boys of Letterfrack used to say that only fish women wear a shawl, in other words, only low class people would appear in public with a shawl. I remember one time a Galway lad asked me if my mother ever wore a shawl. When I answered 'yes', he went round the yard and told everyone and they all laughed and teased me for weeks afterwards. Although the majority in Letterfrack are here because of poverty, few will admit this fact. A boy who is sent to the school for an offence such as stealing, or failing to go to school, is considered a higher class of person than the one who is there as a result of poverty. Only the other day I heard Johnny Comeford from Dublin say to another fellow, 'I was sent here for robbing and not because my parents were paupers'.

The play is now about to start we have been very busy for two days, cleaning and scrubbing the gymnasium. The place is decorated with flags and bunting, and there are many coloured lights. We have to carry down chairs from the back of the stage and place them in position at the front near the stage for the Parish Priests, Christian Brothers and local people who will be there. There are about a hundred expected. The acting is very good, and everything goes off without a single mistake. The band and the singing is good. Now the Parish Priest Fr. Discum stands up and thanks every one for the splendid performance. Everyone is now happy because they know what would happen if something did go wrong. Everyone taking part would be lined up and beaten the next day, and the whole play would be rehearsed very many times, until perfection was achieved.

The next day, Dan Kelly, the old bandmaster came to the school, to borrow five shillings from Mr Hickey, to get married. Everyone was now talking about Dan. He had been going with a girl for nearly two years. Some people laughed at the idea of him getting married on five shillings, but Brother Byrne said it was a very brave thing to come back and marry the girl. Dan Kelly was very small only five feet. He was considered something of a joke by the Brothers because of his height, but he was a first class musician and a good band-master.

My brother Joe now leaves the school. It's almost 2? years since we left home. He is going back to our own village, as my father has found him a job. He hasn't learned very much, because he can't read or write, but he has learned a little about his trade. Joe has not had a really bad time as he went to third standard under Mr. Griffin. He was never beaten by Walsh because he was in St. Patrick's Dormitory. And now he is leaving as Brother Vale arrives. Joe would find it more pleasant at home now, as there are two windows in the kitchen, and the roof has been repaired. I didn't think I would miss Joe so very much because he worked all day in the bakehouse. Sometimes I would see him at breakfast or after dinner, or when I took clothes from the laundry to the tailors shop to be repaired. As I had to pass the bakehouse I would throw a small stone at the window, and if there was no one about he would hand a piece of bread out the window, and I would hide it in the bushes until I came back. I was very fond of fresh bread whilst it was still warm. When I couldn't get bread, I was able to get a turnip or a carrot from the garden at the back of the laundry. Annie Aspel didn't mind me bringing food to the Laundry. She couldn't understand how I was able to eat the raw carrots and turnips. I explained to her that at home we got very little else to eat except what we could pick up in the woods and fields. Annie then said she couldn't eat anything here, because she had no teeth.

I now felt terribly lonely and home sick, a lot worse than when I first came to the school, and added to all this was a new sense of fear. I asked Paddy the other day how long more I would have to remain, and he said it would be almost four and a half years. He didn't think four and a half was very long. Besides he would be going home in another year, and he would ask mother to try and get us out when we were fifteen. Paddy said that sometimes a boy could be claimed by his parents at that age if the P.P. was satisfied that conditions at home had improved. But even at that, it still meant three and a half years with Bother Vale.

6

The Workshops

The superior Brother Keegan was in the tailors shop yesterday when I went there to collect some shirts, and Lydon the foreman tailor asked him if I could be posted to the tailors shop, as he thought I would be a good tailor. Brother Keegan then told me to report to Mr. Lydon on the following Monday. This news upset me very much as I was quite happy in the laundry, and when I explained this to Brother Keegan he answered saying, laundry work was not suitable for a boy. He thought I should learn a trade which would be useful to me when I went out into the world. I then said I should like to be a farmer or anything except a tailor, but there was no choice. I could see he was getting angry, so I went back to the laundry and told Annie Aspel, but she was not surprised. She said that they changed the boys every few months.

My first job in the tailors shop was taking the pressing irons to the blacksmiths to be heated, as the stove in our shop was never working well in the morning. The blacksmiths was three doors away and the boss Mr Moran made us blow the bellows whilst the iron was getting hot. If he was in a bad mood he would chase us with a hammer, but he never hit anyone with it. I think that was his idea of a joke, he was then over sixty years old, and was very well liked by everyone. It was his son the Irish teacher who died the previous year. His daughter teaches darning and knitting. Mr Moran's nickname was 'Knocky' and he did not like it. Another change has now been made. Joe Carmody the Mechanic has been dismissed from the school because he was always late getting up in the morning. Keegan brought the guards to take him away from the school. The children were sorry to see Joe Carmody being taken away, because he was a very good man. He once stopped Walsh from beating the lads, and warned him that he would throw him through the window if he was ever seen beating anyone naked again. Joe Carmody's room was in St. Michael's dormitory, and the screams of the kids kept him awake at night.

The new mechanic was O'Shea from Cork city. He was a good tradesman and was thirty-two years old. I have now been three months in second class, and there is great excitement over the big fight. It is the heavyweight championship of the world between Jack

Dempsey and Gene Tunney. Brother Byrne has come into our school to make a bet with Brother Conway who is backing Dempsey to win. Byrne has backed Tunney to win. Tunney wins, but Conway is not very worried, they often have a bet of a shilling on a handball game. The lads of fifth standard say that Fahy is a bad loser, and he beats the boys more when he loses money. Brother Fahy is a heavy gambler and he lost five pounds last week on a game of handball.

In the tailors shop I am learning how to put on patches by hand. I hate working on old clothes because they are covered with lice, and we can't keep ourselves clean for this reason. Yesterday I had to work under the bench. The bench takes up half the workshop and eight boys work on it. It's about three feet in height, and underneath is where all the old remnants are kept, and there is no light there except when the small door is open. Lydon made me work there sorting out bits of wool material for making patches, but I was terribly frightened because I had been told that there were rats under the bench. I worked for a half hour and brought out what pieces of wool material I could find.

Lydon then told me to go back again under the bench, but I was too frightened it was so terribly dark in there. And the smell of the rats was too much for me. Tommy Hewitt told me they had placed rat poison there a week ago, perhaps it was that which was smelling. I could not go back there again so I ran out of the workshop and continued to run until I had reached the farm yard where I met Brother Scully, and I asked him if I could work on the farm. He said he would ask Keegan. I worked with Brother Scully for two days until Brother Fahy sent for me. Tom Thornton came for me, he was also in the tailor shop. Fahy beat me on both hands and then put me across a desk. I was now beaten so severely with a heavy stick that I was admitted to the infirmary for a week. I was treated by Dr. Lavelle. As I lay in the infirmary I prayed to God for courage to be able to carry on. Tom Thornton was the same age as me or a little younger. He got a similar beating the same day. Thornton had one leg.

I was now back at school, and the workshop in the afternoon. Brother Vale now walks around during meals, and without a word of warning he flogs several boys during every meal. He has not allowed us to talk for more than two months. We never know who is going to be beaten, and there is never any reason given. Vale is about five feet five inches, with dark hair. He usually beats boys between ten and thirteen years. After each meal we say the Grace, and then everyone makes a rush for the door, because the last few are beaten.

During meal times we just look at the table, in case we might be tempted to talk or whisper or smile. We don't look at each other. The most terrible ordeal is the compulsory silence. It is a silence which, I feel sure I can hear. It's like bells ringing very far away. As I sit in silence I think of what the missionary told us last Christmas. The more we suffer on this earth, the greater will be our reward in the next. We must never complain. It is sinful in the eyes of God to complain. The lads in the play and the band have been to Clifden, Claremorris, and Westport. Tomorrow, Sunday, they will be off to Castlebar Co. Mayo. Last week Con Murphy brought me back an orange. I once got a half orange from my mother, when I was five years old. My mother used to put orange peel in the chest of drawers, as perfume, to take away the smell of smoke from our clothing.

It's now September 1927. Mother has written saying Joe has a nice job, he is working for Twohill of Ahascragh. She speaks about the many improvements which have taken place at home. She thinks it may be possible very soon to buy a cow, it would save her going to town every day for a pint of milk. Mother reminds us that the goat has died, she is not sure that it was mentioned in the last letter. The contract for supplying stone for the mental hospital in Ballinasloe will soon be completed. Dad said he has sold three thousand tons of stone at two and six a ton. The contract was a very good thing, because mother has been able to pay back all the money she borrowed, and everyone at home has been able to get new clothes.

Mother ends her letter, saying, 'your dad prays every night for every one of you', your dad often says to me, 'I always knew that my boys would be well looked after by the good kind Christian brothers. When Paddy finished reading the letter, he said, 'it seems that Joe has told them nothing'. I'm glad he said nothing about what was going on, it wouldn't do any good. It's now bath night, and Brother Conway is in charge. We are all lined up in the dormitory to get a clean shirt and stockings. But before getting clean ones we have to hand in the old ones, and a few of the boys have lost a shirt or a stocking in which case they can't get a change.

Brother Keegan now comes to the dormitory with a new white stiff collar for everyone, which is worn outside the cotton of the jacket, and is held in position by a collar stud. As no one has ever worn this type of collar before, we have a lot of trouble the next morning putting the collars on, the result being that we are all late for Mass, and we have to run all the way to the chapel. The chapel is far too small and many of the local inhabitants kneel outside. Fr. Discum[1] says Mass and in his sermon he says that work on the new chapel may have to stop, owing to lack of funds, so he appeals to everyone in the Parish to contribute within their means to get the work completed. He also reminds them that there would be a special collection after Mass, and he hoped everyone would give generously for a new chalice, which would cost ten pounds. After Mass, instead of having our usual fifteen minutes interval to play, Brother Fahy made us march round the yard in silence, because we were late for the chapel.

Brother Keegan came to take charge of breakfast and he talked for half an hour about the shortage of money in the school, and he reminded us of the need for greater economy in the workshops, the farm, the school rooms and the kitchen. We must take much greater care of our clothes and boots. They must be repaired when necessary. He said he wanted a higher standard of work from the shoemakers and the tailors. He said the monitors in each workshop would be held responsible for all work done by younger children. The monitors did beat the younger children, but there is some doubt as to who gave them authority. Brother Keegan added that the workshops must not only pay their way in supplying the needs of the school, they should also build up greater trade with local people. He mentioned that many complaints had been received from customers, about badly made boots and suits which were made in our workshops.

One of the older boys then raised his hand and asked for permission to speak. When granted permission, he asked if the bread ration could be increased as he was starving (present ration three slices a day). Brother Keegan answering said that there was every chance of the ration being reduced rather than increased. Brother Keegan added, we should be thankful to God for what he gives us. Keegan then said that the cost of the suit, boots, socks and shirt, which every boy received on leaving the school was about five pounds ten shillings. He thought any boy with a conscience who really appreciated what was done for him in the school, should consider it his duty to refund that money during his first year of employment.

During the next week I learned how to use the sewing machine, and I made pillowcases and sheets. As I now realized that there was no escape from the tailor shop I made up my mind to try and learn what I could, and if the opportunity did arise I should definitely try to get a change to another trade. I now had to go to the laundry twice a week to collect work which had to be repaired. I liked this now as it gave me a chance to get away for half an hour and besides I could sometimes get a few potatoes because I used to work a lot harder now, and would stay on working when all the other lads went to play.

43

It was now Halloween again and we got the usual apple and nuts. We also got tea with sugar instead of the usual cocoa. We were allowed to talk during meals all that day. We have had a better time lately. As Vale does not beat the lads so much during meal times. He hasn't beaten anyone for almost a week except a few for allowing crumbs to fall on the floor. He beats the boy on 'serve' especially after meals.

After making pillow cases and sheets the young tailors were then taught shirt making. The shirt was a very simple made garment, which could be completed in a half hour. The tailor in charge of us was not a good tradesman, and a poor teacher, so the children under him made poor work, and suffered severely by being punished. Sometimes he would beat the lads himself but usually he reported us to the Brothers. Beatings carried out after such a report were always severe.

I was more interested in shoe making than tailoring, and would often spend an hour in the shoemakers, when our own foreman went to dinner or went to the village drinking. The old shoemaker didn't mind me sitting looking at him, because I would do little jobs, like changing the water or putting the sole leather in the bucket for him. His name was Flanagan and he taught me how to cut out the upper and stitch it by machine. It was also reinforced with one row of hand stitching. I also learned to stitch soles by hand. In exchange for all his teaching I would repair and press his clothes. When the Brothers were away on holidays I could go to his house in the village, and do cleaning and washing up for him and would get bread and country butter. The bread was made with buttermilk, and was nearly always newly baked and the butter was delicious.

It was Halloween again and the usual excitement. As we lined up for the apples and nuts Mr Griffin stood a little distance away. In previous years the superior always gave Mr Griffin several handfuls of nuts because he did not eat apples. But this year Brother Vale gave out the apples and nuts, and he didn't give any to Mr Griffin. The boys quickly noticed that Mr Griffin was left out, and many shared their nuts with him. Some days later as I was on my way to the laundry to collect shirts for repair, I heard very loud screaming from the kitchen, and I climbed up on a pile of wood and looked through the window. What I seen in the kitchen was my brother Jack lying on the floor and he was being flogged by Vale. He was being beaten all over the body with the rubber. Vale was shouting 'get on your feet, get on your feet you pig'. This continued for at least ten minutes. I then ran next door to the laundry to tell Annie Aspel, and she came running out with an iron bar. As we went into the kitchen, my brother Jack was still lying on the floor. He was now very quiet. Annie said he was unconscious. With that Vale appeared with a bucket of water and threw the lot over Jack. Jack had now recovered and when he got to his feet, Annie Aspel pushed at Vale with the bar and he ran to the pantry. As he did his glasses fell to the ground. As he turned to pick up the glasses, we could only stand and stare. Vale looked terrible without the dark glasses, his eyes frightened us. Annie now backed away, his eyes were very red with great rings underneath. I seen Jack at school that evening, and asked him what he had done wrong and he said, he had let 'Nigger' get out of the pantry. 'Nigger' was a black kitten. Stapleton also worked in the kitchen and was subject to the same ill-treatment.

At school we were now concentrating on catechism, as the priest would be coming soon. And after the exam it would be only a few weeks 'til Christmas. We have been promised a big parcel this year from home, and Mother said she would buy us all a pair of gloves, as we get chilblains very bad. We were now going to the infirmary every day after dinner for cod liver oil. Keegan said that no one should have chilblains if they go for their cod liver oil. Yesterday Martin Mullins and I went to the farmyard after leaving the infirmary and 'Festy' the butcher let us see the young pigs. Festy McDonald is his full name. He is very nice when he is not too drunk. They say he drinks poitín.[2] Muddy Gleeson said they have to go to Clifden for this drink and it's made up in the mountains. Festy shouts and swears a lot when he is drunk, and the boys run away from him, but 'bulldog' a boy in third standard told me 'that Festy never hurts anyone'.

Every evening Festy takes his collie dog to Diamond Hill to count the sheep. He doesn't go up the hill himself but stands at the bottom and whistles to his dog. The dog rounds up all the sheep and brings them back. I am told that Festy slaughters one sheep a week, for the use of the monastery. Cattle are slaughtered for the school. Bulldog said 'we will have pork at Christmas', so that a pig would be killed. He also told me he heard Keegan say that we may have geese for Christmas dinner provided the fox doesn't steal too many. So far this year he has stolen four geese and several chickens.

There are about twelve boys now employed on the farm and ten in the tailors shop, and ten in the shoemakers. Four in the carpenters, three in the wheelwrights shop, three in the mechanics, four in the bakehouse, two in the main office. There are two in the monastery under Brother Murphy, and two in the boys kitchen, one looks after the stores. There are usually two in the infirmary, and there are two or three employed in the powerhouses, under the electrician. There is one boy in charge of the fretwork shop. The number of younger children employed in the darning and knitting room now vary between twelve and fifteen. One boy is always available at the chapel to assist the priest when required.

The new priest Fr. Donlon is very much nicer than Fr. Lyons the curate who went away. Fr. Donlon was again caught stealing petrol from the school pump, which is kept locked, but Fr. Donlon has discovered a way how to open it. A lot of petrol has been stolen lately, but when the superior found out it was the priest, he just made a joke of it and said perhaps the good priest borrowed the petrol.

Last Saturday when confessions were being heard, all the boys wanted to make their confession to Fr. Donlon, and no one would go to Fr. Diskan the P.P. because he always shouts at the boys, when they confess to having stolen anything. What they usually steal is potatoes from the garden at the back of the laundry, and what makes the P.P. angry is that most boys confess the same sin. Another reason why we don't like to confess to Fr. Diskan is because he is getting old and is a little deaf so that we have to shout and everyone hears what we are saying.

We have four threadle sewing machines in the tailors shop but only two work fairly well. One is almost new, it is a light dressmakers machine, which will not take the heavy furze material from which the boys jackets are made. So that there is only one machine available for this work, and there are often six of us waiting for the machine, as a result we are behind with the work. When Saturday comes, Brother Fahy sends for the tailors and beats them for not being able to make the required number. I am not amongst those beaten because I have not yet started to make jackets.

It's now almost Christmas. The catechism examination is over. The priest who examined us was very hard. He asked us many very difficult questions with the result that about a third of our class failed. He told Brother Conway 'that he was not satisfied' and added that 'what we required was a good spanking'.

Brother Vale now always takes charge of the Saturday night baths. It's very much colder now, and we have to wait for almost an hour on the stairs before going into the bathroom. We get undressed in the dormitory. We enter the baths about thirty at a time. And as we go past Brother Vale, who is standing at the door, he beats us with the rubber, he doesn't hit everyone, it just depends how quick we can get past him. We now stand in the foot baths fifteen each side. The shower is now turned on and the water is very hot, so the children jump out of the bath, and as they do, they are beaten on the backside. The more they cry and shout the more Vale beats them. I did not jump from the bath, because one of the older lads explained to me that, by standing very close to the wall, most of the water would miss me.

I had an awful experience a few weeks before. The water was very cold and when I ran from the bath, he hit me several blows on the back and head, and as the floor was slippy with the soapy water I fell down and was beaten on the floor. I was terrified of being beaten naked. When we had finished our bath, Vale would give us the signal to return to our dormitory. The signal was, he would hit the door with the rubber. When this happened we would all run for the door because the last few would be beaten as they climbed the stairs. On that particular night I had fallen. I hurt my leg and was unable to run. Vale hit me many times going up the stairs. I did not sleep when I went to bed but lay trembling most of the night. I was assisted to the infirmary next day.

It was now Christmas Eve and the nurse told me I could go back to the school. Each time I left the infirmary it became more difficult, yet I wanted to spend Christmas with my brothers. We had a fine Christmas. We each got the woollen gloves and a rubber ball, as well as sweets and a homemade cake. The breakfast was quite good. We had fried bacon and black pudding. There was plenty of sweet tea and there was extra bread if required. Vale did not carry the rubber on Christmas day. The impression was always visible under the shoulder of his jacket.

The dinner was even better than last year. There was roast pork, goose or duck, with green peas following by plum pudding. After dinner there was several raffles for chocolates or sweets. At Christmas time some of the boys became ill because they ate too much. In the afternoon it began to rain although the morning was fine and sunny. We played games in the school rooms until supper at seven o'clock.

After supper the superior Brother Keegan showed a film of Charles Chaplin. It was the first picture I had seen. It was shown in number two schoolroom, or the one normally used by third and fourth standards. The machine, or projector I think it was called, broke down many times. And new bulbs had to be found. But finally Brother Keegan had to abandon further attempts, as there were no more bulbs left. So after spending half an hour or so looking at the stuffed animals and birds in glass cases, we said the Rosary and went to bed.

We usually went to bed about eight thirty p.m. but on Christmas night there was no rules and no discipline. The Christian Brothers would come round with funny masks on their faces and play games. The masters who lived in the school also took part, so that there was a lovely atmosphere of kindness and friendship. Life was really worth living at this time of year. Almost every Brother spent several hours with the lads at Christmas. I never heard an unkind word during this festive season. Almost every one of the Brothers were now sitting on our beds telling stories, laughing and joking, and giving us sweets. It seemed difficult to believe that only a few days ago I was lying in the infirmary suffering from the effects of a number of severe beatings. I had not understood why this happened, nor was there any reason given.

Today I spend a lot of time with several older boys, McGrath the shoemaker, Stapleton who worked in the kitchen, and big Downes, and 'Bullock' Fanning, who is now over seventeen and he has had at least two jobs, but has been sent back to the school because he is no good at his work. Stapleton and Downes stammer a lot. That is probably why they have spent several years in first class. Two years ago Brother Walsh used to stand behind Downes and beat him whilst he tried to read English. This was done, I am told, to try and cure his stammer. McGrath is due to leave the school shortly. He has come on fairly well at school, and is a good shoemaker. His brother is the electrician. The McGrath brothers are very good to the younger children and often stop them being bullied by older fellows.

7

Fourth Year

The Christmas feeling lasted until the New Year. New Year's day was also celebrated but to a smaller degree. We got what was left over from Christmas, for breakfast there was boiled egg, bread and margarine, and jam and tea. For dinner we had roast beef, roast potatoes, peas and Christmas pudding. Brother Vale was a good cook on such occasions, and would stay up half the night before to prepare a meal. For evening meal we got bread, margarine, marmalade and cake. When supper was over the senior boys played at whist drive, whilst the younger lads played in the school rooms. Brother Keegan promised to show a picture once a month provided the boys behaved themselves. He said he was to go to Dublin soon and would buy films of cowboys and Indians, and Charlie Chaplin's latest film.

The Christmas spirit soon died away when we returned to school. Our own teacher Brother Conway was quiet enough and so was the Irish teacher McLoughlin. But the lads in fifth and sixth classes were having a difficult time with Fahy. He was back to his old form. Although he only beat boys for failure at lessons, or leaving the yard without permission, or when one of his pets told him something. Fahy hated to see any one from his school speaking to one of the other Brothers or teachers. Even to play hand-ball with one of the masters, or to do a message for any one, he immensely disliked what he called shaping or 'acting the man'.

He disliked anyone with spirit or guts. Smoking was a serious crime and carried a severe penalty. As well as being beaten the offender would be made to stand for hours in one position. I know a lad who had to stand all day on the terrace on a Sunday. Another boy who had one leg was made to walk around the square all day. The boys usually smoked in the lavatory and a spy was always there to give information. Fahy did not like to see anyone wearing anything out of the ordinary. A few of the boys whose parents were not too poor may have a cap or a tie sent to them. He did not like them to wear it. He was against fancy haircuts, everybody must get their hair cut completely off except a little at the front. The only exception to the short haircut was the band, because they had to appear in public. One of the band boys told me that when they were on tour last year to Clifden to play at a band concert in aid of our new Church, Brother Fahy asked his girlfriend Lydon O'Neill what she thought of the lads, and she answered saying that 'they looked like a bunch of convicts with their bald heads'. Fahy was of course very upset because he himself had cut their hair. So ever since he gives them a "fancy" hair cut and makes them use hair oil before going on tour. He also bought a comb which they use.

Miss Lydon O'Neill from Clifden has great influence on Fahy. He never takes her into the school unless the superior is on holiday. But he often meets her on the main road, and they drive away together. Brother Fahy wears very expensive clothes and boots. He does not get them made in our own workshops but has them made specially in Dublin. He sent a suit to the tailors to be pressed recently, and Lydon our boss, said that it must have cost a lot of money, it was not the plain black the brothers usually wear but Herringbone. His boots also looked very expensive. He carried a beautiful watch, which was of white gold. He said it was a present from his old school Artane. The boys in his school are always happy when his girlfriend calls because he does not beat them for several days after.

It's now January 1928 and the weather is much colder. Most of the younger lads have chilblains again and their hands are swollen and many of them are broken and are just a mass of running sores. Brother Keegan has now bought ten rolls of the very heavy material "frieze" and has ordered a warm jacket for all the boys in the school. I have now got chilblains in spite of the fact that I take cod liver oil every day. We have now taken down all the Christmas holly and other decorations and the place looks lonely and empty. There is now the awful depression that existed before. Every one hates to see the holly go into the fire. Brother Conway said that if we leave the decorations up after a certain date it may bring us bad luck.

There is now a change over in "serve" duties in the Refectory. During dinnertime our numbers were called out, and my number 151 has been called. The length of this duty can be any time from three weeks to three months. We must report to the kitchen five minutes before the whistle blows for meals. We draw the food and serve it to the fourteen lads on our table. After meals we remain behind and carry out the washing up duties. The boys on serve with me are Tommy Gordon, Matt Feerick, Martin Mullens, the two Giblins, John Power, Joe Baker, Tommy Berry, John Coyne, 'Sharkey' Murtaugh, the two McLoughlins, Tom Thornton, the boy with one leg, and many others. Our first job was to carry all the dishes to the scullery and then get a bucket of warm water from the boiler. My brother Jack and Stapleton washed all the dishes and trays, and also the ladles. We were responsible for washing the mugs and knives and forks and spoons. We then washed down the table and the forms. The floor was then swept, each two were responsible for the part of floor under their own table. The dirt was swept to the centre of the floor. The centre was swept by a different person each day in turn. We then washed under our own tables, by soaking a cloth in water, and just wiping the floor which was tiled with red and white tiles. Then one boy from each table washed the centre of the floor twice a week or whenever Brother Vale told us. We scrubbed the floor on our hands and knees with a brush and soap and water. In this case all the tables had to be shifted to one end and then the other. It was whilst this work was being done that we were severely beaten from behind. As we were in line on hands and knees, we were flogged on the backside with the rubber. We must continue to wash the floor, and *not* stop or even look up. If we did not cry or scream we would only get a few blows but on the other hand, if we showed any sign of fear the punishment would be very much greater, and should any boy jump up from the pain of the blows, it was just agony even to watch the result. When the floor was all washed and scrubbed it would be examined, and very often the same thing would be repeated all over again, and of course the same beating. It was awful to see the children trembling, their faces *twitching*, their faces were pale, drawn and haggard. Most of them were too terrified to cry. Murtaugh and John Coyne would make water on the floor when being beaten.

When the tables were put back in their places we would line up to have the knives and forks examined. The forks were held in the left hand, the knives in the right. We went forward in single file. Vale would only examine the forks. Even though the forks had been washed in warm water they would not be clean enough, because as I found out after a long time it was small particles of fibre which came off the tea towel that were visible. After this inspection almost all were beaten, but this time only on the hands, five slaps on each hand. Vale now used a stick which he held in his left hand. The stick was used to keep the hand in the correct position, that is the stick was held under so that the boys hand would be kept up and not allowed to drop. It was St. Patrick's Day, which was also a day off from school, the work shops were also closed. It was just like Sunday except that we got a slice of cake or currant loaf plus the usual amount of bread for breakfast and the evening meal. After breakfast, Keegan brought us for a walk to Kylemore Abbey, which was occupied by French nuns. It was also a convent where young girls were looked after. There was a priest there also, who was well known in Letterfrack. He often came to the school to play hand ball with Fahy, and they usually played for a pound, but sometimes the stakes would be higher. The priest was about twenty-eight to thirty years old. A few days ago the Kylemore priest came round the school, it was purely an unofficial call. He visited our class for about fifteen minutes whilst we were at catechism. He asked several questions, some of which were not correctly answered. He then turned to Brother Conway and told him 'he was not using the cane enough'. It was the first time I heard a priest speak of beating. Until then I imagined that a priest would not hurt anyone. Kylemore Abbey is a beautiful building high up on a hill. Quite close is the chapel which Keegan said had a copper roof, and there is a lovely waterfall close by. We remained on the road for half an hour before returning to school.

A day or two later my brother Jack came running from the refectory and shouted that there had been an accident. Brother Vale fell from a ladder whilst he was working on the windows. He had fallen on to a table and fractured his leg. After Dr Lavelle arrived he was removed to Galway hospital where he remained for three months. During this time Brother Murphy who looked after the monastery looked after the kitchen as well. Vale returned just in time to go on his holidays, so that we had a very wonderful time for nearly four months. During the whole of this time we were allowed to talk at meals, and we were free to play what was called *half loaves*. The bread ration was one small loaf between four boys, so that no one was satisfied. We were always hungry, so we agreed to let one have half a loaf and the other half was divided between the other three. We would spin the knife around, and who ever the handle pointed to was entitled to the half loaf. The knife was made with a raised band in the centre so that it would make several complete rotations. Brother Vale outlawed the half loaf game, which was considered a very serious offence.

I am now in third standard. Mr Griffin is the teacher. We stand round the blackboard for all subjects except writing and drawing. Mr Griffin sits on a high stool. It is common knowledge that Griffin is one of the most highly educated men in the country. Brother Byrne once said that Mr Griffin was too good a man for the position he held, he ought to have been a Lawyer or a Doctor. Mr Griffin was a very simple and a shy man. He always dressed in a plain blue suit with a cap to match. His pay was one pound a week, and he was a teacher at Letterfrack for more than forty years. It is said that he once taught the senior classes, but now he was getting old, he reads with the aid of a magnifying glass. He is always happy on Friday because it's pay day, and he goes to the village for a few pints of stout, so that when he comes to school in the evening, we have an easy time. He tells us very funny stories. One story I can very well remember: Mr Griffin said, 'when I came to this school, I was about twenty three, and a good footballer. In those days many of the boys were seventeen and eighteen years old, because they were often sent back to the school from their first job and would then have to wait a year or eighteen months for another one. Sometimes they got very contrary, and would try to run the school their way. They usually made trouble during the holidays when most of the Christian Brothers were away. Three or four of them would pick on me on Friday or Saturday night. They would wait for me coming from the village and steal my blue cap. It often took me a whole hour to beat them one by one.' Griffin mentioned two boys about seventeen who he had to fight several times. They were killed in the Boer War. Mr Griffin told us how the senior football teams always tried to get him on their side because he was a good goalkeeper. He told us about all the old tradesmen, who are now in Letterfrack, but were young lads forty years ago. Festy in the farmyard, Moran the blacksmith, Lydon the tailor, and Flanagan the shoemaker and so on.

Brother Vale has now returned to the school. He is much quieter for the first two weeks. He seems to have changed, we are allowed to talk at meals some days. I am on 'serve' again. He sent for me yesterday and asked for my brother Jack, and I said he was now working on the farm, so Vale dismissed me by flicking his fingers. A new pair of trousers were made for Vale because his old trousers were cut up the leg by the doctor who treated him after the accident. Lydon asked me to take the new trousers to Brother Vale, but when I went to the kitchen to deliver them, he could not be found. So I asked Stapleton where he was and he replied, Vale always locked himself in the pantry for an hour everyday in order to pray.

It was now almost supper time, and Mr Griffin asked if we had any questions, he always said that at the end of each lesson. There was no teaching that evening. In fact he told us several stories and he sang a few verses of a song. I can't remember the song now, only a few words which ran 'O, It Aint like it used to be, fifty years ago'. A boy called White put up his hand and asked a question, 'Sir have you ever been married?' Mr Griffin now jumped off the stool, and he looked annoyed. But the boy again asked the question. Mr Griffin got back on the stool again and very shyly told us that, shortly after he had finished college, he met a lovely girl about his own age and after meeting her several times she invited him to meet her parents. He promised that he would, and bought a new suit and cap for the occasion. When the day came he dressed up in his new suit, but was too nervous to meet her parents. That was the nearest he ever got to being married.

My brother Paddy was now in fifth standard, and was due to leave the school in a few months. He was always bright at lessons and was becoming good at his trade. He had been in the mechanics shop for more than two years. The first year was under Joe Carmody a great tradesman, and now under Mr O'Shea also equally good. Paddy's suit was now being made. I can't remember the colour of the material, but it was a good tweed from Foxford Wollen Mills, where we got most of our materials. He also got black shoes which were made to measure. Boys were now allowed to have shoes instead of boots, and the leather was quite good boxcalf. Paddy leaves early in the morning and we say goodbye the night before. He got a haircut and bath before leaving, and Brother Keegan gave him five shilling and Mr O'Shea also gave him 2/–. I missed my brother Paddy a lot more than Joe, because we played together more in spite of the difference in ages. Paddy was the one who received all the letters and read them to us. As well as getting the credit for the small sums of money and the parcels we received he also took the blame if a festival went by without us getting anything from home. We accused Paddy of putting the wrong address on or putting the stamp on the wrong side. I was not so close to Joe because he was older and he could neither read or write. Mother said that Joe has learned to read since he left school. He learned because dad was always calling him 'our Dunce'.

The days are now getting short and it's dark when we go to school in the evenings. Next week will be Halloween and the lads are all talking about it first thing in the morning when we are lined up for inspection, after washing ourselves. Brother Byrne said we shouldn't get so excited over a festival, but should think about what we are doing. When he had inspected everyone, he took several lads away and gave them a good scrubbing, because their necks were dirty. We were now issued with new toothbrushes which had our number on them, and we were told we must brush our teeth every day at least once. Brother Byrne explained that unless teeth are cleaned regularly they would soon decay, and without teeth we could not chew our food. It was now Halloween again and a day of great joy. There was now great excitement in St. Michael's dormitory and almost everyone was up long before we were called. When I awoke and seen the kids running to get washed my thoughts flashed back to a few years ago, when Walsh would beat us for being up before being called. During breakfast all kinds of stories were going about, concerning the apples and nuts. Some said the apples were big and rosy, others said they were small. Joe Baker said they were Australian. But everybody's mouth dropped when we learned that the apples and nuts were still at Clifden ten miles away, and the lorry which was to go for them was out of order.

Better news now reached us. Brother Keegan himself had already left in the old Ford. Everyone was now pleased because the Ford although very slow never got stuck. She was more reliable than the Guy which was bought recently. Joe O'Shea told my brother the Guy lorry was a bad bargain, and was only fit for scrap, and added that if they didn't dispose of the Guy he would leave the school for a better job. Shortly after dinner there is a roar of excitement as the whistle blows. Everyone knows it's Brother Keegan's whistle. He always gives three short blasts, and besides it's much louder than the others. Brother Keegan once said the whistle was given to him by a policeman who was retiring. When we are all lined up four of the old boys or monitors are sent to carry several bags (which are sealed up) from the car, and Brother Keegan cuts the bags open with a small penknife. There is even greater excitement, because as well as apples and oranges there are four different varieties of nuts.

The older boys are now pushing forward and Mr Griffin who is standing against the ball alley comes over, and tells them that there is 'more than enough for everyone', 'Go back and be patient you lucky lads' says Mr Griffin, with that, he pushes them gently back. Brother Vale now comes from the kitchen, he walks very slowly around the yard, still limping a little after his accident. He looks awfully fed up and lonely. No one says very much as Vale walks along. Brother Keegan now calls Mr Griffin 'Tom', and he is now getting all the nuts he wants. Mr Griffin also takes an orange. There are plenty of nuts and oranges left over and anyone can go and ask for more, but it is not considered good manners in our school to be greedy or selfish. Our education is based on self-denial. Although we sometimes get up during the night and steal food from the kitchen if there is a window open, in front of our superiors and schoolmates we try to behave in keeping with our teaching.

Back in the tailors shop we are busy making suits and costumes for those taking part in a new play. The suits were of Donegal tweed and a very old design, which was fashionable some fifty years ago. In the play where boys dressed up as girls in colours of white green and gold, they wore wigs and wore wings which we also made. Wings consisted of a simple wire frame and covered with a thin cotton material. The wings were held in position by elastic bands, which fitted over the arms and were fastened in the centre book, about the shoulder blades by press studs.

The boys jacket we found very difficult to make. They were very long at the back like a frock coat, and were cut away in front. The collar was of a different material. Brother Byrne supervises the making of all costumes etc. He is also responsible for the teaching and training of each one who is taking part in the play. Brother Byrne is quite an expert in this kind of work. He is being advised by a professional man called Mr Jarvis from Castlebar, who visits the school periodically.

I have been chosen to take part in a marching and exercise act, which is done to music, but I never report for training because I am much too frightened. I go and hide in the laundry or under my bed in the dormitory each day until I have been replaced. Brother Byrne who is a very good man understands, and he does not punish me. I now feel terribly ashamed as I am such a coward. I am not afraid of being beaten, but I am afraid of making a mistake, and letting down Brother Byrne who has been good to everyone.

It's only a few weeks to Christmas and everyone is getting himself worked up. The stories are already going about as to what the menu will consist of in our workshop. Ginger Donlon has marked down on the bench the number of days. He has made 18 strokes with chalk or a stroke for each day and every afternoon when we report to the workshop at 2 p.m. all the youngsters watch almost breathlessly, as Donlan crosses out another stroke. As the days go past we are even more excited, and many times during working hours we count and recount the number of strokes.

A few days before Christmas we receive a letter from mother telling us that Paddy has a nice job and comes home each night. She also explains that as the quarry contract is long since finished and dad is out of work we would only receive a cake for Christmas. There is now only a few days to go and the lads spend most of their time climbing up and looking in the kitchen windows. Latest information is that Brother Murphy who looks after the monastery has come to give Brother Vale a hand, who is still walking with great difficulty. On Christmas Eve, the superior Brother Keegan comes around the school, and lines up everyone against the wall and inspects our clothing. He has been to Dublin and bought pants with pockets and lining for everyone. We are told they have been purchased at a bargain price much less than to buy the material from the mills. The pants which are made in our shop have no lining or pockets. On Christmas Eve night we all hang up our stockings, as there is a rumour going about that Father Christmas will be coming. We heard that story last year, but he never came. Anyhow we hang up a stocking on the end of the bed. We are awakened in the early hours of Christmas morning. Some one has seen Father Christmas leaving, and sure enough we all have a present of some kind and sweets.

There is no more sleep for anyone. Most of the children are up and running about. It's still dark, and the night man who normally makes us go back to bed has turned on all the lights. Before Brother Byrne comes to call us we are up and dressed. Most have had a wash already, so there is no inspection. I have a new comb, which I have found in my stocking.

I spend a very long time combing my hair, but the more I comb the more it stands up. We only comb our hair on special occasions, for a play or concert, or when the priest comes for catechism exams. We wander off to mass in our own time. There is no parade, yet there are no absentees. Most of the boys get to the chapel long before the service has started. Brother Keegan is not present at mass as he is ill, and the doctor has been called. We are told at breakfast that his illness is not severe and would be well in a day or two.

The dinner is roast turkey with boiled potatoes and peas or cabbage, with gravy, and plum pudding. The office Brother is present with Brother Vale and Brother Murphy from the monastery. The office Brother doesn't see us very much because he is always up at the farm with his pigeons, and tame rabbits, and chickens. After dinner we go to number two school and say prayers for the superior. After which a picture is shown, but there are so many breakdowns that it cannot be considered a success. The mechanic is present and Brother Vale, so when the machine finally breaks down we have a sing song. And any boy who gives a turn, whether it be a song, a dance, or a piece of poetry or a story, gets a bar of chocolate.

After Christmas we are told that Brother Keegan may be replaced as superior and another man, who had already left Letterfrack would be taking over. There was a long silence. Who could it be? There was Brother Dooley, Walsh, and the older lads were talking about a Brother O'Brien, and they also mentioned a man called 'the boxer', because he never used a stick or strap, only his bare hands.

8

Portraits

The superior (or manager) Brother Keegan is rather tall about 5'–11" aged about forty five has a sloping forehead going thin on top, with dark hair. He is very religious, he is fond of a drink but never to excess. A strict disciplinarian, he is very hard and can be a very cruel man. As already mentioned in earlier chapters, it was Keegan's practice to come to the square always carrying a stick. He often took several boys away, and flogged them severely with their pants off. The reason for this flogging was because of *improper* actions, which are said to have taken place in the dormitories and lavatories. Keegan has a very good knowledge of motorcar engines and can do most repairs, and is a good and careful driver. He is a qualified electrician. He is just as severe on the other Christian Brothers and masters as on the children.

Brother Blake was in the farm for a short time during my first year, before Brother Scully came. He had a bad name amongst the farm hands, he was transferred to Salthill in Galway, where he was tied up and severely beaten by senior boys for alleged ill-treatment. Brother Scully was a small man of about sixty years of age and was bald. He was easily the kindest and most friendly man in Letterfrack. He had a kind word for everyone and was most liberal with his snuff. Tommy Mannion a man on the farm said, 'Brother Scully got more work out of the boys by singing a song than all the other brothers had with their sticks and straps.' Scully was a broadminded man, was well read and had travelled widely. He spoke several languages. Scully carried a walking stick but it was only to assist him when walking through the farm land, it was never carried when he visited the school yard. He was at home with the very young children and it was a common sight to see him walking along with a young child on each side. Whenever we had a problem, we always went to Scully, he was always ready to listen and his advice was appreciated. He never passed anyone by without a few words. During the summer holidays when most of the Brothers were away he would love to come to the square and take charge. This would allow Mr Griffin to go to the village for a pint. If the weather was fine we would go for a walk around the farm, and through the football field, and along the sea front, we could go into the sea or pick black berries.

Brother Walsh was of medium build was about forty years old, with dark hair brushed straight back. He was cruel and cunning. He dressed in expensive clothes and was very religious. He spent most of his time praying, except during school hours. He was ferocious not only in his treatment of young children but all who worked under him. I remember him on at least one occasion attacking our schoolteacher, McAntaggart who was also a bandmaster. He beat him across the face with the strap until the teacher cried like a child. It was awful to see a teacher being beaten. The very strange part of this is that McAntaggart was a taller man, and much younger than Walsh. I should also add that McAntaggart was an ex-industrial schoolboy from Artane.

The Hayden brothers are two bakers, they have been brought up in Letterfrack. They are aged about 28 and 30 years. Joe Hayden was the baker in 1925 and left about 1927 when his brother took over. They change about every two or three years. They are good men, but differ in many ways. Mick wears a hat and is friendly with Fahy, while Joe does not even speak to Fahy. He wears a cap and is an ex-soldier from the Free State army. Sorry they are both ex-soldiers.

Joe Hayden refused to go to mass and the parish priest Fr. Discan came to the bakehouse to see him. There was an argument which finished up on the terrace one Sunday morning about ten o'clock. Fr. Discan threatened to strike Joe. Joe warned the priest, and advised him to go and mind his own business. Shortly after, Joe left and Mick came. Mick is a quieter man and gets on better with the Brothers, and the priests. He spends most of his time in the mechanics shop or with Fahy, and the bandmaster Hickey.

Brother Dooley was in charge of senior classes from 1925 until 1926. A fairly big man aged about fifty, was very bald. He always took the whole school on drill and P.T. every Sunday on the yard, during wet weather we went to the gymnasium. He nearly always carried a heavy cane or walking stick, which he used fairly often to beat the older lads on the back and the legs, for mistakes in drill and exercises. I don't remember seeing him beat very young boys. The lads in top class say that he was bad at sums and he often sent for Mr Griffin when in difficulty. He was very religious. He sold sweets from the small shop under the stairs after breakfast or just before school. He had a good knowledge of music and was a fairly good singer. He conducted the singing with the walking stick. George Gordon, a boy of fifteen played the piano, as there was no regular bandmaster in 1925.

Brother Murphy, the office Brother, is a man of about forty five. He is bald, thick set, round shouldered (from desk work and study), brilliant and highly educated. He is also widely travelled and well read and a very broadminded man. He was very fond of animals and birds, he used to spend most of his spare time on the farm with his pigeons, and pet rabbits which he used to breed. He taught boys fret saw work and how to make models from plywood. He was very good at geometry and maths. Murphy was a very modern thinker. I once heard him say to Fr. Diskan, the P.P. (jokingly), 'I am more interested in this world than the next'. On another occasion when Brother Fahy was pulling his leg about the farm, Brother Murphy said 'I spend my time on the farm because I like animals better than some men'.

Brother Fahy was a conceited, self-centred, arrogant bully. He bullied not only children, but other Brothers, and masters as well. Fahy wore expensive clothes, which were not made in the school. He had a girlfriend from Clifden called Lydon O'Neill. Fahy is said to have used some of the school funds for his personal use and to help some of his relations in Claremorris. His age was about 43 years. He had a gold tooth which was visible when he smiled. He liked a drink. He often complained about the poverty of the Christian Brothers, who worked for their food and clothes, which they would get in any workhouse.

Brother Vale. About forty years old, 5'-5" with dark hair, wore dark sunglasses, he was a very lonely man, and had no real friends. He didn't mix with the other Brothers. He spent most of his time in the kitchen or in the pantry. He cooked a good Christmas dinner, but at other times, the food was disgusting. Vale often put large doses of medicine in the food, to cure skin disease which most young children suffered from. This medicine made children ill and kept them running to the lavatory at night.

Brother Conway was about 5'-7", very young about twenty, very handsome with black wavy hair, brushed straight back, a good teacher, rather childish, likes to play with the children. He plays handball and football very well. When his class are not working well, Conway reads them a story, or changes the subject.

Mr Moran, the old blacksmith, lost his son two years ago who was aged 33. His daughter teaches knitting and darning. Moran is a first class tradesman, he is very popular with everyone. He sings and shouts all day. He is cruel to horses. I have seen him many times hitting a horse with a heavy hammer. He is almost seventy years old. He has worked at the school for many years.

Mr Cummings is thirty years old, wears a brown suit, with a hat to match, he has only one ear they say. He got the other ear shot off during the trouble in 1921. Cummings is the wheelwright and carpenter and he is a fairly good tradesman. He is very quiet, about 5' 6" of medium build. He spends his spare time walking around the school grounds.

Joe O'Shea the Mechanic aged 30, native of Cork city, has been in the school a year, he is 5' 6" tall with fair hair. He is married with two children living in Cork. He is leaving the school shortly.

Brother Murphy, who cooks for the monastery aged about 47 is about 5'-8" in height rather slim build, is going grey, a good handball player. He is also a good carpenter, he made a crutch for Tom Thornton who has one leg. I have never seen him beating the children.

Brother Kelly was the office Brother. He left Letterfrack in early 1927. He sometimes came to the refectory during meals. He is a very good and religious man, and is most kind to everyone. He is about fifty years old about 5'-9" going grey, he is a slim figure. He used to read letters from boys who had left the school, he often gave lectures during meals about the importance of chewing food correctly. He said that "each mouthful of food should be chewed thirty times". The purpose of this lecture was because many children suffered from indigestion and skin disease.

Brother Byrne in charge of number 2 school was aged about 36 about 5'-8", with fair hair. A good teacher, he slapped the boys for failure at lessons, but only on special occasions, i.e. when it was obvious the boy failed because of inattention, or when he was lazy. Only a strap or light stick was used. Brother Byrne's lectures were most educational in preparing children for life outside the school. He said on several occasions, that 'children who were brought up in industrial schools were, generally speaking, *failures*' (It was about this time that *an ex-Artane* boy was on trial for murder.) He went on to say that 'children brought up in schools and convents, were starved of love and affection which is the very foundation of a healthy and happy life'. 'Children with memories of an unhappy early life, very often become a serious problem, to themselves and society'.

Mr Griffin see earlier chapters

Mr Hickey the bandmaster. A short thick-set man about 5'-3" in height 28 years old, fair hair brushed back. An ex-Artane boy, he is a cruel bully. He spends half the time teaching the band and the other half beating them. He beats them with his fists and the drumstick. He pulls them by the hair and the ears. Hickey is full of vanity, he is proud and cocky. He is studying for an exam and if he passes he will be awarded the *A.R.C.M.*

Mr Lydon the tailor is a rather big man, about 5'–9" in height, and about fourteen stone, with dark hair, and about fifty years of age. His son Martin Joe is learning the tailoring. This boy does not live in the school but with his father. Lydon is a very unfriendly man, and a poor teacher because he is not a good tradesman, therefore the children are backward in their learning and when their work is unsatisfactory they are reported to the superior, or to Fahy. Lydon has been the school tailor for eighteen years, and is training his son so that he will get the job when his father retires.

John Cusack is the handyman, who does all the repairs to the property, and he also works on the farm. He is about 48 years old and 5'–6" in height, he is thick set. He wears a blue suit and a check cap. He is very good to the children and often brings them food from his home. During the summer holidays, when the Brothers are not about, he takes lads to his house which is only a half a mile from the school and there they are given food. He is always friendly and has a kind word for everyone.

Tom Mannion works on the farm. He is a tall man of about six foot and about twenty-five years old. He is thinly built and an excellent workman, he is well liked by everyone. He lives at Cleggan. Festy McDonald is in charge of the farmyard and the slaughterhouse (under Brother Scully.) He is about fifty years old of medium build, He is noted for his heavy drinking and obscene language. He lives a mile south east of Letterfrack. He is married with several young children. Festy is responsible for all the fowl and livestock on the farm, and has a very famous sheep dog. Festy once said he would be lost without his dog, because he can't count, but the dog can, and if there is a sheep missing, the dog will go and find it.

9

Fifth Year

It's February 1929, we clean out the tailors shop and the dirty rags, old clothing, and clippings, which have collected under the bench are removed to be burned. The workshop has always been rat-infested probably because it is next door to the bakehouse. Most of the children's clothing we get for repair is alive with vermin. Recently two electric irons have been installed one is seven pounds and the other is ten pounds. The first week we get the irons, one is left on during the night and the next Morning it has burned its way through the table. The play which has been rehearsed for weeks is now on tour. Brother Byrne accompanies them and a bus is engaged from Clifden. Joe O'Shea the mechanic has now left Letterfrack, and a man of about fifty from Dublin takes his place.

Brother Keegan is found one morning lying on the floor of his room. He is seriously ill, and confined to bed for several weeks, and is seen by the doctor every day. Brother Kelly, who was office Brother in 1925 and 1926 has now returned to take over the duties of superior. Everyone is now very pleased because Kelly is a very quiet man, and is fond of the children. We don't have to worry about stamps anymore because those who can't afford them hand their letters into the office and they are stamped by Brother Kelly. But many children have stopped writing home. Some forget about their parents after two years, others blame them for their being in Letterfrack.

I am now thinking of a tailor of about fourteen years, the name is Tommy Hewitt, he never reads his letters. He puts them in the stove in the workshop unopened. Another lad from Galway city, called O'Brien has turned eyes and wears glasses He just tears his letters up without even reading them. To me this seems very strange, something which puzzles me, so I often try to make conversation with them in order to find out what is wrong. Why should a boy of 12 or 13 years forget his mother? Why should they act so strangely? I am now about 12 and a half, yet every day I think of home, and every hour I can guess what is going on. I know that dad will not be up before 10 a.m. and he will sit by the fire until about twelve. After this he will probably go to the pump for water a mile away. He will take the donkey and cart with the barrel, which he will fill to the top, but by the time he gets home, it will be only half full, as the boreen is so uneven and with the jolting of the cart the water will be lost. Dad will get a fair share of water over his clothes and boots, because he stands on the cart to try and keep the barrel steady. When he gets home, he will have to sit by the fire for an hour to dry his clothes. He will then have a meal if there is anything in the house. He had lots of things to do to-day but it was too late to bother starting so he would just wander off to the village to see the time, or would go to the wood to get sticks for the fire.

On Sunday everyone would go to eleven o'clock mass, but would be late as usual. When we were at home it was my job to go to the main road to find out the time. Jack would come with me. As we were a good mile from the chapel we calculated the time like this. If there were people walking to mass it was about 10.30 a.m. If they were travelling on bicycles it would be 10.45 a.m., in which time we would be late. So with this information we would run back home as fast as our feet could carry us. My mother always went to mass in the donkey and cart and before leaving she would warn us to go across the fields to the chapel, as it was late, and this was a shortcut, and another reason was so that the people would not see our shabby clothes.

It is almost Easter 1929. There is quite a lot of excitement but nothing like what it is at Christmas. It has been terribly cold all winter. We don't get much snow in Connemara, but a lot of frost. Most of the very young children have been ill with chilblains, but I don't get any this year, or at least my hands don't break out like they did the first three years. My brother Jack is now working on the farm and is having a better time. Vale gave him a hell of a life. Vale's leg is now a lot better, and he just limps a little. He has started beating the boys again just as bad as ever. The other day he flogged every one on our table because there were crumbs of bread on the floor after breakfast.

He is back again on his old perch, he stands on the hot water pipe which runs along by the wall about nine inches from the floor. By doing this, he gets a good field of view, he can now see everyone in the refectory, and by turning around he can see the school clock which is over the door of number one and number two schools. He also keeps an eye on the steps leading down from the terrace, because Brother Kelly the new superior often comes down to see the boys at meals.

Vale doesn't seem to like the superior and always gets out of his way quickly when he arrives. It's Good Friday and there is no mass to day, but we go to the chapel just the same. We go again in the evening to kiss the cross. We all file into the chapel and take our usual place and as Brother Fahy walks piously to the altar steps to where the cross is laid, he kneels down and kisses the cross. We all follow and do likewise. After a breakfast in silence, we go to the dormitories to make the beds, and sweep and polish the floor. There is no school so we spend the morning cleaning the windows and polishing the washbasin taps. As I am cleaning one of the back windows I can see the 'Gough' coming up the road, with a horse and cartload of fish for the dinner. Every two weeks we get fish, it's always mackerel. When it's not fish, we get rice and rhubarb mixed or rice with raisins in it. The food always gives me terrible indigestion, no matter what I eat in the refectory, but I do not suffer from indigestion when I get potatoes from the farm and roast them in the stove in the workshop, or the bread which Mr Hayden gives me from the bakehouse. We must always finish our food, if we leave any we get beaten. We always get soup on Monday and Wednesday, and very often there is far too much salt in it. It is in the soup the medicine is usually put. This happens about once a month and Vale comes round at the end of each meal to see that every boy has finished his soup.

Easter passes without very much excitement. I get a letter from home and a homemade cake. Mother says that my sister Norah has gone to the States. She is eighteen, a relation has paid her fare, and has found her a job. For breakfast on Easter Sunday we have a boiled egg, with tea and an extra slice of bread and marmalade, and margarine. There is roast lamb boiled potatoes and turnip. Supper the same as for any other Sunday plus a slice of cake. There is a whist drive that evening in the library for the senior classes, and prizes of sweets and chocolates for the three highest scores and the lowest score.

Back in school again we are doing well under Mr Griffin. He only beats boys for cheating, and at the end of each lesson boys who get all their sums wrong, or get *Poor* for any subject are slapped once with a light rod or stick. For the last fifteen minutes each evening Mr Griffin reads a chapter of a book called 'Sinbad the Sailor' until the whistle blows for supper.

The new mechanic has left the school as the work is much too hard for him, and he is over fifty years old. A man called Joe Kelly has taken his place. He is a relation of the superior Brother Kelly and everyone is talking about the big wage he is getting, three pounds a week. Mr Griffin who is now 42 years in Letterfrack is only getting a pound a week. Joe Kelly is known as the mechanic who always carries the book of knowledge, so that when anything goes wrong with a car or lorry he looks up his book. He is also the man who brings the new style of suit to Letterfrack. The black jacket which is very short, and the black trousers with a white stripe which are worn very wide at the bottom, 24 inches. The next to copy the new style is the bandmaster Hickey, who has now gone to London to sit for his examination in music which he has passed, he is now an A.R.C.M. He has returned to the school and is paid a higher wage. He is now a right pain in the neck. He has always been proud and cocky but he only speaks to the great people from now on. He no longer dines with the masters, they are not good enough for him. He dines with the nurse in the monastery. He spends all his spare time with Brother Fahy in the Library they often leave the school together in the late evenings, and go for a drive with their girlfriends. Fahy now takes advantage of the new superior, because he is not as strict as Keegan, who did not allow the Brothers to go with women. Brother Kelly has now bought a new car called a "Desota" it is said to have cost three hundred pounds. The mechanic said it is very fast, it can do eighty miles an hour, and it is the latest model.

The mechanic is now courting the carpenter's daughter, and they are going to be married very soon. I do not know this man the carpenter well as I have only been in the carpenters shop a few times. It was in this shop a few months ago that John cut a wooden plank (the saw is worked by electricity). As Cummings could not switch off the saw he jumped up and caught the belt, to try and stop it and he lost a finger.

In the tailor's shop, work is more interesting, as the superior bought a long roll of blue serge material, and a number of the local people are having suits made at £4–15–0 each. It's very much more pleasant working on good material. Up 'til now I have only done work for the children, and the material used is a very cheap cotton.

Bob Donavan who is the oldest tailor in the shop leaves the school. He is over sixteen but had to wait until a vacancy occurred. He is going to a job in Westport and he will get five shillings a week and his keep. Donavan was a nice fellow and taught me quite a lot. We always envy a lad who is 'going out', that is the expression used for leaving the school, and on such an occasion every one becomes anxious as to when he will be going out. This time I have a friend called Bob Haywood from Galway city, he is my own age, and he works in the office with Brother Murphy. Haywood has promised to look up the rule book and find out for me when I shall be going out. So one afternoon I go to the office and as Haywood is alone we go through the book and find out that my time is up on October 1932. I have another three and a half years to do, so we work it out in months, weeks, and days. It seems a lifetime under such conditions.

It's now the first week in June and I am on serve again, with all the same lads as before. Vale now beats us almost daily when scrubbing the floor. It is a habit of his to come up and look at the bucket of water we are using, and say 'that water is dirty go to the kitchen and change it'. But when we go into the kitchen we find he has followed us in. As he wears rubber heels it's difficult to hear him, and we dare not look back, to look back is a sign that we are afraid, and he always beats lads more when they are afraid of him. He has now got a lot worse than before the accident, we had a good time while he was in hospital, and for a few months after he came back.

I went into the scullery a few days ago and there were two boys washing dishes in the sink, Stapleton and Sharkey, and as they worked he flogged them from behind, as usual I asked Joe Baker, why it is that the rubber is so terribly painful and he explained that the rubber which Vale is using is the *rim* of the tyre, and is reinforced with wire which is running through it (steel wire). I have now been beaten several times daily for weeks, and when I go to the refectory for meals my hands are sweating. My sight is getting blurred and I am unsteady on my feet. I feel hungry but when I eat the food will not stay down. I am now weak, and as I walk along find it difficult to keep my balance.

I now get bad dreams in my sleep, I am always running away, but there is a man behind me, and he is getting closer and closer. I want to scream but I can't. I now wake up and I am sweating all over. I want a drink of water but am afraid to go in the dark, I try to keep awake because I am terrified to go to sleep. I do sleep again but there is an even worse dream. I am flying over water there is no land in sight, I am now losing height, as I touch the water I wake up again more afraid than before. It's now only a few days until the holidays commence and Vale is standing at the organ, he appears to be looking towards our table, he is swaying slightly from side to side, like a cat about to spring at a mouse. He is swinging the rubber and hitting the leg of his trousers, we are well used to this, everyone knows he is about to beat someone, but who? That is the question. We are now having breakfast and as I drink the tasteless cocoa, I am thinking of previous years at this time. Vale becomes a savage brute during the last few days before going away on holiday, some of the lads say it's because he does not go home, but spends his holidays praying at a monastery. He now walks fairly quickly towards the kitchen. We dare not look to enquire where he is going, it would just be too bad if we did. All of a sudden there is a scream of agony as he attacks two boys. One lad we call 'Redskin' and John Kelly, they are both about twelve years old. There is no doubt as to who he is beating. I can always recognise the voice of 'Redskin' as he cries 'please sir, forgive me sir' this is repeated every time he gets a blow. They each get about twenty blows on the back and head. Kelly is now being flogged. He is very brave and doesn't cry very much. I have seen this boy being savagely beaten on many occasions. He goes snow white in the face. Vale always gives him several terrible blows on the backside when he is scrubbing the floor.

Vale is now standing on the water pipe again. I glance towards him, and he is, or I imagine he is looking at me. I hope my face does not start twitching again, because he may think I am talking. This has worried me terribly of late, the left side of my face shivers and trembles, and my left eye closes and opens very quickly. In order to try and stop this twitching I sometimes bit into my upper lip real hard, until the blood comes from it.

The breakfast is over and we are now doing the washing up. Vale calls a lad called Murtaugh, who is small for his age, he is about eleven. Vale sits on the ———[3] and puts the lad across his knee and pinches him first playfully, now harder, until the lad begins to cry and shout. Vale is now using the rubber. He is flogging him. Murtaugh is in a state of hysteria, he is laughing and crying, he is now allowed to fall on to the floor.

This is a terrible method of punishment, which I have suffered many times, but it's not as bad as the bathroom treatment. Having experienced this kind of beating it's even more horrifying to watch, than the actual beating. In other words the victim in this case is better off than the onlooker. We are all lined up now for inspection with knives and forks and spoons (sometimes the spoons are not inspected). We are standing by our tables for inspection and Vale is back on the water pipe. He looks out the window towards the clock, usually he walks around and looks at the floor under each table but not today. He hits the wall with the strap, which is the signal for attention. As we look towards him, he signals with his head towards the door, this means we can go, but he does not follow us. Usually he beats the last one or two.

The first day of the holidays is simply wonderful. As the new car, the Desoto, takes the Christian Brothers away to Clifden station there is a great sigh of relief. Brothers Fahy, Conway, Byrne, and Murphy all leave. Everyone is sorry to see Byrne leaving, and Brother Murphy, because they are real good people. There is no visible sign of happiness or excitement. On this day there is no laughing or shouting or singing as on Christmas, even when one looks the children in the face. One may still see the frightened look in their eyes, only sometimes an occasional smile and from a close friend, one's own age. It is not unusual to find a boy huddled in some corner crying. I have seen lads on this day standing in small groups without saying a single word. We are lost for words, the change has been too sudden. We are caught unawares as it were. It takes time to learn to be happy after this quick change from unpleasure to pleasure.

Six whole weeks of freedom. We have to go to the workshops each day, but it's different. We work just as hard, and even better than before, but we can talk now and play around a little. We know that the old boss Lydon will report us when Fahy comes back, but we don't care, besides, if we behave ourselves during the last week or two, Lydon may forget that we have now gone a bit wild. He is a terribly mean person, his daughter Bridie brings his lunch to the shop each day, it's a very big lunch – a lot more than we get, he always turns his back to us while he is eating. Bridie his daughter is a nice girl of about fourteen, she used to speak to us, but now she doesn't say a word, he must have told her not to talk to us. His son Martin Joe is twelve. He is learning the trade, but he is not allowed to come to the yard to play ball with us. Lydon has finished his lunch and he has a slice of bread left over. We are hungry and hoping he will give it away, instead, he puts it back in the paper bag and hands to Bridie to take home.

I am now sent down to the power house for the electrician because one of the irons is not working. On the way there I have to go past the glasshouse (or greenhouse) outside the glasshouse is Mr Griffin's little dog Toby. He barks as I approach, and I stop to stroke his head, but he backs away growling. I know why, because some of the boys beat him with sticks. I have seen them do it, so I advance and explain to him that he will not be hurt. As I touch his head he snaps at me, he is still growling a little, but I now have my arm round his neck and telling him about our own little dog at home, his name is 'Rusty'. I now sit down and lean against the wall, and Toby has his head rested on my knee, he is not afraid anymore. The sun is warm and I go to sleep. I suddenly wake up, as Mr Griffin speaks, saying it's bedtime.

The superior was present at breakfast next morning, and we remembered that Brother Kelly did not mind us talking at meals, he only asked for silence when he was reading a letter or making a speech. But today he just spent his time going about and talking to the older lads. He had been away over two years during which time many things had changed. After breakfast I went to see the electrician to ask him to repair the electric iron, and I was surprised to learn that I hadn't even been missed the day before from the workshop.

Most of the older tailors have now left the school – Martin Connelly, Tommy Hewitt and his brother, Mick Bob Donavan, and 'Sykey', the lame boy with the crutch – so that I am now doing the special work making suits for the school staff and the local customers. I also teach the younger lads how to put on patches and other repair work. We also make suits and soutanes (*or cossacks*) for the Brothers who now keep us very busy. Most of them are having a suit made, as Brother Kelly is easy going. Keegan would not have allowed them to get a suit unless the old one was badly worn.

Mr Griffin has been measured for a suit, it's always blue serge for him, and he does not hurry us very much, until it's almost paid for. He pays 5/– a week, as soon as it is ordered. Mr Griffin has one made every two years and it's always the same style, a single-breasted jacket button and full back (that means there is no seam in the centre). The trousers are plain bottoms.

After supper we go to the football field every evening. We are not compelled to play, we can just wander off to the stream, to look for eels under the rocks, or go to the well, where there is nice spring water. It's the best water I have ever tasted, and is surrounded by rocks, and is shaded on one side (the south side) by a bank about three feet high. This water is always cold, and is very clear. I have often spent a whole hour looking into this well. The next best water I have tasted was on Diamond Hill when Brother Scully took us up there one Sunday, and told us stories and sang songs.

We are in the school rooms now, playing around, and there is no one watching us. We will soon be off to bed, it is past eight thirty, and we are usually in bed at this time, but we are free, entirely free. We run about and jump over each other's backs and we wrestle each other. We take full advantage of our freedom, so much so that there is danger. I remember the second year in school, just after the Brothers had gone on holiday, the boys went really wild. They pulled the pictures off the walls and damaged some maps, they spilled ink on the floor and they threw some books into the fire. They were all boys from Brother Walsh's class, who had been subject to ill-treatment every day. Mr Hayden the baker, comes and tells us it's almost ten o'clock, and tells us that we would have to be up at 6 a.m. He tells us that he is going to put the lights out so we run off to bed in a disorderly manner.

It's good to go to bed knowing that we will not be flogged the next day, or the day after, or the day after that. Life is really worth living. After going to bed we can talk to the boy next to us, and the night man tells us to go to sleep, but we don't take any notice, so he just wanders off to the other dormitory. I am a lot better now. I have had several fairly good nights. The dreams are not so terrifying.

It's the second week of the holidays and Mr Griffin takes us to see the coal ship, which has arrived. It's the same ship and the same crew as last year, and we are allowed to talk to the sailors from Scotland, who speak very strange English. Mr Griffin can understand them, but I can't. Mr Griffin said they will start unloading tomorrow and the job will take four days. We have two lorries and one is borrowed from Coyne of Clifden. The Guy is a very big and heavy one, and the old Ford which is tied together with string and wire, is still in humming order. Big Val Connelly drives the borrowed lorry and Mr Kelly the new mechanic, the Guy. Dick Hunt, now a lad of almost sixteen, drives the old Ford. Hunt is the boy with the cauliflower (*frost bitten*) ears. There are twenty lads loading the lorries and another twenty unloading at the coal yard, but there are very many more looking on. Val Connelly takes off his cap and makes the sign of the cross, as Dick Hunt almost backs the old Ford off the quay into the sea. Val now warns Hunt to go slow and drive more carefully. He tells the boys to keep clear as Hunt drives his load of coal away. Val says a prayer as the Ford is driven away, at speed.

Everything went well until the last day. As the last load was being driven from the ship, some of us started to walk back to the school, and we seen in the distance several hundred yards in front, the old Ford which had broken down and was stuck, and would not take a small hill, so when we reached the lorry we gave her a push and she started off again. There was too much coal, so we unloaded about a half ton on to the roadside. When she got stuck the second time, she failed to take the hill near Lydon's house (the tailor's) and was now running back down the hill again. The driver had lost control, but managed to apply his brakes before running off the road. Had he run off the road anywhere along here he would have a drop of over twelve feet and may even finish in the sea.

Several of the lads run forward to give a hand, to push the lorry back up the hill. John Kelly also a mechanic who is travelling in the front with the driver is now pushing her and now she is climbing the hill at a fair speed when something dreadful happens. As John Kelly runs forward and tries to climb into his front seat he tries to jump on the step or running board, and he misses the running board, or his foot slips off which is more probable, because it is loose and breaking away. He falls underneath and is run over as the rear wheel passes over his chest.

John Kelly is dead one hour after the accident. He is laid out in the small room at the road end of the infirmary all the following day as we go into the room to kneel and pray. Brother Kelly the superior is there. He hardly leaves the Room of Death. All day he cries and prays. I have not seen a man cry since the time about three years ago when Mr McAntaggart the bandmaster, and our teacher, was hit several times on the face by Brother Walsh. Brother Kelly is now crying loudly, and between sobs he is praying. He is really genuinely humble and sincere. Brother Kelly is my interpretation of a saint.

We should be going to Tully Strand next week, but it has been cancelled, as the school is now in mourning. As I looked at the face of the corpse, I was amazed at the contented and relaxed appearance and I felt relieved that this boy's sufferings were over. And for just a moment a sinful thought came to my mind. I too would like to be dead. This thought now worried me more every day and I wondered if I should tell the priest, but I was always afraid. I would leave it until the Missioner came on Christmas Eve, or perhaps I might ask Brother Kelly when I go to the office for thread and buttons.

The holidays were spoiled by the accident. We did not go to Tully strand which was an awful disappointment to every one. All the other lads went last year but I did not go because I was ill in the infirmary. Back at school I am in fourth standard. I am awful sorry to leave Mr Griffin, who was so good and kind, and taught us so much. At the exam before the holidays I got second highest marks, Danny Shields got the highest score. My brother Jack does not go to fourth, as he is due to leave school in a year and he works permanently on the farm except for an hour which is spent at school in the evening.

Brother Byrne is now our teacher and he often sends 'Bulldog' (a boy in our class) to the bathroom to get a wash because he has been working with the pigs all day. Bulldog has been a long time at the school because he has been here since he was six, and he has a hard and difficult time. He used to be often beaten by the monitors or bullies, who were lads mostly overage who were sent back to Letterfrack because they were failures outside.

Brother Byrne is a good Irish speaker, and teaches us all subjects so there is no need for the native Irish teacher McLaughlin to come to our class, (his nick name is *adhmad* or the Irish for timber).

It is Halloween and there is the usual excitement. We do not get oranges, because they are too expensive and Brother Kelly speaks of the growing need for economy. But we get very good apples and nuts which have already arrived days ago, and many of the boys write letters, and take them to the office. This gives them a chance to see for themselves the big bags of apples and nuts. This year there is less excitement because everyone knows in advance what they will receive. Brother Kelly has had to go away on business so Brother Fahy and Vale give out the fruit. For supper we get a slice of sweet cake, and a whole pot of strawberry jam to each table.

I have not been on serve now for two months and my state of health is better than before the holidays, but my hands are trembling and sweating just the same, so that my writing is not good, and although I wash my hands several times daily, my writing book and drawing book are dirty. John Power and Tommy Berry and young McLaughlin are all the same as I am. My head aches most mornings during breakfast but it's better when we are permitted to talk. There is now a great atmosphere of tension during every dinner hour, as there is about to be a change over in serve duties. We never know when the change will take place. Sometimes it may be after a month, or six weeks, but it may even be as long as four months before we are relieved of duty. The meal is now almost over, and we sit in nerve breaking silence, until one of the very young children drops a spoon or something on a plate, and I jump. The noise that spoon makes is as if the whole roof had fallen down. I did not notice any of the others jump, and after the meal I wanted, very much, to ask some of the other lads how they felt when the spoon dropped but I thought they would laugh at me, and to be laughed at, was even worse than a beating. I worried terribly what everybody thought about me. If I made a stupid mistake at school, or got the lowest number of marks, it was something to be ashamed of, and the remark that old Lydon made last year upset me quite a lot. He said my 'work was getting worse every day, and a good thing it is for you, the manager is away'.

The change over has now taken pace. After weeks of tension, the worst has happened. We are back on serve again. For almost a week he does not beat anyone except those working in the kitchen. Cunningham is in the scullery washing the dishes and we can hear awful cries coming from there. I want to go in to change the water, but am terrified. I know that if I am found using dirty water, I shall be in serious trouble. So I just grab the bucket and go to the kitchen as quickly as possible. I go to the boiler and get clean warm water, and as I am leaving, a little water is spilled on the floor of the kitchen which has been washed and dried, so I take the bucket back as quickly as possible, and return with a cloth to dry the floor. Luckily

I am able to wipe it up without being caught, because it is considered a terrible thing to allow anything to fall on the floor after it has been washed. The next two months go by with little change. The same anxiety and tension prevails. The constant beatings go on as before, and we are relieved from some duties during Christmas week

The missioner has arrived. As usual it is a Redemptorist Father, who preaches about little else only the fear of hell. He tells us awful stories about children who die in a state of mortal sin. This missioner tells us about a boy who died recently. He was called to give the last sacraments, but on arrival found the boy to be dead, so the following morning as the missioner was about to offer mass for the boy, he felt a tugging on his garment as he was about to climb the altar steps. As he turned around he observed the boy in flames, who begged him not to pray for him as it was too late and would only add to his torment. The priest told us many such stories, at least one every day for a week. This particular missioner in December 1929 also told us the exact depth of hell and the thickness of the walls. He also explained in detail, how a condemned soul would be chained and the exact position of the chains. He also told us that it took a soul three seconds to reach hell. These stories frightened me so much that I prayed almost all the time, for many weeks after.

I lived in a state of terror. I can remember very little of Christmas that year, because I was ill with fear, and suffered from what Brother Byrne said was a false conscience. I imagined that everything I said and done was a sin, and punishable by hell. It was at least a month after before I found the courage to explain my fears to the priest Fr. Donlan. I then asked him if he thought it was true that the missioner had actually seen this boy in flames. He did not answer my question. He merely laughed and said 'Do not worry about such things'. 'But I am worried', I said. 'Please tell me father was the story true or untrue?' And he answered saying, 'You must not doubt the word of a priest.' I asked Brother Kelly and he answered me saying 'There is a good reason why the priest talks to children in this manner'. 'Go away and forget about it', so that I started the year 1930 with a doubt in my mind as to whether or not the priest was speaking the truth from the altar.

10

Sixth Year

The year 1930 is no better than any of the previous years. I now have very grave doubts, concerning my religious education. When I go to confession I often ask questions many of which are answered in such a manner as to leave me in greater doubt than before, so I often go to Brother Kelly for help. He tries to help me, but his words prove nothing and I tell him this, and he gets a little angry. He advises me to believe what I am told without question. He then goes on to say that my religion is based on the Holy Bible which is the written word of God.

He reminded me that the good men responsible for my spiritual education were sent by God to simplify his word in keeping with my intelligence. I then asked, is it not true that many other religions are based on the Bible. Brother Kelly said that the other people's interpretation was incorrect. I then reminded him that those good men whose work it was to simplify the teachings of the Bible, had been unsuccessful so far in my case, and that I was dissatisfied with many of the answers even from the priest. He then advised me not to think too much about such matters as I was too young.

Although the new superior is a very good and sincere man his knowledge of economy is very limited, and the school is getting into financial difficulties. He has warned everyone that there would have to be many cuts in the purchase of food and materials, and that the wages of all employees would be cut by four shillings a week, irrespective of present earnings. I did not realize the meaning of this until I went to the office for materials for the workshop and Mr Griffin was being paid. His weekly wage was one pound, and with four shilling deducted, this left him with only sixteen shillings.

Mr Griffin refused to take his wages. With that the superior said your wage is sixteen shillings take it or leave it. Mr Griffin had been a teacher in the school for 43 years. It is a known fact that Mr Griffin is one of the best teachers in the country. His day starts at 6 a.m. and he finishes at 9 p.m., after school he is in the yard looking after the children, and he also looks after the greenhouse. Mr Griffin was always clean and tidy but now he couldn't afford to buy a shirt, instead he had a piece of calico, which was fastened to his waistcoat each side with pins. He didn't wear socks because he had none and he was almost blind trying to teach as they wouldn't buy him a pair of glasses. The Bothers used to laugh at him, because he was getting old, yet he had a smile for everyone and would always lift his old torn cap when the brothers came along. Mr Griffin always addressed the Brothers properly. Mr Griffin, who was a brilliant and highly educated man, and an excellent teacher, who had given a lifetime of hard work under the most trying conditions, was now rewarded, by reducing his weekly wage of one pound, to sixteen shillings and his keep.

Mr Griffin had never taken a holiday away from the school, nor had he taken a single day off during the years I spent at Letterfrack. When he was not teaching in the schoolroom, he was present in the yard, or in St. Patrick's Dormitory. Wherever the children were you could always find Mr Griffin. He took them to mass everyday and back again, he accompanied them to the football field and for walks during the holiday time, he wrote their letters, and read to them any they might receive.

About this time there was a catastrophe just off the coast of Connemara and only a few miles from Letterfrack, when 45 fishermen lost their lives as a terrific storm arose suddenly and without warning (or it may have been the year before). We were confined to the school rooms and were not allowed into the yard, because there were a lot of slates blown from the roof, and on one occasion a slate came through the window of number 2 school. There was widespread damage to the little houses in Connemara most of which were thatched and whitewashed.

In spite of the critical financial position of the school, the superior had engaged a physical training instructor, who took us on P.T. for a half hour daily. He also taught step dancing, and assisted Brother Byrne in teaching the boys a new play. A barber was also employed. He came to the school once a month, and cut everybody's hair, until now, one of the older boys cut the children's hair, but hair cutting was not done regularly, and it would often be two or three months before we would get a hair cut, the result was that many suffered from dirty heads full of vermin and sores. The children were often blamed for this state of affairs, and of course beaten. We were now in the new chapel which was more than twice as big as the old one, which was now being used as a store. The chapel was built on fairly high ground, which in 1925 was a wood. There were many and varied opinions as to the architecture of this building, Brother Byrne thought it was a 'beautiful jem', Brother Kelly said it was the 'most modern chapel in the county, Brother Murphy the office Brother thought it was like a 'bloody barn'. Although it has only been completed, the recent storm blew half the roof off, and there are several gaping cracks from top to bottom. It has been constructed of concrete with dashed walls, the roof is made of red tiles, the altar is built from green Connemara marble, one end of the chapel, or the altar end, is only twenty yards from the Brothers monastery, the other end is about eighty yards from the old chapel. The cemetery is in the wood, half way between the old church and the infirmary, and about a hundred yards from the road.

In the tailor's work shop we are busy making suits for the Brothers and a few outside customers. Our customers outside the school are mostly fishermen or farmers. They wear a very simple suit called a *báneen* which is made completely by machine. The jacket is made without a collar, the front is shaped like a waistcoat, it has sleeves, but is usually without pockets. The trousers have plain bottoms and are made with or without pockets. The *báneen* suit is of plain light grey flannel. The customers in Connemara are not difficult to please, they only want a strongly made plain garment with plenty of room to work in it. The natives are a very simple, almost primitive, and kindly folk. They take very little notice of fashions and the style of dress never changes. They are religious and superstitious, and many of the older people do not speak English.

As the land is terribly poor, most of them earn a living by fishing. Mackerel is the most common fish in these waters. Val Connelly the very big young man, who lives in the thatched house in the village, just outside the school, is in the mechanic's shop most days. He is often engaged to drive the Guy lorry to Westport, and Foxford woollen mills where we buy most of our cloth. Val, is better known as 'the Bolshie' on account of his escapades during the trouble. He gets no regular wage but is often allowed expenses. He may go two or three weeks without getting anything and then will probably get anything from one to three pounds, but only after he has reminded the superior of the dreadful circumstances at home. I always know when he is paid expenses, because Joe Baker tells me. He also tells me when Val is due back, and I manage to get out of the yard by climbing over the wall at the back of the lavatory and hang about the garage until he gets back, because when Val gets any money he goes drinking and does not eat his sandwiches, which he brings from home. And if I can stay around long enough, and he does not forget, he will give them to me. They are made of home baked bread and butter or jam, and once he had bacon and egg sandwiches.

It is now St. Patrick's Day which is a holiday and we wear our best clothes just like on Sunday. We are allowed to talk at meals. Breakfast is the same as on Sunday, tea with bread and margarine. Dinner consists of roast beef, potatoes and cabbage, after dinner Brother Kelly comes to the yard, and as the weather is fine he takes all the boys for a walk along the Tully Strand road. Normally we should line up and march in our own divisions or tables, but Brother Kelly is not very strict, and I manage to work my way back to the rear of the parade where Brother Kelly is, because on such occasions he is very free and easy, and likes to make conversation. There are several questions I would like to ask him provided the opportunity arises, but when we are about a mile from the school, there is a donkey and cart coming towards us. The donkey is very small, and looks quite young, and there are two men sitting on the cart. As the donkey is unable to climb a fairly steep part of the road, and as the load is too much for him, he falls on the road, and is beaten by one of the men with a stick. On seeing this I turned to Brother Kelly and asked, 'Sir is it a sin to ill-treat an animal in this manner?', surely the correct thing to do is to help the donkey to his feet instead of hitting him with a stick. Brother Kelly just laughed and answered, 'the animal has no soul, like us.' After a pause I then said, the children have souls, yet, they are flogged almost every day. He looked at me and seemed to be angry, and asked, 'is that a complaint?' I did not answer, Brother Kelly then went on, 'I have never heard you complain before. It is very sinful in the eyes of God to complain'. He then added, 'I thought you were a good boy and was about to teach you how to "serve Mass". But I can now see that you are not suitable for this duty, as this is your first complaint I will let you off, but you must never make this mistake again'.

For supper we have tea, bread, margarine and sweet cake. After supper there is a concert, and many clergy are invited. There are Christian Brothers from Salthill in Galway, and about a hundred paying guests. All the children are present, and everyone enjoys a good evening's entertainment. The band plays very well. There is also step dancing by Matt Feerick and Christy Long. There are also some fairly good singers including Tommy Gordon, and young Hunt, but Hunt is so nervous, that he breaks down completely. This seems very strange in view of the fact that Hunt has been the school's best singer for two years. We have another good tenor from Galway called Cooney.

The following day Hunt is asked in front of the class to give an explanation for his failure at the concert. He is now out of favour with the bandmaster and Fahy, and has been Fahy's favourite pet for more than a year. Matt Feerick is now in Fahy's good books and is nearly always in his company. Fahy always has one favourite, who spends long hours in his private room. Unlike most of his other pets Feerick does not carry stories.

In the tailor's shop I only work on suits for the staff or outside customers. I no longer make clothes for the children, but am responsible to Lydon for any work done by the young lads, and have to teach them repairs and the making of the children's suits as well as shirts, pillowcases and sheets. I also go to the office and store for materials for the shop.

Brother Scully has left and Brother Rairdon takes over the duties of farm Brother (Brother Blake was the farm Brother in 1925) Blake and Rairdon have much in common. They are about the same age 40. They both have a red face, and dark hair brushed straight back. They are religious and equally brutal to the children. Brother Blake went to Salthill on or about 1926, and it is said that he was so cruel to the lads that the older ones tied him up one night and flogged him severely. The boys who done this were sent to a reformatory.

In school there is almost half our time spent on Irish, and catechism, with the result we are behind in other subjects. Brother Byrne thinks teaching of Irish is a mistake, in view of the fact that most of the boys would find it necessary to emigrate before they reach the age of eighteen, due mainly to economic conditions at home. Tommy Ward then asked why do such conditions exist. Brother Byrne answered saying, our country is under-developed, because it was the policy of the British who occupied it, to keep it that way. But that is not the only reason, Ireland is poor in mineral wealth, Brother Byrne then added, but we are also poor in great leaders. 'We have not a single leader who is worth his salt, and another very important reason for our poor economy is, because the Irish have always been reluctant to do anything for themselves'. The Irish have done great things abroad, they have built the railroads in America and they have played a great part in the building up of the British Empire. They have fought and won wars for other people, but at home they can't even feed themselves.

The nurse who left and married Mr Hogan, has come to Letterfrack for a holiday. They are very happy and every one is glad to learn this. Mr Hogan was a boy in Letterfrack many years ago. He was a blacksmith to trade but has since become a cook. They have settled down in England. Mrs Hogan is working in a hospital and is now a fully qualified nurse. Mrs Hogan has always walked with the aid of a stick and it is said that she has an artificial leg.

The waste ground at the back of the drill hall or concert hall, is now being levelled off, and a tennis court is going to be built there. Brother Fahy is in charge of the job and we all work there for an hour every day. Brother Keegan intended to grow vegetables there, but never got round to starting the job.

It is now Easter week and there are great preparations for a dance to be held in the hall on Easter Sunday. We are washing and scrubbing the floor and putting the chairs in position, the entrance fee is 5 shilling. The children will not be there of course. It is a tea dance, which is good news for everyone, because we will have to do the clearing up the next day, and shall be able to get the food that's left over. I can't remember the last tea dance but the lads say there was lovely meat sandwiches and all kinds of cakes left over.

Tom Donlon said he found a half crown on the floor when he was sweeping up after the last dance, which he gave to Brother Vale and got a penny for himself. A very large crowd is expected as the dance is well advertised. The boys all look forward to a dance or a whist drive, because the Christian Brothers will be busy with their girlfriends. Brother Byrne has a lovely girl with black hair, she is only 22. Brother Fahy sees his girl two or three times a week now, she always comes in her car and waits for him on the road outside the avenue. The boys in Fahy's school say they have a good time when he is going with the girl, but when they fall out he beats them much more.

In the refectory we are still being beaten by Vale. I have not been beaten during meal times for nearly three weeks, but we are beaten on serve usually for three days, and then he leaves us alone sometimes for a whole week. I have now discovered a very good idea. I have made a double seat for my pants which I have stitched on the inside. It is a very heavy material, and I find it most effective. When I was beaten two days ago it didn't hurt very much, and I am not so much afraid anymore. I have promised to put double seats in for many other lads, as soon as I can get material. I am going to pad the back of my jacket as well especially around the back of the shoulders, as that is where the rubber hurts most. I forget my own fears when I see the faces of some of the other boys, John Power, Martin Mullins, the two Giblins, John Coyne, Tommy Berry, Murdoch, the two McLaughlins. I have heard that John Power and big McLaughlin will be going to another home unless their condition improves. John Power goes about talking to himself and laughing. Sometimes he cries when there is no one near him. Tommy Feerick is also taking the beatings badly. He is at present in the infirmary with skin disease from which many are now suffering.

We often get nasty sores on the head and face, and the backs of the hands. John Coyne, this boy's father killed his mother when he was six years old and he was admitted to the school shortly afterwards. I remember the day he arrived, he was a very shy and timid child. I was older than him about two years, and everybody was wondering if he really realised the terrible thing that had happened, although he never smiled he didn't appear too unhappy. He was a really handsome boy with a lovely round face, dark hair and brown eyes. There was that searching look in his face. Every time he looked at me he seemed to be asking, 'Do you really know the dreadful experience I have had?', 'Do you really mind very much?', 'Do you condemn me for what has happened?' and 'Will you hold it against me?' I was extremely fond of this little lad, and although he is younger than me I often play with him, and share what little I get from home with him, because he has never received a letter although he has been here three years. I have never mentioned anything to him about his home life, nor he to me. Very few of the other lads bother with him and they often talk among themselves about his parents. I sometimes wonder, has anyone ever said anything to him about the past. It would be an awful thing if they had. I can well remember when he was only about a week in the school, seeing Brother Walsh holding him by the hand and beating him. Walsh always done that to children of seven or eight, he grabbed hold of their hand because they didn't hold it in the correct position, to be slapped.

Vale has beaten this unfortunate boy terribly during the last year. His lovely face seems to have changed an awful lot, that roundness has vanished, instead his face is long, his check bones stick out, his eyes just glare (or stare) and there are dark shadows underneath. His cheeks were once rosy but now they are chalk white, with several spots.

Con Murphy has always been my chum. He plays in the band, and never forgets to bring me back something nice when he has been on tour, an apple, an orange, a bag of sweets, or a piece of cake. He was very young when he came to Letterfrack in 1923. He couldn't have been more than seven years old. His health has failed terribly, he works beside me in the tailor's shop, his mouth and gums are diseased, and by pressing his gums he can bring puss and blood from them, and like many of the children here he smells real bad, it's like a stale smell of sweat. We sweat a lot when we are in the refectory. I have noticed many times when I am having a meal in silence the sweat just pours off my hands, and from under my armpits. I can feel it running down my sides, and when we are lined up to be beaten I can smell the sweat of the others, everyone a little different. If I closed my eyes and just walked along a line of children I imagine I could recognise each one by their particular odour. This is very strange to me. In spite of the fact that we take a bath every Saturday, and our shirts and socks are changed, most of us smell. Perhaps that is why Vale puts medicine in our food. We have not had any medicine recently because the last time it made many of the kids ill and they were up all night.

I have noticed too that many suffer from catarrh of the nose and throat. I can hear many of them sniffing, and they have great difficulty in breathing. I can hear them during the night fighting for breath, as it were. I have the same complaint, my nose is always stopped up on one side, and it's hard to breathe and my face feels hot and it gets flushed. I get pains between the eyes and when I try to blow my nose, I get a sharp pain over my left eye.

They call big McLaughlin 'Kangaroo' because the day he came to the school Walsh said he looked like one. He has long legs and big ears, he is very backward at school, and has been flogged a lot more than anyone else. Boys who are not good looking, or are in any way deformed, are laughed at, and ill-treated. Tom Thornton a big lad for his age, has one leg, and is made to do serve duties, and washing up and scrubbing floors etc. I have seen him been beaten by Vale on the stump of his bad leg. He works in the tailor's shop and is a good tailor, he plays handball very well, and he can beat me easily.

Matt Feerick a band boy plays a flute. He is very good looking lad of fourteen years and is now Brother Fahy's pet. He has always had favourable treatment, he appears to be in good health, he is a nice lad and does not carry stories like the other pets.

Tommy Gordon, like his older brother George is a good musician, he plays the piano and the clarinet. The Gordons from Belfast are good looking and very intelligent. They have had better treatment than most, probably because their mother comes to see them periodically. They get lots of toys and sweets. The younger lad is very nice and good natured, he gives most of his sweets away. But his big brother George was a bit of a bully. He used to take half a slice of bread from me at breakfast during my first year, in exchange he would give me half his margarine, but it was no good without bread. He was the monitor in charge of the table. The Gordons have not suffered as much as the others, and they are in better health

Charlie Haywood, now works in the office. He comes from Galway city and his mother sells fish in the market. He is my own age and is rather good at school. He suffered a lot under Walsh and is suffering under Vale now. Yet he is standing up to the beatings fairly good, and looks in fairly good heath.

Murtagh, this lad frightens me to look at his face. He is very small for his age. He was in great spirits when Walsh left, and was doing well at school, but now he is backward at school, and he screams terribly when being beaten, he cries even before he gets one blow. Brother Vale has given him a bad time, and hardly passes him without hitting him. Murtagh like Con Murphy has bad teeth and his gums are all festered and look sore. He is now in the tailor's shop. He has never received any letters and they say he has no parents.

Tom Berry, also small for his age, is very pale, and does not look strong. He gets bad colds and suffers with a cough. He is a tailor. He does not cry when being beaten and he has no parents.

Cosgrave, a Galway boy, is a very good singer. He is now fourteen. His mother came to see him once about two years ago. He is a mass server with Charlie Haywood.

It's Easter and we are all given a new red handkerchief, because the priest is annoyed with us for sniffing at mass. He said we should blow our nose. He also complains about our coughing and said it's just a bad habit. We have a fried egg for breakfast, and there is an extra loaf to each table of twelve. There is marmalade and tea. For dinner we get roast beef, with cabbage and steamed potatoes. After dinner, we have boxing, which is organised by Fahy, and he often matches the contenders badly with the result that several get hurt. Fahy likes boxing but the other Brothers don't. Brother Vale, who is looking on, gets upset when he sees a boy bleeding from the nose. This is very surprising for him. For tea we get currant buns, with bread and jam, and there is a whist drive afterwards in the hall. There is an entrance fee of 2/6 but the boys who are able to play and wish to take part, are allowed in free. It's quite an exciting evening, as several of the local men who take part are a little drunk, including Festy McDonald the butcher. He is always swearing as usual. I take part in the game but make many mistakes, by going to the wrong table. There are prizes of cash and a box of chocolates. Young Hunt wins second prize and the bandmaster gets third. The first prize is won by a very tall man called Joyce. He is a school teacher from the Joyce country, and is the tallest man I have ever seen. He is six ft. three inches.

On Easter Monday, we get a surprise. As the whistle blows at about ten o'clock the superior tells us that we are going to Tully strand. Easter Monday used to be the day for the trip before Keegan came to the school, but he thought it too cold and changed it to the summer holidays. We had a most enjoyable day and played football on the beach, and Brother Murphy the office Brother organised racing and games for the young children. Afterwards there were paper bags of bread and jam sandwiches and cakes distributed. It was much too cold to bathe so we continued with our games, after which there was a sing song, and all those who entertained got prizes of sweets. On arrival back at the school there was a hot meal prepared of stewed meat and vegetables.

There is very little change until the summer holidays, which is always a time of joy and bliss. It is a time and almost the only time, when life is worth living. The warmer weather adds to our pleasure and happiness. The winter is the most unpleasant time of the year, because not only are we cold, but hungry as well. We are not very hungry during the holidays, because we can get potatoes from the farm or from the back of the kitchen and roast them in the forge or our own work shop, and we can also get blackberries and straw-berries in the football fields.

The holidays is a time of complete relaxation, when we enjoy every minute of each day. In the evening we go to the football field or go swimming, but we are not compelled to do either. We wander about the farm or go fishing for eels in the stream. We can go and climb trees near the haunted house or just go across the road from the haunted house where we always get the chestnuts.

After supper we play handball until it's almost dark, and the night man chases us off to bed. The weather is blazing hot and I fall asleep in the yard, and Tommy Gordon calls me to go to the workshop. Mr Griffin takes us for long walks up Diamond Hill, which is about a mile east of the school. Mr Griffin is almost seventy and is getting bad on his feet. We stop for a rest, as he fills his pipe, the tobacco smells wonderful. Mr Griffin never smokes in the school or the yard. The tobacco smell reminds me of when I went with my Dad for the first time to gather sticks in the wood. It was a day just like now, warm and sunny, we went further on up the hill and took a drink from the stream.

After a rest Mr Griffin looks at the sun and says it's time we went back for tea, he can always tell the time by the sun. I asked him if he had a watch and he said he had, but it stopped twenty years ago. In the workshop I am making a suit for my brother Jack, who is due to leave the school before Christmas, he will be only fifteen and a half and is lucky to be able to get away so early. McGrath the shoemaker is also leaving soon. Cunningham the boy who used to make the toys has now left. He never learned to read or write and Jack is the same.

A great number of lads never learn to read or write, and Brother Murphy said 'it's because too much time is spent on learning Irish, and beating the lads.'

The holidays are over and I am in fifth standard. We don't do much the first day. We are given new books, pens and pencils. Brother Fahy explains what is expected of us during the coming year. There will be an exam in catechism shortly and he asks every one a few questions to find out what we do know. He is not satisfied with many of us and explains that we must work very hard during the next few months.

After a few weeks when we are finished our breakfast, it is discovered that there is a fire in number 2 school (or Brother Byrne's school). There was a box of coal left in front of the fire and the box caught alight and quickly spread to the floor, and the wainscot, or the wood work along the wall, which goes up about 3 ft 6 inches and Vale orders the boys to bring buckets of water from the kitchen to extinguish the fire and as the lads get excited at the sight of the fire he beats them, and as they are running to get water he chases after them with the rubber swinging to make them hurry. After twenty minutes the fire is under control, and there is very little damage. Brother Kelly now comes around all the schools and orders all inflammable materials to be moved well away from the fire.

At lessons Fahy is very severe on those who fail, especially at sums and catechism, and we are lined up after each sum and slapped, usually about three slaps with a very heavy stick. He always aims for the thumb or high up on the wrist. Writing is usually the next subject and my hand is so painful that I am unable to write. We are usually beaten about four times a day for failure at lessons. When I go to the tailors shop I am unable to do my work, and am sometimes reported for that. The beating is severe if we are reported for bad work.

It is now Halloween and the usual excitement, but this year I am not very happy about it, because we are beaten at school and sometimes after meals as I am back on serve duties, so that life again is almost unbearable. This goes on until Christmas week. I failed at catechism when the priest came round, and now I have to stay behind when the other lads are at play, to learn catechism. The missioner is now here and is preparing us for the happy event of Christmas by frightening us with his awful stories. He is a Redemptorist father. As usual he always talks about hell. This time he tells us about a young couple who committed a sin and were found together dead the next day.

I am again terrified as I was last year. I go to confession again and again, as well as confessing I also ask questions which have been puzzling me. The answers sometimes put me at ease for a while until I start thinking again, usually in bed and I remember that I asked that question before and got a different answer from another priest. I am now completely confused, and my imagination is playing tricks with me. When I go to sleep I have terrible and frightening dreams, the same dream as last year. There is someone running after me and I can't get away. It's always dark, and I can't see anybody, I am terrified to look behind because I know there is somebody there. I wake up sweating and I try to remain awake, by pinching myself, and biting my lip, it's no good. I sleep again, but am more afraid this time. I am up a great height and falling. I wake up screaming. I am now really worried because I have never screamed before.

It is Christmas day and I try to pull my self together. My brother Jack has left school and I am alone, really alone. Never have I felt so lonely and miserable before. There is someone speaking to me, it is Con Murphy he is wishing me a happy Christmas. I am dazed and he repeats, what he has been saying. As I look at his face, he is smiling, and I can see his gums. They are in a sickly condition, his teeth are discoloured and decayed, his gums are just full of mucus and I advise him to go and see the nurse, but I know he won't go, because I told him before. Many of the children have this complaint or disease, others have running ears. Many suffer from sores on the head and face and in the ears, the legs and the hands. Many walk with their heads down, and some are very round shouldered.

Dr. Lavelle a man of about forty, comes to see us about once a month, but he just walks around the yard with a dog at his heels. The dog is the biggest I have ever seen. Lavelle always wears a plus-four suit of tweed, and I have never see him without a cigarette in his mouth. My younger brother Laurence has been in the school about a year, but I do not recognise him. He was too young to come to Letterfrack so was sent to the nuns at Kilkenny. He is a year younger than me, but is now much bigger than I am and is good at school. He was in the infirmary six months ago with poisoned hands and had to have both lanced in several places in order to let out the puss. This was due to chilblains which became septic.

The Christmas dinner is really good. Roast chicken and roast pork, green peas, followed by plum pudding and custard. There is less excitement than last year as Father Christmas did not come. I am now feeling a little better than for the last few days. It's most remarkable how the Brothers change at this time of year. Vale has been up half the night preparing the dinner, and it is really good. Brothers Fahy and Byrne, Murphy and Conway are waiting on the children. Vale, his clothes dirty and full of grease, is bringing out the trays of chicken from the kitchen. His face is sweating and he looks tired. Brother Kelly is going about giving everyone sweets from a very big tin.

I have not received a letter this year because I have not answered the last two. Now I know why many of the others lads stopped writing. I now feel bitter towards my parents. I want to write home and tell them everything, but always change my mind the last moment. I now feel glad that I never wrote. I think it's much better that my parents forget about me. I shall soon be fifteen and will then have only a year to do. However bad the last year is it can't be any worse than the last five and a half years, so I make up my mind to try and have fun for the next few days like the other lads. I tell myself that I am not going to worry about the awful and terrifying things the missioner has been telling us, besides they may not even be true. I find it hard to believe that the priest has seen a boy who is in hell, and I remember the last year how the missioner explained the exact position of the chains on the condemned boys legs.

After dinner, we go into the village. Martin Mullins and Tommy Gordon have some money and we want to buy sweets. We come to the post office and it is shut. We go across the road to the pub, and Mr Griffin is there, so the lads give Mr Griffin a shilling for a drink. He is now looking old and shabby, since his wages were cut down to sixteen shilling he has not been able to get any new clothes. We asked for sweets in the pub but they didn't sell any, but they had bottles of lemonade and ginger beer, so we had three bottles of ginger beer. Mr Griffin now teaches infants because he is unable to read the third standard book owing to his failing sight.

We stood at the door drinking the ginger beer straight from the bottle. When John Cusack and Tommy Mannion arrived with another farmhand who I do not know, they bought a pint for Mr Griffin and asked us to have something, but we thanked them very much and said no.

We walked along the road towards Kylemore. We were making for Rankins, because they were always open. Martin Mullins asked Gordon if ginger beer would make us drunk, and Gordon admitted he never drank any before. I didn't know because I had never been in a pub before. Just before we came to the sweet shop we met a lady who smiled and spoke to us. Tommy Gordon said she was the Protestant woman Brother Byrne used to talk about, and I then remembered a sermon a few weeks before in the chapel. It was the priest from the convent at Kylemore Abbey who said a Protestant had as much chance of going to heaven as would a rowing boat crossing to America in a storm. This made me think a lot because this lady, although I never met her before, was very good and kind. I could not remember what Brother Byrne said but I should like to find out, and feel certain that he would say nothing wrong about her.

After buying a lot of canned sweets we made our way back and found the boys having supper. After which there was a picture show. It was the same picture we seen about two years before, when it broke down several times. It was Charlie Chaplin.

1. Tyrrell's parents with his eldest brother Mick on the right. Man second on the right is unknown.

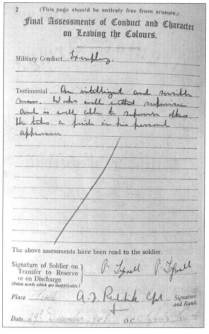

2. Tyrrell's 'Certificate of discharge' from the British Army.

3. Tyrrell's 'Final assessment of conduct and character' from his British Army papers.

4.. *Punishment in Our Schools*. A pamphlet from 1955 published by "School-children's protection organisation" including a collection of letters from parents whose children had received excessive corporal punishment.

CORPORAL   PUNISHMENT
IN
IRISH   PRIMARY   SCHOOLS

THREE SENATE SPEECHES

BY

OWEN SHEEHY SKEFFINGTON

JULY, 1956.

These extracts from the Official Senate Reports are reprinted by per√
mission of the Controller of the Stationery Office.

5. A pamphlet published by Owen Sheehy Skeffington containing the text of his speeches in the Senate including an exchange of views with the then Minister for Education Richard Mulcahy.

NEWS OF THE WORLD, LIMITED
TELEGRAPHIC ADDRESS:
"WORLDLY, FLEET, LONDON"
TELEPHONE:
FLEET STREET 8030 (8 LINES)

News of the World.

30. Bouverie St. Fleet St.

Ref: 34

London 21st April 19 58
E.C.4.

LARGEST CIRCULATION IN THE WORLD

Dear Mr. Tyrrell,

You make some very serious complaints about the Christian Brothers but all your complaints appear to be based on your own personal experience during one particular period and in one particular Home. On those experiences you seem to have started a general compaign but have so far not had much success. I rather think you may have been guilty of generalising and assuming that what may have happened to you must have happened to everyone similarly placed.

Generalisations are always dangerous and rarely get people anywhere. I am not suggesting for a moment that you had no good cause for complaint in the early 1930s. If action was to be taken, however, it should have been taken then, when a specific complaint against a specific Christian Brother could have been properly investigated. Quite frankly, I fear that it is too late now for anybody to be able to investigate your particular charges. All this happened well over 20 years ago and the Christian Brother or Brothers concerned may even be dead by now.

I fully sympathise with your wish to try to put things right when you feel they are wrong, but any action of that sort, to be successful, must be taken at the time things are known to be wrong; not over 20 years later.

Yours sincerely,

For the JOHN HILTON BUREAU.

The Editor presents his Compliments and begs to state that, while every care is taken to ensure accuracy, this information is given on the strict understanding that no legal or other liability is thereby incurred, and can only be used on that understanding.

6. Response from *News of the World* to a letter sent by Tyrrell to them in April 1958.

ARCHBISHOP'S HOUSE,

WESTMINSTER,

LONDON, S.W.1.

3rd March, 1958.

Dear Mr. Tyrnell,

His Grace the Archbishop has asked me to
thank you for your letter of 28th February
and to tell you that as the matter to which you
refer is outside his jurisdiction, it is not a
case in which he can intervene.

Yours sincerely,

Private Secretary.

Peter Tyrnell Esq.,
18 Balford Road,
Highbury,
London, N.5.

7. Another letter found in Skeffington's papers, this time a response from the secretary to the
Archbishop of Westminster – at the time Cardinal Nicholas Wiseman - dismissing Tyrrell's claims.

8. Photo of Senator Owen Sheehy Skeffington at home.

9. The only existing photograph of Peter Tyrrell. On the right is Peter's brother with one of his sons.

36 Caledonian Rd,
Leeds 2.

July 22nd 1958

This is to certify that I Peter Tyrrell witnessed & suffered torture and severe beatings, from 1924 until 1932. at the Christian Brothers School Letter-Frack Co. Galway Eire,

I was an inmate of this school through unfortunate happenings at my home owing to my extreme youth, I had no control, the reason being poverty, my parents could not support me.

Three of the Christian Brothers were sadists one was a Pervert; boys were lined up several times daily to be beaten, this. was not for committing any offence against the school rules, but was normal routine

P. Tyrrell.

10. Peter Tyrrell's first letter to Owen Sheehy Skeffington. For Skeffington's response see Appendix.

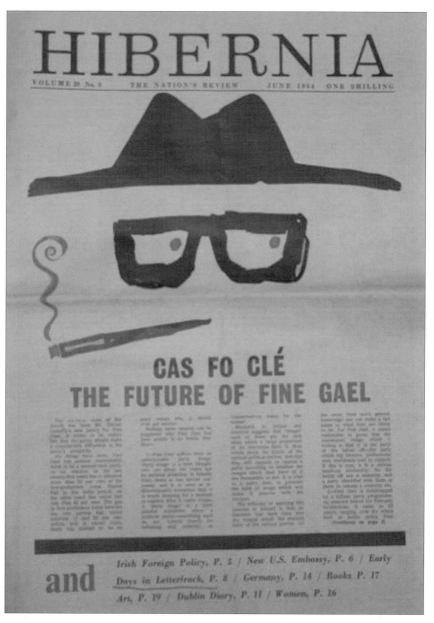

11. The cover of the edition of *Hibernia* magazine in which Tyrrell's brief account of his time in Letterfrack – "Early Days in Letterfrack"– was published.

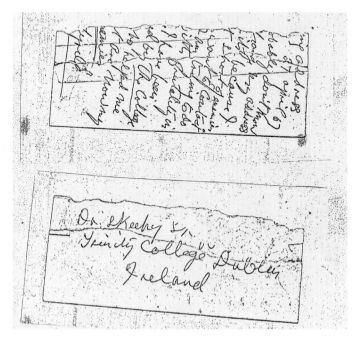

Address any reply to
THE COMMISSIONER OF POLICE OF THE
METROPOLIS, NEW SCOTLAND YARD, S.W.I

quoting:—

/201/67/91(A.4)

POSTAGE MUST BE PREPAID

Your Reference No.......................

NEW SCOTLAND YARD,
LONDON,
S.W.I

01-230 1212

TELEPHONE

Ext. 2545

3/ᵉˢᵗ May, 1968

Sir,

Body found on Hampstead Heath
on 28.4.67

I am directed by the Commissioner to return
as requested the letter from Peter Tyrrell, which
you kindly forwarded to assist enquiries,
together with a photostat copy of the pieces
of postcard found near the body. As positive
identification of the body has not been
established the original pieces of card will
be retained.

Your assistance in this matter is
appreciated.

I am, Sir,
Your obedient Servant,

12. Letter from Scotland Yard to Owen Sheehy Skeffington.

13. A photocopy of the torn postcard found near Tyrrell's body on Hampstead Heath.

11

I leave Letterfrack

My term is up about June 1932. Although it's only January 1931, I call this my last year, hoping they will let me 'go out' before I am sixteen. About one in three manage to 'go out' before their time is up. This can be anything from three to six months early. So far two of my brothers managed to get away before their time. I have known lads to leave school when they were fifteen. The P.P. at home just drops a line to the superior, I am told that a few pounds change hands. Some lads are claimed by their parents, and of course the priest must call to see if the home is suitable for the boy's return. The essential thing is that the parents attend mass and contribute generously to the priest when he calls.

Almost all the old bullies have now left, that is the kind who ran the place when I first came. They were usually monitors who sat at the end of the table in the refectory. They distributed the food, and after everyone was served then went round and demanded a portion of food from the young kids. These monitors were usually fifteen, but George Gordon, our monitor was only fourteen.

The monitor often copied the Brother who was in charge of him. That is in respect to beatings he beat the younger children under him in the same manner, as he had been beaten himself. Ackle a boy of about fifteen and a half in 1925 was a monitor and even worse than any of the Brothers. He was in Brother Dooley's class, and Dooley used a heavy cane walking stick, so Ackle got himself a cane. Cavanagh, who had been several years under Brother Walsh, used a leather strap because Walsh used one. When I was ten I was polishing the floor in St. Michael's dormitory one day, when there was a boy left in charge of us. He was only about thirteen. He worked in the shoemaker's shop and he used a strap to beat us exactly the same as the one Walsh used. He had made this strap himself, it consisted of two pieces of sole leather sewn together by hand. This boy was with Walsh for three years. Not only did he beat us in the same manner as Walsh but he pulled our hair the same. In 1925–26 it was not an uncommon sight to see a lad of twelve to fourteen having five or six very young children in line and beating them with a stick or strap. At that time it was fashionable for boys of over twelve to carry some kind of weapon. During my first few months at the school I can faintly remember seeing monitors using three heavy leather laces which were plaited together. The night man of that time used a number of leather laces which he used to flog the kids when he put them across the bed. Another method used was to lift the child off the ground by catching the hair just in front of the ears with the forefinger and thumb of each hand.

In the yard the band is practicing marching to music. I don't remember seeing them marching before, and every few minutes Hickey stops them to hit some with the drum stick. This Hickey seems to love beating the youngsters, but he does not beat anyone over fifteen, because he is afraid. Instead he sends them to Fahy, who makes a good job of it. Hickey has now become a real swelled head. He gets a lot more money since he became an *A.R.C.M.* He gets four pound a week and he has only been here three years. Yet Mr Griffin who was a schoolteacher many years before he was born, earns 16/– a week because he is an old man and can't get another job.

Several of the staff are now over 65. Mr Moran the blacksmith, Mr Flanagan the shoemaker, and the carpenter whose name I can't remember, Festy McDonald the butcher, Annie Aspel is also looking much older. She said she was 48. That was about three years ago, but I think she is much more. Lydon the tailor is over fifty. He's getting big and fat now and can hardly climb on to the table. He used to sit with his legs crossed but now has to stand. His son Martin Joe has stopped coming to the workshop. He is finished with tailoring and is now running a Ford car. He said tailoring is only a trade for cripples. His father is very angry because his son was a good worker. Tom McDonald has now left and I am the most senior tailor in the shop, and Lydon wants me to work full time in the shop instead of going to school in the morning at nine, but Fahy has chosen Tom Thornton the lad with one leg because, as Fahy puts it, Thornton needs a trade more than me as he is handicapped.

I am back on serve duties again and the beatings still go on. But Vale now beats the younger lads more. As I am now almost fifteen, he leaves me alone and concentrates on the little boys between ten and twelve, using the same methods as before, pinching and beating with the boy across his knee. We are allowed to talk more often now, about three times a week. Vale talks to himself a lot now as if he is praying. He is always swinging the rubber and hitting tables or the wall. He hits almost everything he comes to. He had a lovely black cat called 'Nigger' which he carried on his shoulder, and he looked after the cat for about a year and then got tired of it, and started to beat it, until the cat went wild and used to scratch anyone who touched it. Eventually it left and is now wandering about the wood. 'Nigger' sometimes comes to the tailor's shop at night, and sleeps under the bench, and I have not see any rats lately.

Fahy has fallen out with his girlfriend, and he is always in a bad temper now. When he was meeting her we had a good time. We could always tell when she was coming. It was usually after dinner or late in the evening when the horn of her car would blow, and he would look through the window. He always shaved the day he had a date and he would put oil on his hair. Fahy was getting grey at the sides but some days we couldn't see any grey. Joe Kelly said he used to blacken his hair with boot polish. Fahy always came back with a very red face after being with the girl, some of the lads said he used to go to Clifden drinking.

It's St. Patrick's day and a special service is being held in the chapel. The P.P. usually conducts the service on holidays, but is now ill with his leg, and Fr. McDonald takes it. The priest reminds us that it was St. Patrick who brought the Catholic faith to Ireland. He tells us that Ireland before St Patrick came 'was a country of pagans –what a terrible place it must have been then, when the people adored idols. The pagans were savages and barbarians, but today we are a great people, we are known the world over as saints and scholars, "the island of saints and scholars"'. The priest, now in a loud voice said 'We must thank God to-day for that great honour he has bestowed on us. There are still very many nations which are backward like we once were. But one day my dear brethren the whole world will be united in the faith, our faith in the name of Christ Jesus.' St. Patrick's Day was cold and wet, so we remained in the hall. In the evening after supper we played whist. The band master was my partner and I played badly so he blamed me because he did not win a prize.

Joe Baker is now a very good mechanic and a good driver. He is also the best writer in the school and the other Brothers often came to look at his writing, and they take his old books away. Fahy who does not like Baker often says that good writing is a fool's accomplishment. Fahy often reminds us that a Christian Brother gets no wages. He devotes his whole life towards the welfare of the children, and all he gets in exchange is his food and clothes, which any pauper gets in any workhouse. I remember him saying exactly the very same thing once before. It's Easter Monday and the weather is too wet to go to Tully strand, so we just spend the day reading books in the library.

The superior has now gone away on business and Fahy is looking after the office for a week. We spend a lot of time now on catechism with the result that we are backward in other subjects. This is Fahy's favourite subject, he just loves it. I can't learn catechism because I have no time for it, and I am beginning to feel the same way about religion, because the people who do not go to church (we have had two in Letterfrack) are better than those who go every day. I have now made up my mind to go abroad and study religion, not only the Catholic, but other religions as well. I can't believe that Brothers Walsh, Vale and Fahy, have a better chance of going to heaven than the protestant lady who lives outside the school.

There is very little change until Easter. The same brutality continues. Fahy does not like anyone in his school speaking to Brother Byrne, or indeed any of the Brothers, or masters. Fahy has a violent temper and when any of the other Brothers get the better of him he spends a whole hour talking about them to his school. When Brother Murphy comes to the yard or school, Fahy encourages the lads to jeer and laugh at him and the office Brother is such a nice man. Brother Murphy was not afraid of Fahy, like many others. One morning at breakfast when Fahy was present some of the boys started to jeer when Murphy arrived. Brother Murphy then addressed the boys saying that 'he would open Brother Fahy's eyes for him', knowing that the pets would tell Fahy what was said.

As we are on 'serve' after dinner, Brother Kelly the superior came to the kitchen, and called Vale and asked why a boy with one leg should have to wash dishes and scrub floors. He then turned to Tom Thornton and told him to go the yard and not to do any more serve duties. I have not been beaten in the refectory for a long time, or in the bathroom, except an occasional blow on entering or leaving. Fahy lines us up four or five times a day to be slapped. My writing is now very poor and the paper is always dirty as the sweat just runs off my hands. I carry a large piece of white cloth to dry my hands but they are wet again in a few minutes. I fail at most subjects because I cannot concentrate on what I am doing. My mind is on other things and my imagination just runs riot. I am again sleeping badly and the awful dreams every night frighten and terrify me.

As we are preparing for bed one night after saying the rosary we are kept behind for a talking to. Fahy often does this, he loves to give a lecture or a sermon. He usually starts by reminding us of a coming festival, or he might talk on the life of a saint – a very holy man who when tempted to commit a sin, would cause himself great physical pain by wearing a very tight chain around his body which cut into the flesh, or another who would lie on a bed of thorns or nails, and another when tempted would undress and throw himself into a clump of bushes, or into icy cold water. He often finished up by saying very nasty things about people. On this occasion he told me to stand up and he told the boys for a whole hour, about my home, about how I was brought up in a dirty filthy pigsty. He explained in detail the dreadful circumstances of my family. He called me a dirty tramp and a beggar. He said I was a common tinker, who had come from the gutter and would go back to the gutter. I was supposed to have said something about him, which I cannot recall. I most probably did say something, because we were always talking about him and his girlfriend, and wondering why she wasn't coming to see him.

Micky Comeford and I often go to the farmyard where there is a big boiler of potatoes turnips and carrots, which has been boiled for the pigs. It's really lovely, and we enjoy it much better than our own food. When we have eaten enough we fill our pockets with potatoes, provided they have not been mashed up with the other vegetables. Festy McDonald caught me one night eating the pig food. He had been drinking, and he swore at me, and shouted 'no wonder my pigs are so skinny, you hungry devil, eating all their grub'.

At Easter there isn't very much excitement. We get a boiled egg for breakfast, the usual Sunday dinner, with a slice of cake and bread for supper. There is a band concert in the evening. There are dances held about every three months, and Fahy's girl has started coming to see him again. She visits him several times a week, and everyone in the school is talking about them. The P.P. has sent for Fahy and there is a great argument and they do not speak to each other for several months. About this time the Bishop of Galway visits the school. After this, Fahy does not see his girl anymore.

We are preparing for the summer examinations and the dunce's hat is ready. This is a very big paper hat with the word 'dunce' written on each side, and is worn by the boy who gets the lowest score. Joe Baker who sleeps in the bed next to me has just returned from Clifden where he has been with Joe Kelly the mechanic for two days. As he gets into bed, Fahy comes to Baker's bed and without a word drags the clothes off his bed and beats him with a very big stick. He is beaten all over the body, and is bleeding from the mouth and nose. Joe Baker's nose is broken and he has great difficulty in breathing and becomes worse. Baker who has always been good at games and very bright at school now looks ill, he is green in the face and his health is failing. There was never any reason given for this beating.

Fahy can be very nice at times, he often reads us a story in the evening instead of the usual lessons, but when he is in a bad temper he is just a savage brute. He often uses a stick nearly as thick as a broom handle. He is very strong and hits with full force. He beats the old boys and Vale the youngsters.

The exam is over and I get the second lowest score. Tom Thornton is the lowest, but as he is in the tailors shop in the mornings, and does not get a chance to study for the exam, he is excused, and I have to wear the dunce's hat. This is an awful and embarrassing experience. I have to stand with my back to the wall wearing the paper hat and the class is expected to laugh and jeer. Fahy gives the signal to cheer and clap hands every year when anyone is crowned. It was Fahy who introduced the dunce's hat, it was unknown before he came.

The summer holidays have now commenced and everyone is wild with excitement. We are expecting to go to Tully strand next week, but the weather often lets us down, and the trip is postponed. There is a Christian Brother here who just came for a visit. He has returned from Australia where he has spent many years. He talks about the great opportunities for emigrants in that thinly populated country. He said there are large areas of Australia not yet explored, and much of it is desert because there is very little rainfall. It's not unusual he said to be without rain for eighteen months during which time many thousands of cattle and sheep are lost. The natives of Australia are coloured, and they are very primitive, and probably the most backward in the world. It is very difficult to educate the natives he said, as they are of very limited intelligence. Many of them can only count to ten. The climate is very warm, especially in the interior.

We are off to Tully strand and it's a very warm day, and we all go into the sea. There is cycle racing on the beach, some of the local folk compete against the Clifden lads. For lunch we get a lemonade and sandwiches, and there are prizes of cakes and sweets for those who win an event in racing or the long jump and the high jump.

The following Sunday we are taken for a walk to Kylemore Abbey, and are permitted to wander about in or near the convent grounds. As I am walking with Matt Feerick we make conversation with one of the convent girls. She is fifteen, and is a very pretty girl. We sit on the grass and ask each other questions about our respective schools and I am horrified to learn that this beautiful girl is beaten in the same manner as the boys at our school. I could not believe her story when she said she was often beaten by the priest and the beatings were often severe, so to prove her story she showed marks on her arms and legs. I know this priest well as he often comes to our school. I now know she did not lie to me, because she looked at me straight in the face. When I tell a lie I have to drop my eyes. Besides why should she want to tell a lie about the priest, of all people? I am now very upset, because whatever doubts I had about religion, I still had a great respect for a priest. I always believed he would be the very last one in the world to hurt anyone, least of all a girl. I could never have the same respect for a priest again, and whenever I see one I am reminded of what the girl told me.

The coal ship has arrived from Scotland, and I speak with one of the crew about the possibility of finding work in his country. He did not think there was much chance in view of the fact that thousands of his people were emigrating every year, but he thought I could join the army or the navy, and would get an opportunity to go abroad.

The holidays are now over, and I have less than a year to do, with a little luck it may only be nine months. Perhaps after another three months I will be working full time in the workshop, and will not report for school in the mornings. Martin Mullins has now left to work in a convent at Marseilles in France. He has promised to write to me as soon as he gets settled.

My father has written to say that he can get me a job in Ballinasloe. The wage would be 10/– a week. He thinks the superior may let me out earlier if I have a job to go to. I reply saying that I shall be willing to go home at the earliest opportunity. I am not anxious to see my parents any more. I should be happier if I did not see them, but there is a chance that I may leave earlier by going home. It is not the normal procedure for the parents to find work for the children. The authorities are against it, because they say the parents only want their boys back because they are now able to work and earn money for them. I wish to see my brothers, as I want to know what they now think of Letterfrack, what their reactions are to having been starved and beaten, and above all I want to know their state of health. Joe and Paddy were not long in the school, and have not suffered nearly as much as Jack and I, but I wish to see them just the same.

Young McGrath, a chap of seventeen, has now finished school and is employed on the school staff at a weekly wage. He is the electrician and like his older brother is none the worse for his many years at Letterfrack. Another chap Frank Kelly, also on the staff in the shoemaker's shop appears to be quite well and happy, but as they are older than me I can't say how they have been treated. Brother Byrne often said that the boy who is brought up in an industrial school is usually a failure, because he is starved of love and kindness which, only the parents are qualified to give. But Byrne never mentioned what effect the regular beatings had on a child. Probably because he did not know that this was going on. He never beat anyone severely himself, and therefore did not know that it was taking place. I have never seen a Christian Brother beat children in the presence of another Brother.

There is a boy in the infirmary at present suffering from the effects of a severe beating. His name is McLaughlin or Kangaroo. If he had not been admitted to the infirmary, no one would know about him. This is a very strange thing. He has been beaten by Brother Conway, yet I was in Brother Conway's class for a year and he never beat anyone. I have heard that Conway may be expelled from the Brotherhood. This lad McLaughlin is the quietest boy in the school and yet he has been beaten more than anyone else. He is now suffering from a stammer and cannot read nor write. His brother is very good at school, but has become very nervous lately.

An inspector is visiting the school and our class is on Irish history, which tells of the terrible things the British have done in Ireland. But the inspector tells us that 'Much of our history is greatly exaggerated, besides he added many of our own people have done more harm to Ireland than ever the British.'

Fahy has now got a shotgun and he goes about the farm shooting rabbits and other vermin. Brother Murphy borrows the gun to shoot 'Nigger' the wild cat which is worrying his pigeons. He chases the cat to the tailor's shop one evening after the shop is shut. Murphy has asked us to leave a window open so that he can shoot 'Nigger'. But as he fired through the window he only shot the coal box. It's Halloween and Fahy gives out the fruit. We get an apple, an orange, monkey nuts and walnuts. And there is a concert in the evening, and a professional singer has been engaged. He is a tenor and said to be one of the best in the country. There is also a Christian Brother from another school who plays the violin. Several of our lads are quite good singers, Matt Feerick, Christy Long, and Cosgrove from Galway. The bandmaster thinks Cosgrove may well improve as he grows older and has advised him to go to Dublin for further training after he leaves the school. Young Hunt was a lovely singer, but he has lost his nerve and is unable to sing in public.

The mission is now on as it's Christmas week 1931, but I am determined not to let the missioner frighten me, as he did last year. We are all given new rosary beads, which are blessed by the missioner personally.

We don't do any work on Christmas Eve except to put up the decorations. The young children make long chains of holly and ivy leaves, and there are balloons as well as small coloured bulbs. The refectory has been newly painted. There is a very big glass case at the end of the refectory. It is full of musical instruments. This is called the organ, which I am told used to play during meal times before I came to Letterfrack. This has also been painted. For Christmas dinner, there is roast turkey, roast potatoes, green peas, tomato sauce, and plum pudding.

I receive a letter from mother saying they all hope to see me home very soon, as dad has written to the superior saying that he has found me a job at 10/– a week. The very young children have each received a present from Father Christmas. In the evening we attend a picture show in the hall. There is also a whist drive in the library for those who wish to attend.

It's January 1932. Brother Fahy reads a letter from a man who said he escaped from Letterfrack nineteen years ago. He slept on Diamond Hill during the day and ate pig food from the school farm during the night. This man is at present living in Canada and he hopes to visit the school next year.

The superior has sent for me to say that I will no longer attend school, but will spend the next six months in the workshop. But he thought I would be better off to remain another year, or six months over my time. It would be to my own advantage to stay as long as I could, and if I wished to do so I should inform him.

I am certain that the superior Kelly did not know what was going on. If he did realize that children were being beaten for no reason, I am sure he would have stopped it. I am also sure that Keegan (the first superior) did not know that Walsh and Vale simply tortured the children. Keegan himself was a hard and cruel man. He beat the boys sometimes severely, but there was always a reason. He beat them for having lice and sores on their heads. What he really beat them for was not going sick, when they had sores or skin disease. He said lice was due to laziness and dirt. The most terrible law in Letterfrack was we must not complain. In the words of Brother Kelly, 'it is sinful in the eyes of God to complain'.

The months go by fairly quickly, it's Easter and the kids go to Tully strand. But I am too busy making my own suit, so I don't go. It's now summer and I am due to leave any day but am not terribly excited because I know that my troubles are not over when I leave Letterfrack. I have been warned many times by Brother Byrne. I can remember his words, 'there is no one who is qualified to replace your own mother'. 'The industrial schoolboy is usually a failure' and 'you will always be identified by your *sheepish look*'. I say goodbye to Mr Tom Griffin, he is now 45 years in Letterfrack as a school teacher.

12

I Return Home

It took almost two hours to travel by car to Galway, where the driver and I had lunch at a restaurant. The lunch of liver and onions, boiled potatoes and tea with biscuits was good. Brother Kelly had given me ten shillings to pay for the meal, but the driver (mechanic) insisted on paying.

Brother Kelly left us for an hour, and returned to see me off on the train to Ballinasloe, a distance of thirty miles. The train journey was pleasant and I had a whole compartment to myself. The day was fine and warm, the land here was rich and perfectly flat, unlike Connemara on the west coast which was mountainous and almost barren. The corn had not yet been cut, and it looked rich and beautiful in the fresh breeze. The cattle sheep and horses were all so different here in the Midlands, they were much bigger and stronger and healthier than the poor half starved creatures of Connemara.

This was my first day of freedom for more than seven years, and so far it was nice. I was sorry to leave Brother Kelly as he was one of the best. He made one mistake which I could never forget, and that was cutting down Mr Griffin's wages. That was an awful pity, apart from that he was a really good and genuine person, he was very religious, and one of the few good ones. Usually the religious people were savage and brutal, mean, cunning and ferocious, Fahy, Vale, Walsh, Blake, Reardon and to a slightly less degree Keegan the superior. All these Brothers turned a school into a terrible prison. They made life unbearable for innocent defenceless children. These men were all between thirty eight and fifty years. What damage have they already done, how much more destruction will they be permitted to do? The amount of pain and suffering perpetuated by such evil creatures must be enormous. As the train comes to a halt at my destination I learn that the town is more than half a mile away from the station.

My father is at the station to meet me and I can't recognise him, but as there are only a few passengers getting off the train he quickly picks me out. I did write in advance telling him that I would be wearing a dark blue suit and black shoes. I wore long trousers for the first time and hoped that people would not laugh at me. My suit had been made several months and was already too small for me. Dad took me home in the horse and cart, the horse was called Charlie, it was not difficult to remember him because he had a bad limp, due to an injury when he was a foal. The distance to our village was four and a half miles which took three quarters of an hour. Dad knew most people we met and of course we stopped to have a chat. The old boreen was very familiar and had not altered very much. It was barely wide enough for the cart wheels.

Mother was outside the old house, which no longer looked like the stable which it was first intended to be. Two small windows had been built into the front wall, and there was a new front door. The roof had been repaired and there was a new concrete floor to replace the cobble stones. The chimney was still smoking a bit but dad said he was thinking of building a new one at the other end of the kitchen. The same old dad, still making plans and promises. It must have taken him ten years to put in the two windows from the time he first mentioned it. My eldest brother Mick was still in the same job in Connolly's butchers for thirteen years. He also done the milking and worked on the farm as well. Jim the next eldest and my sister Norah had gone to the States, several years ago. This was the normal thing in those days, almost every family in the country had one or two members in the States, which was about the only place they could earn a living. Their fares were paid by relations already out there. Norah and Jim were doing well and often sent home a few pounds. Jim recently had an accident when he was knocked down by a car, he has since recovered.

Paddy and Joe who were first to leave Letterfrack are now at home and they work in the small village of Ahascragh a mile away. Joe is talking of leaving the country and going to England. Paddy is now qualified to do any running repairs to any vehicle and is employed at Brennan's garage. I have two younger brothers at home, Martin who was with the nuns at Kilkenny for three years and Christy who was too young to leave home.

When I have been home a week when Dad takes me to Ballinasloe to meet my new boss, who has promised to employ me as an improver. But we are informed that Mr Smith is shortly closing his workshop and his cutter who is starting on his own soon will employ me. His name is Mr Evans. Evans is a first class tradesman who has just returned from the States after spending twenty years there.

I buy an old second hand bicycle for 30/– payable in instalments at 5/– a week. I am now working and get on fairly well for about six months. But as I try to mix with the local chaps I quickly discover that I have very little in common with them. An industrial schoolboy is considered low class, within the same category as a pauper or a prisoner. And I am a tailor to trade which is considered the very lowest profession. A tailor is sometimes called a tramp – a tramp tailor is a common expression.

There is another boy from Letterfrack who works down the street, his name is Cunningham. He sometimes calls to see me at closing time and we walk along to the crossroads at the ash tree. He introduced me to some lads my own age the other night, and also to some girls. I noticed one called Peggy. I liked her a lot, she reminded me of another girl, the one from the convent at Kylemore, who said she had been beaten by the priest, yes that's the girl, the same long hair, the same eyes, and the same freckles. I was beginning to think it was the girl from the convent, and intended to ask her when I got an opportunity. So that night Cunningham was waiting at the corner of the bank next door. As I reached him he said, we must hurry along, the girls want to see us at the ash tree. This made me strangely happy, I can't explain how I felt exactly, except that it was a new and strange feeling, almost like the feeling I used to experience on a Christmas Morning when I was in the school – the very first second I would open my eyes and like a flash I would remember that it was Christmas, or similar to the first morning of the holidays – at the very moment of awakening. I would be fully aware of the fact that the Brothers would be going away today and I would not be beaten for a whole six weeks, unless of course I done something wrong. We had reached the ash tree and the girls were waiting, Peggy kept looking at me, and I was embarrassed and hoped I would not blush again like I did last time. I remembered to ask her if she had been to Kylemore, but not in front of the others. We were having a very friendly conversation all the four of us, when Cunningham turned to me and said 'you will soon be a year out of Letterfrack'. Peggy looked at me and said, 'were you there?', when I answered, 'yes' she said 'oh, I didn't know you were one of them'. I could then see she was fidgety and seemed to be restless. She didn't look at me any more, so there was no need to ask if she was from the convent. Had she been at Kylemore, I feel sure that she would not hold it against me, as she was in similar circumstances. I said 'good night' and went home.

We always had several visitors in our kitchen at night and they were getting on my nerves, with the result that I would go for long walks and not get home before midnight, only to find them still there sitting as though it was mid-day. I had been attending mass on Sunday until recently just to please my mother, but now I felt I did not want to go any more. The people made me sick all standing outside the chapel talking nonsense. So I gave up going to church, and on Sunday would wander through the woods.

I hardly ever spoke to anyone except my mother. I was anxious to have a good talk to my brothers, that is those who were at school with me, but as time went on it became more difficult, so in the end I decided not to say anything. It would be useless, they had not been there very long, and they seen very little, and have now forgotten all about it. They are just like the rest of the people in the village. They go dancing and sit at the crossroads talking and laughing. I wonder what people talk and laugh about?

I have now noticed how dirty the people are. None of them have ever taken a bath, because it's unknown in my part of the country. My father once said he never had a bath in his life. They wash their hands and face religiously on Sunday, but not any other day. The sufferings of the animals here is appalling. Only yesterday I seen a horse that was very lame and trying to pull a heavy load of peat, and some time ago I seen a pony with its back badly cut due probably to an ill-fitting harness.

There is a man in the village who is about seventy years old and is said to be a simpleton. They call him Cliss. He rides a pony to the fields daily to milk the cows for his boss, and on his return the young men of the village throw stones at him, and often throw him off his pony and spill the milk. Most of the villagers congregate to see this and seem to enjoy watching it. For these reasons I have no time for the people, I don't care if I never see another man, I want to get away as far as possible. I now get twelve shillings a week. I give mother ten, and I will save the other two until I have my fare anywhere out of this island. We will soon be busy and am going to ask my boss to put me on piecework and I can work until midnight, and work on Sunday as well. If he does this for me, I should save five pounds in three months.

The boss, Mr Evans, has a daughter who has just returned from England where she has been training as a nurse at a hospital in the midlands. She is a most attractive and intelligent girl of nineteen. She was educated in the States. Betty is her name. Once she said she had never been to a country dance and would like someone to take her, but I did not realise that she wanted me to ask her along, until several days later her mother was a little angry when she learned that Betty was going to the dance with Joe Kelleher the footballer. Mrs. Evans looked at me and said 'you missed your chance'. 'Why didn't you want to take Betty?' I answered that she had not asked me, and besides I had never been to a dance except to look in the window. I did not say that I once paid 2/6 but was afraid to go inside.

The boss now agreed to put me on piece rates, and I done more work because I worked later in the evenings, and sometimes worked on Sundays. My eldest brother Mick, now left his job where he worked for fifteen years, and looked after things at home. He applied to the Government for a grant to assist him to build a house. The new one-storey house was completed in three months from the time we received the material. Dad was reluctant to move into the new house but was persuaded to change his mind. During the building my trade got slack, and I worked only two or three days a week, so that I was able to assist my brother and dad, but I could not climb the ladder, as I got dizzy after about ten steps, and had to climb back down.

A new tailor was now employed, he was a very interesting chap who had spent many years abroad. He gave me information on where to find work in England and the different towns, where my chances were better in my trade, but he thought I should be better off to leave the trade and try something else. He was always broke after Monday, and I was able to lend him a little money. But he insisted on paying back more than I gave him which I did not like.

There was a mental hospital in the town, and we done quite a lot of work for the male nurses. One day we were making a first fitting for a chap from the hospital. And as he was sitting waiting for the garment to be tried on, he was telling my boss something of the general routine of the mental home. I became very interested when he said that they had several patients from a Christian Brothers school, who were troublesome and difficult to handle. The boss then asked what happened when the patients got out of hand. The male nurse laughed and said, 'we have our own methods of dealing with such a situation. Of course we are not allowed to beat them, *but there are other patients, who do the job for us.* In my ward I have two fine big strong lads, who can handle anyone'.

I now felt ill. I was sitting at the machine, and was afraid to stand up in case I should fall. Breathing became more difficult and the perspiration was simply running from my hands and my armpits. I thought I must go out into the yard for air, my table was close to the machine, and I was able to stand and walk to the door by holding on to the table. They were so interested in the conversation that I don't think I was noticed leaving. After walking about half an hour I was dry and went to a pub and bought a glass of stout which I couldn't drink, so I bought a bottle of whiskey and took it away, and drank it in the field just past the ash tree. I lay down and fell asleep. It was dark when I awoke and it was very cold. I then realised that I had forgotten my jacket so went back to the workshop to collect it.

Mrs Evans got out of bed to let me in and I explained that I had been drinking. Betty then arrived with her boyfriend. They had been dancing and we all went into the workshop and Mrs Evans made tea, and after a while came out and said there were some sausages if we were hungry. Betty said she liked sausages and invited me to go to the kitchen and help her to fry them up. In the kitchen we found cold potatoes and onions and we fried the lot. Betty talked about a doctor in the hospital in England, who loved cold potatoes and onions. The light was bad in the kitchen so we took the food into the workshop. We found Joe Kelleher all worried. He explained that he had been in hospital for a year, with his back, due to an injury playing football. Betty asked me what it was like in the country, as she would like one day to see what it was like. I told her that in the country, or village where I lived, life was very much different. There was no gas or electricity, and no water, except at the well, and sometimes the well was dry and we had to go to the pump, which was almost a mile away. She then asked me if we had any baby ducks and chickens, or goats and donkeys. I told her we had ducks, chickens, geese, a small donkey and an old horse. She then asked me to promise to take her out there soon. I told her that she would not like the country very much, and it was not advisable for a visit now, as my mother was not well. Betty then told me that she was a qualified nurse and would love to meet my mother. I then promised to take her out at the earliest opportunity and added that we had no bathrooms or toilets. Betty then laughed, and shouted to Joe Kelleher who was asleep.

The following week Mrs Evans became ill, and Dr Rositon who lived a few doors away called and said that she was to remain in bed for ten days. She must not do any work of any kind. She was not suffering from a disease of any kind, only overwork and worry. Several things happened in the next few months. My elder brother Joe left home, and shortly after Paddy had an accident when he crashed his motorcycle, he was not badly injured and was back at work after a week. My sister in the States had left her job and went to a convent to become a nun.

Mrs Evans was now up and able to get about, but her husband started drinking heavily. About every three months he would spend a week on the drink and would have to go to bed for several days. Another tailor came to work with me. He had been in an industrial school about twenty years before (Salthill). When he heard I had been to Letterfrack he asked me if the Brothers still took the boys trousers off to beat them. When I answered yes, he told me that he was in jail during the 1921 trouble and had a far better time than at school. This man's name was Maye. He was married with three children, and his wife had often taken him to court for drunkenness and beating her, and non-maintenance. Another tailor in the town also from Salthill, called Duggan, was a heavy drinker who neglected his wife and kids and eventually left them to become a tramp.

My brother Jack had now come home. He was sent from Letterfrack to a job in Mayo in 1931. Jack was now extremely nervous and could not do any regular work. He had now become most irresponsible, and got drunk whenever he got any money. Jack had been to Letterfrack for more than six years and never learned to read or write. He was subject to severe beatings almost daily for several years.

Its now June 1934 and its two years since I came home, and am becoming more unsettled every week. Trade has been quiet and am finding it difficult to save any money, so I shall probably have to remain here another year. I am now subject to severe colds, about every three months, which leave me ill and weak and I get headaches and dizziness and spots in front of the eyes. My memory is now very bad and when I am sent on an errand, even for one item I must write it down or I shall forget.

Betty is now going steady with Joe Kelleher, and I am very glad because he is a good chap, one of the few nice fellows here. Betty is so lovely and so childish, she no longer talks about the visit to the country and I am very pleased. She often tells me about when she was a little girl. She has a wonderful memory, she had just started to go to school, and is not more than five years old, she has a dog called 'Prince', and together they walk along a river bank and the dog walks between her and the river in order to ensure that she does not get too close and fall in.

There is now a football match in Ballinasloe. It's Sunday and I go to see the game, the first I have attended since leaving school. The game is between Galway and Tuam. The first half is played very well and without any serious incident but during the second half several of the players get injured and the game comes to an end with several fights. On my way home from the game I met a Letterfrack lad called O'Brien, better known as 'Redskin'. He told me he works for ten shillings a week on a farm, near the bog road. He seems to be doing fairly well, and does not appear to have suffered greatly from his experience at school. He is a rather jolly lad and fond of games. Redskin was sent to Letterfrack because he had lost his parents, he said he was saving up to emigrate, because there was no future in this country for an industrial school lad. He said his boss does not trust him and when anything is missing he always gets the blame.

It's now October, and the big cattle sheep and horse fair is on. It's held on the first week of October every year, and during this week there is plenty of trade. We usually get enough customers to keep us busy for a whole month. There are cattle dealers from the north, as well as gypsies, tinkers and fortunetellers, street singers and musicians. The gypsies are the most difficult to do business with. They usually supply their own cloth and we charge a pound for making up which takes us twenty hours really hard work, yet the gypsies always argue for more than an hour to have the work done for a shilling or two less, and then invite the boss to the local public house and spend 5/- on drink.

After the fair there is always a circus and other entertainments at the far green. During this period we finish work early, around about 5 pm. The farmers, jobbers and dealers spend money freely and there are a number of hangers on or beer thiefs, i.e. those who hang around the pubs for a cheap drink. I have known farmers to stay in town for a whole week after the fair. A few names I find it difficult to forget are Jim Coen and Charlie Green, they are good customers of ours. Another is 'Bookie' Higgins. They make the October fair and the week after an annual holiday. Its drinks all round when they come to town. Higgins is a bookmaker, and he has a bad name amongst the punters, because he is a bad payer, except in the pub. The street singers come from all over the country at this time of year.

There is talk of Betty getting married and I am a bit upset, as I am very fond of her, but would not try to stand in her way marrying Joe Kelleher, because I think she would be doing the correct thing, but am worried in case they go to live in Joe's home. There would be no fun in the workshop if Betty left. It's good to see her cutting out her dresses and frocks without a pattern or even the use of a measuring tape. She often asks me to press up her costume or coat on a Saturday, and I refuse at first, saying that I am too busy but would willingly do it on Monday. She then walks away slowly, and returns and whispers in my ear saying it's no good on Monday, the dance is tonight. I think for a few moments and say, 'o.k. Betty, I will try my best.' With that she runs away singing.

On the way to work the other day, the frame of my bicycle just broke across the middle, it was a ladies bike and therefore not as strong as if it had a cross bar. I simply threw it over the ditch into the field and walked the rest of the way. It's a long way to walk, and back home again at night. There is a lad who comes to the shop. He is the assistant postmaster's son, and he has an old racing bicycle for sale and he wants me to have it for 30/– but he must ask his father first of all. His father said it's none of his business, so I bought the bike the next day and it was a treat, I could now get to work much faster and with less difficulty. It was a fixed wheel and took some getting used to, but was a pleasure to ride. With the racing bike I was much happier and was no longer anxious to get away in a matter of months. Besides I had 30/– less now and it would take at least three months to save that. I then made up my mind to try and stay another year.

It was almost Christmas, but I no longer looked forward to that festival. I remember last year at home when there wasn't too much excitement. We had a good breakfast and dinner, and then neighbours came and stayed half the night, talking about subjects which just bored me, until I just wandered into the wood. The people around here don't interest me in the least, probably because their conversation is limited to local gossip or to their own personal affairs. They laugh too much and too loudly. Whereas I could listen to Betty or her Dad all day. Betty would often ask me, how many chickens we had, their age and their colour, how many cocks? What time they would wake up in the morning? How old is the calf now, and so on. Betty is now twenty and such conversation would seem to some to be childish but to me it's not. She was very fond of animals and would walk for miles to see sheep and lambs. I once remember her cycling seven miles in the rain to see a mare and foal. She spent several years training to be a nurse and spent no end of money on books, yet when she finished her training and became fully qualified she just decided not to do anymore nursing.

It's Christmas 1934. The new de Valera government has been in office for two years, and some favourable changes have taken place. The land is being taken away from the wealthy landlords, and distributed amongst the poor farmers. Grants are given as well as loans to anyone who is willing to build his house. There is talk of new industries being created, which it is hoped will slow down emigration. The main cause of our poverty and backwardness, is, in the words of a candidate at the last election, emigration. 'It would be a blessing', he thought, 'if Britain refused permission for Irish men to work and settle there. Then perhaps they would be compelled to develop their own country'. 'Our country', he said, 'was the most under-developed in the whole of Europe'.

My eldest brother Mick has bought a shotgun and we often go out in the early hours of the morning shooting rabbits, and wild duck. It's a wonderful entertainment, as well as being able to provide food. We are able to buy all the ammunition we require, as we sell most of the duck in the town. We also manage to shoot an occasional wild goose, but it's very difficult to get within range of the geese. Pheasants too are fairly plentiful but we have to travel a long way to find them.

My mother's sister is home for Christmas and she has brought her son with her. He is about nineteen years old. He is learning photography, and they are settled in London. My aunt tells me there is plenty of work for tailors in London and has invited me to stay with them if ever I decide to go. She married a Mr Green, and they are very happy. Charles her son likes the country here and would like to remain, he enjoys going to the well for water. We brought him to see the peat bog yesterday, and he thinks it's wonderful, he thinks peat is much better and cleaner to handle than coal.

We have been terribly busy in the workshop for the Christmas, and made thirty suits in two weeks. We had a tailor off the road to help us. They call him Tom Gray, and he goes on tramp for three months each year. He is an old industrial schoolboy, he is now almost sixty and he told me he would retire soon. I asked him what he would do on retirement and he answered, 'like all good tailors, and like my father before me, I am going to the workhouse'. 'Surely', I said, 'wouldn't it be much nicer to have a place of your own'? 'Indeed no, the worry and responsibility would kill me'.

One of our best customers is Mr Kernan an old 'Peeler' (R.I.C.). He comes to the workshop nearly every day, spends hours with us, and talks about his twenty two years in the police. He told us of when he was stationed in Limerick he was called out one night because there was a lot of shooting going on, and discovered that it was the Black and Tans who had occupied a building, and the last man in bed had to shoot the light out. He told us another about a man who had gone mad and was running down the street naked. His job was to go and arrest him and bring him back through the town, and the people all turned out to cheer them.

During Christmas week most men play cards, for chickens, ducks, geese and turkeys, and very often they play all night. This may continue until New Year. Dances are held in a barn or at the cross-roads. We now have a dance hall in the town a mile away, so that the barn dance is getting out of date. Silent pictures are also shown in the Dance Hall. The picture show is operated by the local mechanic Tom Brennan.

My trade is now very quiet and I only work two days a week, so that I spend most of my time at home, assisting my brother to build a wall around the new house. We are also planting new trees, in a row just inside the wall. Paddy the mechanic has now left home to work in London. He hopes to join the R.A.F when he is a year in Britain, as the air force do not normally accept recruits from the twenty six counties until they are resident in Britain.

I have been two years at home, but have failed to settle down. I am unhappy and discontented. I catch colds regularly, about three or four each year, after which I get severe headaches. At meal times I become restless and am subject to attacks of trembling, especially when there is any one behind me. The other morning as my mother was passing she happened to brush against me from behind and I jumped and almost screamed. I am terribly worried lest I should be noticed. Even in the workshop when there is anyone behind me I am very uncomfortable. Probably it's because I was beaten so often from behind, so that now whenever possible I sit with my back to the wall, by this method I feel more at ease.

For many months now I have been observing my brothers one by one. I am looking for symptoms of a nervous nature, similar to that which I am suffering from. I want to find out if my complaint is a general family disorder of a hereditary background. So far I can find no evidence of any nervous trouble, amongst any of my brothers except Jack (my father and mother are not nervous) who was ill-treated even more than I was, but Jack reacts in a different manner to me, he shouts and swears and becomes quarrelsome, or he gets moody, and leaves home just after breakfast, and may not return until bedtime, he will often leave home every day for a whole week during which time he will do no work of any kind. He has become very unpopular in our own home and with most people outside. I am liked better than Jack because I agree with everybody, even when they are wrong, I agree with them because I am afraid of them. I have never met a bad woman. I have not known many good men. I dislike and fear men. I do not trust them. In the workshop I cannot work on black material because I can't see it well, the Reverend Brothers all wore black. I always liked and trusted a Catholic priest, until the girl from Kylemore told me she had been severely beaten by one. I can no longer trust them.

It is St. Patrick's day and everyone goes to mass, and those who have any money get drunk afterwards. We are busy at the workshop and in three months I shall be away. I am almost as anxious to get away from here as from Letterfrack. I want to get away from my people, my home and my country. What a people, what a home, and what a country.

There are two neighbours in the house when I get home, and they are talking about the wake tomorrow night. 'Who's dead asked Martin Cosgrove?' 'Didn't you hear, said Jim Tulley, old Tom Larkin who lives on the bog Road.' 'O' that should be a good wake' said Martin, 'we had a great time when his brother died last year, there was lots of drink for everyone, and when the porter was all finished we went out into the garden, and pulled all the apples and threw them into the house.' 'That wasn't the best wake I've seen', said Martin, 'it was when Mick Byrne died, 'the Lord have mercy on him'. 'We had a whole barrel of porter and plenty of tobacco, and when everybody had enough to drink, we took the corpse from the room and laid it out on two thin planks, the planks we laid on two stools. The planks of wood were twelve inches in width, and the stools were placed one at the top and one at the bottom. But when we got a chance we moved the bottom stool to the centre so that if anyone should sit on the end of the planks, the planks would tip up, and the corpse would appear to stand up. It was almost morning before a man sat on the planks, as he did the whole thing tipped up and he fell to the floor with the corpse on top of him'. This behaviour is very common in my part of the country. The wake is considered a great occasion. A wake without drink and tobacco is no good, and the people are thought to be mean if at least a half-barrel is not supplied.

Paddy has written telling me that there is lots of work in London. He found it difficult at first. He got a job in a restaurant for a few days and last Christmas he plucked turkeys, his next job was washing up dishes in a café. He said if I liked I could stay with him until I found my own place.

Betty is now planning to be married in the coming year. I am glad. I will be away before it takes place. There have been two weddings in our village in the last year. It was all so wonderful during the celebration and before, but six months after there was a different story to tell. Young Mrs. Morrisey next door to us was a very beautiful and happy girl less than a year ago, now she looks years older, she works fourteen hours a day, feeding pigs and looking after the cows, travelling almost a mile for water. She has to look after her husband and his mother who is almost seventy. She is only 23 and her husband is 50 years old. There is a baby a few weeks old, and she will probably have another nine or ten children.

There is Mrs. Cosgrove who got married at nineteen to a man of 45, who earns 25/– a week. She has been married less than two years and already has two kids. She not only looks after her husband and his parents but five of his brothers as well. I often wonder why a girl ever gets married in this country, because after a few months she is no more than an unpaid servant. I suppose the answer is that they made the mistake before they are old enough to realise what they are doing. I sometimes think, there ought to be schools for parents, rather than for children, the parents should be taught how to bring up their children correctly and also give them an elementary education. The school as I have known it is no place for any child. No child of mine will ever go into any school in Ireland.

There is a Letterfrack boy now employed by Jim Coen, only a mile away. He left the school only a week ago, the neighbours say he is silly and daft, so I am anxious to go and meet him. On my way home from work I have to pass the house where he is employed, it lies just off the main road. As I approach the house, there is a crowd of lads, laughing and joking and making fun of the Letterfrack boy, it is none other than big McLaughlin, better known as 'Kangaroo'. I remember this lad, when he first came to Letterfrack, he was about ten years old and a perfectly normal and healthy boy. I used to play handball with him and he beat me several times. But because he had fairly big ears and long thin legs, the brothers used to beat him and call him an ass and a fool. Now he looks ill, he is very pale, with very prominent cheekbones. His head moves up and down quickly as he tries to speak, as he has a bad stammer. His boss complains that the lad is unable to do any work, and is being sent back to Letterfrack.

It's June and I shall be leaving home in a few weeks. I managed to buy a piece of cheap material and have made myself a suit. Naughton the tailor who spent many years abroad has now returned from Galway where he has been staying with his sister. I have told him that I will be going away. When he discovered that he can't make me change my mind, he has given me the following advice. No matter where you go abroad you must always be polite. Always say please and thank you. The less you say the further you will go, and the less mistakes you will make. He then went on, it is better to be silent and thought a fool, than to speak, and remove all doubt. He said he learned this saying from an officer in 1918, when the officer was trying to impress on his men the danger of giving information to the enemy.

13

I Join the Regular Army

I left home about the second week in June 1935. I only carry a very
small suit case, the contents consist of a shirt, one pair of old shoes
and a few collars, as well as my tools, and an extra pair of trousers.
I travel to Dublin by train, and catch the night boat from the North
Wall to Liverpool. Standing next to me on the boat is a very young
woman with a baby in her arms and her husband. As the boat sails
away the young woman who was looking towards a small group of
people on the quay turns about quickly and faces out to sea, and said
quietly, and very slowly, 'I never want to see that island again as long
as I live'. She was definitely Irish, her husband did not answer.

I did not remain any longer than was necessary at Liverpool. I
travelled to London where I had lunch just after one o'clock. What
struck me most about this country was how thickly populated it was
in comparison to my own country, where it was possible to travel
twenty miles without seeing a single house. The people did not talk a
lot. They just sat reading papers. London, unlike Liverpool, was
terribly busy. I got into Euston Station which was almost as big as my
own village. I soon found out that this was only one of the many
stations in this massive city. It then dawned on me that I had no
address to go to, and could not remember where my brother lived,
except the name of the garage where he was employed. But on
making enquiries it was discovered that there were many garages of
the same name (R.A.C.). I tried several without success, so decided
not to bother anymore. I then began to tell myself that it probably
was a blessing in disguise, finding my own way would do me more
good than being led by the hand. By this time I had wandered miles
from Euston and had no idea where I was going. It wasn't much use
asking anyone unless I had somewhere to go to. So I just kept on
wandering about. It was a very warm day and I kept on drinking tea
which made me still warmer. I had no idea of the time except that the
pubs were open and I know they had been shut for several hours.
Most people had stopped work as there were a lot of people working
on the road, and they have gone home. My feet were getting sore so
I strolled into a fairly busy pub. I didn't know what kind of drinks
the customers were having so thought I would listen to hear a few

giving their orders, and ask for the same. It would be a terrible thing to ask for something not on sale in case people thought I was stupid or silly, or in any way different to themselves. My ambition was to get along without being noticed. The barman served me a pint of beer without anyone even glancing my way. I was now sitting on a small stool by the door and it was lovely and cool. The beer tasted wonderful and it was quite cheap at five pence a pint. The stout or porter at home was more expensive and I never could drink it. It was the colour that put me off. It reminded me of cascara, a medicine my mother once gave me. I was much happier and contented now. Fancy being able to walk into a pub and buy a pint of beer without people staring at you. If I bought a pint at home everyone would be wondering who I was, where I had come from and where the money came from. London seemed a good place and I was getting to like the people. What I hated at home was whenever I went up or down the boreen, morning, noon or night, the people always came to the door to see who it was. This annoyed me so much that I stopped using the boreen, and would carry my bicycle across the fields to the main road. When the neighbours hadn't seen me for a whole week they came and asked my mother what was wrong. 'Was I ill?' 'Had I left home, or did I get the sack?' On hearing this from my mother, I just went mad and burst into a rage and told my mother, 'in future she must tell them to go to hell and mind their own business.'

It was the first time I lost my temper in front of my mother. She was worried. I could tell by the way she sat down, looking into the fire and not saying a word. She always done this when dad quarrelled with her. I know I should have said I was sorry but I was trembling all over, and didn't want to let her see this. So I just cleared out of the house and into the wood.

I must have wandered about for several hours as it was now quite dark. I finished my beer and went out into the street, and called a taxi, and asked him – the driver – to take me to the nearest lodging house. He looked at me and laughed. He was an awfully nice chap, and he explained that there were a few cheap places in the district, the Rowton House, the Salvation Army Hostel and the Church Army. He said I would probably have to sleep in a dormitory and people who stayed in such places didn't normally go by taxi. I advised him that I had no wish to sleep in a dormitory but would try anything else. He dropped me off at a small hotel, which was nine and six, bed and breakfast. The taxi cost 3/– which put a big hole in the four pounds I had left. The following day I made up my mind to find work and accommodation.

I tried several firms where I might find work but there was nothing doing. I hadn't the faintest idea where or how to look for a place to live. I now discovered that I was in Westminster and a different district to the one I had been in yesterday. I also remember that my brother Paddy said in his letter he could see Big Ben from where he works so I made inquiries as to where the nearest R.A.C. garage was and sure enough he was working in Lucas Street, Pimlico. He brought me to his digs where we shared the same room. I managed to get a few days work here and there at 6/– a day. But after a month I called at the recruiting office at Whitehall, and enlisted in the Regular Army, to serve for seven years with the colours and five on the reserve. I reported each day to do about two hours work and collect my pay. It paid 1/3 for living out, 3/3 for two hours simple work like sweeping a floor or cleaning a window and during this few hours working we got ten minutes to go the canteen and buy tea, at a penny a cup. Previously I had to work hard 9 hours for 6/–. After a week they informed me that my character had arrived from the police of my village at home, and I was to report to my Regimental H.Q. at Berwick on Tweed on the border. I was posted to a Scottish Infantry Regiment. About a dozen of us were brought to the station the following day where we were put on our respective trains. At the station we all gathered at the saloon bar and treated the sergeant to several glasses of beer. Already I could feel a sense of comradeship, and friendship, which was new and strange to me. Here was I a few days in the army, I hadn't even got my uniform yet and I am drinking beer with a sergeant who has served in the Boer War who, after all, is my superior, yet he is sharing a drink with me and has just offered to pay his turn. I am a little out of touch with things. Everything has been happening too quickly. Some kind of solution is beginning to emerge. But no, I can't believe it, it's just a dream only this time it's a pleasant dream.

They are all talking now, and I can't follow the line of their conversation. All I know is that they are happy and I am not unhappy. It's just that I am a little slow witted. Yes I think I've got everything straight at last. For the first time in my life I am somebody, a human being, previously I have been neglected, beaten, insulted and humiliated by my own people in my own country, and all this by a most highly respected religious order in the Catholic church. Here I am amongst strangers and foreigners yet I have seen nothing except plain simple goodness, kindness and friendship.

Surely there is something bad and rotten about the society into which I was born. At school I was forced to steal food because I was hungry. I had to tell lies to try and avoid being beaten. I am bound to believe that it's sinful to tell lies and steal, yet it's all part of a corrupt environment which was forced on me.

We were all saying goodbye and I was to travel alone. My train was first to leave and the sergeant and the other lads were waving. 'Jolly' Rodgers had forced a neat little parcel of sandwiches on me, which his mother had given him. He said he wouldn't need them as he would only be on the train for two hours.

I am travelling north. There is a lady and a little girl in my compartment. The child has a white pup, about three months old. It's called 'Snowball'. As we go further north the weather is much cooler. There has been a heat wave in London for the past month. I have never known such heat, and I had been outdoors all the time, and now there is a little colour in my face. My brother said so last evening. My other brother, Joe the Baker, lives a long way out of London and I didn't see much of him. Paddy said he spends most of his time with the girlfriend. Yes last evening was most pleasant. We had a meal of pork chop and onions, and then walked all round Hyde Park. Late in the evening we had a drink. I promised to come to London for my first holiday, which would probably be Christmas. Joe was now saying goodbye as I should not be seeing him the following day.

The little girl was now feeding her puppy with a saucer of milk. The lady, her mother, was telling me about the climate in Scotland. She said she comes from the mountains and they often get snow in the month of May. The further north you go the colder it gets, and the further south the warmer it is. When I said I had joined the Kings own Scottish Borders she thought it was a good regiment, and added 'that the soldier boys often do training on the mountains, and they carry their beds up the mountains because they often remain up there for a week'. She thought the time would come when the women would be fighting side by side with their men folk. If we lost as many in the next war, as we did in the last the women would have to put the trousers on. She carried on and on. I was listening but, as usual, thinking on other matters as well. I was thinking about my mother. I hadn't told her about the army. There was no promise that I would return at any special date. I merely said I was going to Dublin. There was no mention of catching the boat to Liverpool and I don't remember having written home since I left. But I know Paddy did write letters, because I knocked a bottle of ink over one night, which he was using. I stayed up and washed the table cloth, but only made it a lot worse, and bought a new one next day. We were lucky it was only a small table.

I was thinking about Betty, and her mother and father, and hoping he was not drinking again. Although Betty didn't mind it so much because when her dad had a drink he would dance with her and often bring the gramophone into the workshop. This made Mrs Evans mad. Mr Evans was an easy going man when there was any little trouble. He would send me along to the pub for a drink of whiskey (on the book of course) after which he would sing a song and talk about life in the States and about the money he lost and won on the horses. When business was real bad he would just go across the road to the egg store and bring back a customer. The farmers always came there to sell their eggs. He understood the farmers. He knew they would cut him down to the last penny, so he put the price up a few shillings and by the time the deal was made, he got his original price. The farmers loved him because he would listen to their troubles. The farmers were always in trouble with their next door neighbours and were always seeking legal advice so they came to Evans. It was cheaper to buy a drink or two for the 'master tailor' than to pay a lawyer's fee. Not only that, it was a better atmosphere in the pub. They didn't like to see books and papers in an office, which cost money, their money.

The little girl came to offer me sweets, which I accepted. They were long hard caramel sweets wrapped in paper, and others she called butterscotch which were delicious. I had been dreaming a little, and explained this to her mother, and asked to be forgiven. She said she understood, as her husband was always day dreaming, that is why she left him at home. He doesn't get lost there, except when he goes out to buy the paper. He meets someone, or wanders off to the club to see what won the last race.

We are now slowing down. I am getting ready to get off at the next stop which is Berwick on Tweed. I had no luggage as a lad in the digs said it wouldn't be any good to me, as it would just be parcelled up and put into the store until I was finished my training of twenty weeks.

A rather serious looking corporal was waiting for me at the station, and I imagine he had been given a good description of me, because he had no difficulty in picking me out of about two dozen passengers, and I noticed there were several lads my own age. He looked me up and down with his trained eye, and asked, in a broad Scotch accent, 'may I see your identification papers?' After having read the documentation carefully he said 'I will take you to your depot'. As we walked through the cobble stone streets in step he asked, 'Have you had any experience of the army before?' I answered

'No'. He then smiled a little and said, 'The first ten years are the worst'. I then asked if he would like a drink, and his answer surprised me. 'I never refuse'. We had two pints of Scotch ale, which was stronger than the London beer. I asked if I should wear the same kind of uniform as he had on, 'exactly the same' was his answer. I wasn't very keen on the tartan trousers, and the short khaki jacket, and the Glengarry headdress, but I didn't say this. He told me something of the general routine. Reveille at 6.30 a.m., first parade 7 a.m. until 7.45, breakfast 8 a.m. until 8.30. After breakfast we make our beds and clean the barrack rooms. Next, parade 9.30. We do three parades of one hour each, with ten minutes break between parades in order to change from one dress into another. Lunch at 1 p.m. There is one parade from 2 p.m. 'til 3 p.m. in the afternoon, after which we clean equipment, rifles, etc. until tea time 5 p.m.

We may leave the barracks after 6 p.m. and return by 9.30 p.m. except at the weekends when we are allowed out until midnight. We should be properly dressed at all times outside our barrack rooms, except when going to the dining room where we are allowed to go without a headdress. When walking out from barracks we must carry in our right hand a cane or stick, which is carried parallel with the ground.

When I entered barracks I was given a bath and haircut, and then had a meal in the canteen after which I was shown to my barrack room where there were four other men, and one N.C.O. in charge. I found them a mixed lot. One from Manchester, two from London and one from Wales. They were all very friendly and helpful. The N.C.O. was Scotch, from Edinburgh. Men from other rooms came and sat talking. Most had only been there a week or two. People who came from big cities didn't like the routine and discipline and often complained mainly about the food. An officer came to the dining room each meal time and walked to every table. It was the practice for the man at the head of the table to stand up and answer for his table. After being a few days at the depot I had to answer for my table. When the officer asked if there were any complaints, I answered, 'No Complaints Sir.' The officer was surprised because everyone else had complained.

I found the first three months most enjoyable. Our squad sergeant was a London chap and was a real nice man who had recently returned from Hong Kong. He was absent one day and another sergeant took his place. This man terrified me, when he shouted at me for making a mistake and I became worse, and he used to rush over and lift his hand as though to strike me, but never did. I am told that he used to hit men from his own squad. He was a heavyweight boxer and had been once a brigade champion.

Up 'til this time the training had been simple and I thought easy. We done drill, P.T., musketry education and bayonet fighting. We had been firing miniature rifles (202) but now we were firing the service rifle on the open range. I was afraid to jump over the wooden horse to do a hand spring. I couldn't walk along a 3 inch plank at a height of 3 feet. I was getting no better however hard I tried, and the P.T. instructor gave me a bad report and said that he didn't think I was going to be any good, and on several occasions he reported me to the adjutant. One day he lost his temper and told me to leave the drill hall and not to come back the following day. He advised me to desert the army. I had now given up all hope and expected to be discharged before my twenty weeks training period had been completed.

I thought and still believed that the army would do me good. It was the kind of life, the only kind that suited me. I would one day be able to cast-aside my fears and live a normal carefree and happy life like those around me. Soon I would forget the torment of my unhappy schooldays. I should be able to go to bed and sleep at night instead of being afraid to sleep, terrified of those frightening dreams which haunted me. The fears of being followed. I am always trying to get away from someone who wants to kill me. I try to scream and can't. During the day time I am like a coiled spring, unable to relax, like an animal always on its guard.

The other young soldiers are now talking about their holidays, before joining the Regiment. There is a passing out parade, which is not bothering them. We are now at P.T. and there is an officer watching us, and at the end of the parade he sends for me, and said 'I have heard unfavourable reports about your work'. 'Now listen here soldier, many have tried this game before you. You find you don't like the army and you're trying to work your discharge. But it's not going to work. You will join your Regiment even if you go under escort.' I was lost for words. The officer hesitated as if waiting for me to speak. But I said nothing.

The following week we're firing on the open range at distances up to 500 yards. It is a cold day and is snowing. I failed to hit the target at 3 and 400 yards. But at 500 yards we are firing with the rifle rested, there is a fresh wind blowing across our front. I manage to get two bulls out of five shots by aiming at the top left hand corner of the target. On seeing this, the officer said that anyone who could hit the target under such conditions is not a bad shot, and he overlooked my other failures. I go north to Glasgow for my holidays.

After a quiet holiday in Glasgow I return to the depot, and we are issued with tropical kit, and are now preparing to join our battalion which is stationed in Malta. We leave the depot and travel south to Tilbury by train. We are given a good send off, and the adjutant says goodbye to each man personally and gives us a packet of cigarettes and chocolates. We now get a pleasant surprise. We embark in a P & O passenger liner instead of the usual troopship and we travel as first class passengers. The first few days are rather pleasant, but on the third day the sea is choppy and gets worse on the fourth day and most of the lads are seasick. It's still rough on the fifth day and by now very few attend for meals. I have had nothing to eat for two days. But the sixth day is wonderful. The sea is very calm, without even a ripple, and it's very light blue in colour. There isn't a cloud in the sky.

We stopped at Gibraltar for two hours yesterday, but did not disembark. This has been a most enjoyable voyage except for two days when I was sick. The weather is beautiful and a sailor told me that it's like this most of the year. We sleep in cabins, and are waited on during every meal. This is real luxury and I never imagined that life could be so comfortable. Malta is now in sight. It just looks like a tiny rock. I can feel a kind of loneliness and imagine that many others feel the same way, as the voyage is almost over. We have been happy since we left the Bay of Biscay. It's now only two miles off, and looks a light brown, roasted with the sun.

We are now getting ready to disembark, and a sergeant who is going to be in charge of us has come on board. He is very brown and looks very strong and healthy. We are going down the gangway and one of the lads has dropped his rifle into the sea. An officer of the ship goes away and returns after twenty minutes with a diver from one of the warships. He dives and comes back up with the rifle and everyone is now pleased. The diver is now cheered for his wonderful work. We march to Floriana Barracks to the music of our battalion pipe band.

As we go through the streets of Valetta, there are plenty of goats and a few horse drawn vehicles for carrying passengers. Here and there we find a man sitting on the pavement and leaning against the wall fast asleep and by his side is a basket of fruit. He is usually in his bare feet, and wearing an open necked shirt with trousers and waistcoat. Most of the women wore a black hood over their head which I am told is called the hood of shame. Napoleon is said to have compelled them to wear this because they would not entertain his soldiers. The people of Malta are very religious and are all Roman Catholics.

This was once a barren island or just a rock until a law was passed which compelled all ships calling at the island to carry a percentage of soil or earth, which now covers the island and has made it fertile. There are great quantities of grapes, tomatoes, figs and perhaps a few dates.

We are now in our barrack rooms, about twenty men to each room. After a week at the barracks we go to a camp twelve miles away on the other side of the island, to do advanced recruits training. We finish parades at 3 p.m. and spend the rest of the day cleaning equipment, and swimming, and hiking. The food is not as good as it was at the depot. But it's quite cheap in the canteen and we can buy a meal each night, for 6d.

There are no licensing laws here and all the cafés sell drinks. There is at least one hostel in every café. But some have as many as five or six, whose duty it is to entertain the customers. The hostess drinks a small glass of wine called Ambeit, but is often only coloured water and costs 6d. The customer is expected to pay for her drink in exchange for her attention.

There is a good price paid for woollen garments, and the soldiers often wear extra shirts and cardigans which they sell outside (we are not allowed to carry a parcel). The Abyssinian War is now on, and it is thought we may intervene, as maps of that country are being studied by the officers. We are now on manoeuvres and are doing intensive training with the navy and the R.A.F. and we watch a demonstration by the radio controlled Queen Bee Aircraft which is said to be the first pilotless plane. During manoeuvres we are taken by a destroyer to the small island of Gozo, the other side of the Leper's Island. On the ship a lad who was in the Navy Cadets two years ago told me that he watched a demonstration on Gibraltar when the anti-aircraft gunners tried to shoot down Queen Bee. King George V was present and after firing at it for two days and failed to get a hit, they placed a time bomb in the plane to impress His Majesty.

In August 1936 we are moved to Palestine where there is trouble between Arabs and Jews. We are in Carmel Camp 3 miles from the capital, and are being sniped at during the night from Mount Carmel. I move to a Jewish settlement at Beersheba. The people in this settlement live on a semi-military basis. They start work at about 5 a.m. and are detailed for their different jobs in much the same way as the army, i.e. there is a notice board where orders are posted, and they are changed to different jobs weekly. The people are nearly all young, between 18 and 40 years. Men and women dress very much the same, in light khaki shirt and short pants and shoes. They wear a light toppee. They are mostly German Jews and are all armed with German weapons of superior quality. They do guard duties in the same way as we do them. The men and women are on an equal footing. There are no wages paid. But everyone is well provided for and all expenses are paid. Children are not brought up by the parents, but are kept in the infirmary, and looked after by experienced nurses. There is a doctor in each settlement.

The farms are beautifully kept, and are watered by revolving sprays, the water can be turned on or off. The cattle are well cared for and are spotlessly clean. The fruit is delicious and every day we are given several grapefruits and oranges. Dances are held periodically and we are invited. We are often invited to their tea parties. Their tea is not like ours but is very weak, and sometimes they have black tea with fresh lime or lemon squeezed into it.

We are now posted to Tiberius near the Sea of Galilee. This is not in fact a sea but a fresh water lake. We are now living in a two storey school which is surrounded by barbed wire entanglements. There are a few shots fired occasionally but there is no serious trouble.

I am now suffering from malaria and go to a hospital in Alexandria Egypt. I go by Red Cross ship from Hefa. After two weeks I am well and return to Palestine by train. We travel through the desert, and the train catches fire underneath and the Arabs jump off screaming. We cross a river by ferry. On the ferry the money is changed. We board the train for Hefa and catch a bus to Nazareth. I am walking through the bazaar at Nazareth when I am stopped by two Arabs, one shows me tricks with a pack of cards as the other one goes through my pockets.

After a few weeks my battalion returns to England and we arrive home for Christmas 1936. During the Palestine campaign we suffered only three casualties, one killed and two wounded. Our task was to protect the Jewish settlements and the railways. We provided escorts for all trains for all road transport. We also guarded the oil pipe lines. We are stationed at Catterick Camp where I have a course of driving and maintenance. After which we go north to Leeds to prepare for a military tattoo which is very interesting. My battalion gives a physical training display. The tattoo is quite a success and everyone is satisfied with the result.

After a weeks holiday I embark for India in September 1937. We sail in the troop ship Dorsetshire, which takes 21 days. There is a storm after ten days which lasts 24 hours. But there is no further incident. There are plenty of games and other recreation. There is a dance and a concert. We disembarked at Bombay and after two hours caught the train to Calcutta which took almost four days. The troop trains are not comfortable with their wooden seats. In each compartment in addition to the seat each side there are two shelves or racks over the seats so that six persons may lie down at once. The trains are larger than at home and the engines are bigger and more powerful so that they can travel great distances. We don't take food on the trains but stop three times daily between stations at pre-arranged places where a meal is usually ready. We have an aluminium plate and mess tin, which we always carry, together with a knife, fork and spoon. There is no fence or railings each side of the railways as at home, except in a few places, so that very often buffalo, goats, etc. can wander on to the lines. I am told that there was once a fence but the natives took it away for their personal use. At home wooden sleepers are used under the lines. But in India metal sleepers are used because of the white ant which can eat through wood in a very short time. We carry everywhere when travelling a small bundle of bedding which we call a 'Blue Bundle'. This consists of a blanket or two, and an outward covering we call a 'Dunny'. Sheets are not normally provided but we buy them as well as a small pillow, remembering that all this has to be carried in addition to a rifle and other equipment, and if we want a comfortable bed, we must suffer a little discomfort in carrying it about in this hot climate.

At every stop there are children selling bananas and small tangerines, monkey nuts, and 'Bombay Oysters'. This is an egg broken into a small glass or cup with vinegar, pepper and salt. There are also the *char wallahs* (tea men) who carry a large tin container of tea which is kept warm by a small fire of charcoal underneath. The tea is never good due to the fact that the best tea is exported, and the water is terrible, and is always full of chemicals. Where the tap is exposed to the sun, the water must be allowed to run for several minutes, as it's too warm to hold one's hand underneath. There is an enormous sale for these minerals which are quite cheap.

The natives do not use a cup and saucer as Europeans do, but many carry their own metal cup which has no handle. But there are many different religions and castes, each with their own customs and habits. Most eat with their fingers which should be washed after the meal. The staple food is rice and many of the very poor eat nothing else. The most common diet is curried rice with beef, mutton, fish, or chicken. The rice is boiled separately but the curried beef etc. is cooked with chillies which are small pea shaped, and may be red or green. The green chilli is very bitter and once eaten can be tasted several hours after. Water is usually taken with the meal.

We arrive at Calcutta, about 12.30 p.m. and march to the fort about two miles away. We are accompanied by the pipe band. Fort William has several entrances. Two are guarded day and night and a third is guarded at night only. The wall around the fort is very substantial, and is about nine feet in height and is surrounded by a moat.

We are directed to our barrack rooms after *tiffen* (mid-day meal) and I am surprised to find almost everyone in bed. At first I imagine they have just returned from manoeuvres, but soon learn that those not on any special duty go to bed every afternoon. There are about 90 beds in each room, and it's picturesque to watch everyone lying on top of a sheet covered bed with nothing on except a pair of white pants, and overhead many very large fans. There are about ten big double swing doors leading out on to a veranda and at one end of the veranda there are stairs leading up on to the roof which is flat like most buildings in the east.

At 4 p.m. tea is served in the barrack rooms with a biscuit, after which everyone takes a shower bath and will then play a game of football or hockey, or just watch a game. Many go for a run or walk around outside the fort. Many will have another shower bath on return. We take a shower after every parade, if time permits. It's not terribly warm here usually about 108 degrees in the shade. But it's the awful humidity, and our clothing is always wet with perspiration. Most get prickly heat which is thousands of tiny red spots and cause a terrible irritation. We have dinner at 6 p.m. after which we may go to the canteen where beer is served, and the day canteen for tea and a hot or cold meal and minerals.

There is a cinema inside the fort. Most walk into the city until 9.30 p.m. and midnight during weekends. Reveille is at 5.30 a.m. We do two parades before breakfast which is at 8 a.m. There are three parades before *tiffen* and we finish parades at 12.30 a.m. We do about one 24 hour guard and one 12 hour guard a week. As well as guarding the fort we have to guard the gun and shell factory about four miles away at Cossipore. After three weeks at the fort we go about fifteen miles away to fire the rifle and the Lewis light machine gun. We live in tents for ten days. On my return, I am transferred to the signal section, and after two months go to a hill station in the Himalayas. We climb the hills to Darjeeling about nine thousand feet in the small mountain train. From there we climb another thousand feet (on foot) to Jalapahar, where we live in wooden bungalows. It's very much colder here and we have to light fires. We do guard duties on the married families quarters at Katapahar about 900 feet higher.

From here Mount Everest and Känchenjunga are visible at about 4.30–5.30 a.m. It rains a lot, almost continuously for two weeks. After parades we can hire a pony for one rupee an hour, and go down to the tea plantations, or climb higher to Tiger Hill.

As I stand on guard one morning at Katapahar and look across towards Tibet, I think of many things, first of all the wonderful protection which the Himalayas affords to India, and then again I wonder and think an attack through Tibet would not be impossible. I ask myself who or what lies on the other side of Tibet. One of the lads in the guard room has told me that China is the other side and that the Chinese people were friendly towards us. But what if the Japanese ever conquered China. I often wonder why there are so many Japs in Calcutta. Is it not possible they are there for reasons other than normal trade. There are quite a lot of dentists amongst them, and they run a few cheap restaurants. I used to visit one a mile from Calcutta at a place called Kidderpore, which was out of bounds, and I went mainly because it was out of bounds. If there is a desire to hide something there must be something which is worth hiding. There is danger in these out of bounds areas. In this particular street I go to, it's said that many people have gone there and never left it. It's called Watjun Street. But the greatest danger as I see it is entering and leaving without being caught by the military police, which makes life exciting.

Most food, including fruit, is most expensive with the exception of pineapples, due to the cost of bringing it up the mountain. We can get a medium sized pineapple for one and a half annas (1?d). An anna is about a penny and there are sixteen annas in one rupee. There are four pice in one anna and four pies in one pice. The pie which is 1/16 of an anna is not normally used by the Europeans. But I have seen the poor Indians buy a small cup of tea for two pies in Kidderpore near Calcutta. This cup is made of very thin reddish earthenware material, which is a kind of clay. The cup has no handle, and is never used a second time but is broken on the roadside outside the tea shop. Therefore the amount of business or trade may be calculated by the number of broken cups.

In Jalapahar it is still raining, and most of our training is done indoors. We are taught how to use the heliograph. This is a mirror used to transmit messages if the weather permits, i.e. there must be plenty of sun and the sky should be clear of clouds. A double mirror is used when the sun is at the back of the sender. We are taught hand signalling which is more effective at night. We are also taught telephone work. Ours is a D.3. As well as sending messages by speech, we may use the Morse code. There is a key attachment, similar to that used in the post office. Flag signalling is another method. Code is also used, as in all other kinds of signalling except semaphore when two flags are used. Our D3 telephone makes a buzzing sound when using the key, unlike the post office key which is a knocking sound.

It is the indoor training that worries me because we stand in a half circle around a blackboard and it is so much like being back at school, and I feel nervous, and when I am asked to go to the blackboard I am trembling and my writing is poor, when I speak I stammer. We have a corporal called D. Lloyd and he likes to make fun of me and some of the lads laugh. They think it's fun seeing me so nervous. It's remarkable how I can't get over this fear of making a mistake. In the old days it was fear of being beaten, but now it's the fear of looking foolish or being laughed at. I often wish I was getting beaten again. It would be much more bearable than being laughed at. One of the instructors is very nice and I think he understands how I feel and tries to help me. Some days I think I have made a great mistake by joining the army, because there is no escape route. The other morning when there was no mist or cloud, I borrowed a telescope. It was a very good one as it magnified 30 times. I wanted to study the mountains and valleys. I was thinking of deserting the army if I ever felt any worse. But of course things would have to be much worse than they are at present. My headaches are not too bad and I sleep a few hours each night. I still dream of flying across water. But I am not being followed. I dream that I may fall into the water and be drowned. But the fear does not terrify me. I will probably never desert the army. But if I ever do, it will be to Tibet, or to Afghanistan. The lads are talking about our battalion being transferred to the northwest frontier, which is in Afghanistan, where it snows in the winter. Troops who serve at the frontier get a medal, but a medal is just something to let people see when one goes back home, something to boast about. But I never think about going home besides I have to do another five years yet. After three months we go back to Calcutta. It's better here. There is more life and I have now made two pals, Reilly and Hannigan from Glasgow. Their parents come from Ireland. We always walk out together. We drink iced German beer on Friday and Saturday, and spend the remainder of the week reading papers and playing billiards. The beer is one rupee four annas (or 1s 8d) a bottle which is slightly more than a pint. But it's a high gravity beer, and the alcoholic content is higher than our beer at home. Cigarettes are about half the price at home, or 6 annas for twenty best brand. Calcutta is in the province of Bengal and the language spoken is Bengali. But as it's a cosmopolitan city there are many languages spoken. Almost anyone of any importance can speak English and Hindustani. The natives are mostly Hindus.

We are now transferred to Jabalpur in the central provinces. It's much warmer here and the people are darker. They are slightly bigger than in Bengal. Their religion is mainly Muslim and Buddhist and Mohammedan. The people of different religions have little or nothing in common and do practically no business with each other, and they do not even converse with each other. There are many riots in India starting with some petty incident, for example one person touching another as they pass on the street or seeing an animal being slaughtered. But the soldier does not mix very much with the natives, and therefore one learns so very little about the people or their customs.

Here, as in Calcutta, few of the men shave themselves as the *nappy* (barber) comes around each morning, and shaves them in bed between four and five am. We have a 'boot boy' between every dozen men, who brings us char (tea) from the cookhouse each morning. He cleans our equipment, boots, etc. He washes our toppee, makes beds and runs errands. We clean our own rifles and guns. We each pay him eight annas but for a rupee he will wait on us hand and foot the whole day. The *dhobi* (laundry man) calls each evening to collect the soiled laundry and return it the next day. He comes to the barrack room to collect it, he is called the 'free of charge' but it means tying up the laundry and carrying it a hundred yards to the Company store. But in this country nobody likes work and anyone who can earn ten rupees a week will employ a boy or servant.

There are two kinds of servants, the honest and dishonest, and they are equally efficient at their work. The dishonest one will sometimes wait a whole year before he robs you. But then he does it on a grand scale. When I arrived at Calcutta they were talking about a servant who was trusted so much that they allowed him to come to the Company store each day and clean and oil all the spare rifles. The store man would go drinking to the canteen and leave him in charge of the store. He done this for more than a year until Christmas 1936. He was missing on Christmas day and so also was a box of twelve rifles. He was arrested at the northwest frontier but the rifles were already sold and were never recovered.

In Jabalpur we do a lot of outdoor training but nobody takes it seriously. We go fairly long distances to signal with the heliograph. We do manoeuvres and long marches. But it's all a joke and if we don't want to do a route march we just go sick. On a training exercise one day our platoon officer offered a packet of cigarettes to the first man back to camp a distance of six miles. But when we came to a river we decided to travel a mile further down where it was shallow. L. Henderson wanted the cigarettes badly and tried to swim the river but was drowned.

It's 1938 and life has been tolerable. There is a cinema in camp and a library, a billiard room and canteen, and a bicycle shop where we can hire one for eight annas an hour to go to bazaar or village where we may buy cheap spirits or native beer which tastes like cold coffee. We also buy underwear, bed spreads and sheets. Many of the lads have cameras and they develop their own films. Many have pen pals in the States and photographs are exchanged. Some of the lads write letters to many parts of the world mostly to girlfriends. Some chaps fall madly in love with girls they have never met. In this part of India nobody thinks of going out with a girl because there isn't any. In the big cities, Bombay and Calcutta, there are many half caste girls who go to dances and in many cases marry their soldier boys and they make good wives. There are six men in my Battalion who have married coloured girls.

Many of the men who marry half-caste girls are very conscious about the colour of their skin and will spend no end of money trying to make the skin fair. They go to native quack doctors and purchase paints, powders and various chemicals and after a few days trial will take their wife's photograph which they will study and show around to all their friends for their opinion as to whether or not there is any improvement in their wife's complexion. These women are so colour conscious that they will not leave the house before sunset in case the sun makes them darker.

I am transferred to Nagpur 30 hours train journey from here, on a three months tour of duty. There is another signaller with me. Our job is to keep in communication with the Rajput Indian regiment using heliograph during the day and the signal lamp at night. The reason for this is in the event of riots or disturbances we will be able to assist each other. Most people in Nagpur support the Congress or Ghandi party. They are more aggressive than most other Indians and unlike the timid Bengalis. There is more entertainment in the town of Nagpur and we have some very good sports grounds, football fields and hockey grounds.

I am back at Jabalpur and there is a lot of talk about the possibility of war. But it doesn't cost me a thought. I don't believe we shall ever go to war again in Europe. I can't imagine our army going to war with anyone because we should be lost without the *nappi*, the *dhobi* and the bootboy to bring us tea in bed. I fail to see how we could win a war. It's true we have a good rifle, probably the best in the world. But most of our other equipment is obsolete. I can't imagine using a heliograph at the front, or a pair of semaphore flags, or a lamp. Besides we should not be able to go to bed at the front after our mid-day meal. We have mule transport which can hardly be said to be modern. It's true that some of the mules we have are the fastest things on land, but how can we keep up with them? The last time we done manoeuvres we just managed to load our signalling equipment on the backs of the animals when they decided to stampede. Much of our best equipment was lost or broken and it was several hours before all the mules were recaptured.

War has been declared and we are informed by our C.O. that we are on active service. But we carry on just as before, except that nobody leaves the Regiment. About twenty who are due to be transferred to the reserve were on their way home but they have returned to India. All leave is cancelled. The war does not affect us in the least until well after Dunkirk. Our failure in Europe did not surprise us. I remember once asking a sergeant of the tank corps, in 1937, whilst we were on manoeuvres at Catterick Camp how many tanks we had which were serviceable. He said 'there were about three hundred modern tanks, and about two hundred of an older type which could be considered obsolete'. This was in the whole of Britain. The Germans used three thousand tanks in a single battle.

The training is now more realistic. There is no more going to bed in the afternoons. The army at home lost two-thirds of all their war material and are now training with broomsticks. The authorities are now getting worried. We have only 28,000 troops in the whole of India. So we go on flag marches to many parts where no troops have previously been stationed. We travel about two hundred miles by train and march through villages, and in many cases the natives run away from us, because they have not seen white men before. I am told the reason for the 'flag marches' is to let the people know that the British are still in India, because recently it has been said at public meetings that the British have lost the war and gone home.

It was on one of these marches we came to a place called Asigor. It was 200 miles south of Jabalpur. Here in Asigor was the most magnificent sight I have ever seen. It was a fort built on top of a small mountain by the Mongols 2,000 years before. We had marched about fifteen miles that day. My pal Reilly and I, when we had erected the tents, decided to take a look at the fort. It was erected of stone and the walls were fifteen feet thick. Many of the stones must have weighed a ton and even more, yet how did they get the material up the mountain? My guess is that the fort was built around a stone quarry and the material was found on the spot. The building was still in perfect condition. The architecture was good, and yet buildings which had been erected by the East India Co. about 120 years ago had in many cases fallen down. In the fort was a graveyard where a company of British troops had been buried. There was a well of delicious spring water, still intact. We saw several dungeons, the sight of which was frightening. There were chains in the walls and the floor where it is said the prisoners were held.

In 1941 there is talk of a great battle being fought in North Africa, and the Italian 10th Army has been defeated. There are several ship loads of prisoners on their way to India. My battalion is now attached to an Australian unit at Bombay. We are to escort the prisoners to Bangalore in the South. It is not a pleasant job. I have to look after 26 prisoners packed like sardines in a train compartment. They have come straight from the desert. They are unwashed and it's very warm. The prisoners are seated but I have to stand on guard with my rifle. But they are a rather timid and childish lot. What strikes me about them is that most of them are very fair skinned, while others are dark. There is a senior N.C.O. amongst my prisoners who can speak a little English and I ask him who the dark lads are, and he answers saying 'they are the dirty Arabs from the South', and most of them sleep out. They don't give much trouble except during meal times they rush like hungry wolves, when the food is brought. They get good food, in addition to the normal ration of the British soldier, they get dates and figs and a bigger sugar ration. They are very industrious and are always making something like cigarette lights and cigarette cases. They take away the lavatory seats and make picture frames, etc. At each station they are trying to sell to the Indians clothing and blankets which we have given them. I have just stopped a man selling a new pair of boots for a 20 packet of cigarettes. I call the N.C.O. and explain that the cigarettes cost 6 anna and the boots cost 12 rupees, and I tell him it's a very serious crime to sell government material. The N.C.O. explains that this man is uneducated. Instead of going to school he went to church. Bangalore is called the garden of India. But we don't see the town. The camp is several miles outside it.

It's June 1941 the Company commander has sent for me. I am to travel to Calcutta to work in an Indian army ordnance clothing factory, as I am a tailor. After a trade test I am promoted to the rank of sergeant. After a few months in the cutting section I am transferred to the 'inspection' to supervise finished uniforms, which are made by

24 different contractors, who have their own small factories outside. After a few weeks in the inspection department, it is discovered that the standard of work is far below that required. I am in charge of twenty Indian examiners and one day I am sent for. Lieutenant Payore wants to know why the quality of work was so poor and I inform him that most of my examiners are taking bribes from the contractors so that their work is passed.

A week later I am transferred back to the cutting shop. Cutting is far more interesting. But we work much harder, 12 hours a day for six days a week. We work a week on days and a week on nights. The controller of the factory sent for me one day and told me he had made a mistake by employing me, without having passed a cutting test. This was good news because my infantry battalion were stationed at 'Rasmen' at the northwest frontier.

I just had a letter from my old pal Ginger Reilly. He said it was snowing every day, and I thought how wonderful it was. I always wanted to see the northwest. I had heard so much about it from Naughton a tailor who worked with me in 1934. He told me about the 'Pathans' who used to come from the hills at night to steal food and rifles. He explained that they had no quarrel with the soldiers. All they wanted was their rifles, and in many cases took only the bolt of the rifle. They could make a rifle but could not make a bolt as good as ours. The secret was in the bolt *head* which was made of a very hard material.

I now realised the major was talking to me, and asked me how long it would take me to learn to draft patterns. I told him it was not possible to learn quickly. Besides there were no cutting school in Calcutta. I did not know who would want to teach me. He advised me to speak to Mr L. Milston who had just arrived in the factory. He was a cutter and designer.

I asked the major to allow me to go back to my regiment. I was a soldier and a signaller. I would be more efficient at the work which I was better qualified to do. The major dismissed me saying that I was a sergeant and there were great possibilities. He said if I can pass a cutting test in three months he would personally recommend me for further promotion. This word frightened me a lot. *Promotion* meant further responsibility for which I was unsuited. The very thought of more promotion instilled me with a new sense of fear. It simply made me freeze up.

I remembered at school I would be beaten for a mistake. Later on in the army in Malta or Palestine or in the Central provinces, the lads just laughed, which hurt plenty. But now the position was entirely different. A mistake now would make trouble for others. When I failed my driving test in England my pals joked about it, saying you are a clever fellow, you didn't want to drive so you just failed deliberately. I liked them to think that way. I done like the major said. I did learn to draft and design. It was good learning. It took my mind off other matters. I was promoted to Warrant Officer Class I. I was assistant foreman, on civil rates of pay at 450 Rupees plus expenses and overtime which made my pay about 600 a month (100 Rupees £7–10).

We were at war with Japan. They had taken Singapore and were advancing rapidly through Burma. There were air raids, as the American ships unloaded thousands of tons of war material only two miles from where I worked.[4] I went down to the docks one Sunday and talked to an American officer. I told him I didn't think there were so many tanks and trucks in the world. He said there was much more out at sea. They had another 20 ships in the Bay of Bengal, but were short of parking ground in Calcutta. He said 2000 drivers were arriving the next day to take some of the material further north. I said I hoped they could clear the dock area before the next air raid. There were thousands of vehicles parked bumper to bumper. I hoped there was no fuel in the tanks. He laughed, and said 'Full right to the top fella. These babies got to be driven a thousand miles north, and not pulled by your mules and oxen'.

I wished him luck and kept my fingers crossed. There was an air raid the same night but the bombs missed by a 1000 yards and killed 500 Indians. There was now a stampede. The roads were blocked. More than half a million natives left Calcutta during the next week.

The Japs were less than 50 miles from the Indian border. We had three fire engines in our factory which I looked after and was also responsible for the training of crews to operate them. These engines were petrol driven but had to be manhandled to the scene of the fire. I was responsible for all fires on the Alipur side of Calcutta. As the Calcutta fire brigade was not able to reach us during air raids due to the fact that the Kidderpore Swing Bridge over the River Hugli was now open in order to allow ships to escape if necessary out in the Bay of Bengal. When this bridge was open to shipping it was closed to the road traffic. Hence the need for our factory fire fighting appliance.

Capt. Simpson who was our deputy controller sent for me one day to explain why I had not filled in my monthly report book on fire appliances. I informed the Capt that I was more interested in the fire fighting appliances than in writing about them. He became angry and thought I was being insolent. He jumped to his feet and asked me if

I knew there was a war on. I assured him I did. He asked me if I knew the Japs were only 20 miles from the Indian border. I corrected him saying they had reached a point 20 miles from the border a week ago and had advanced a further ten miles since then. He told me he had received his information a few hours ago. He told me to go back to my work.[5]

The situation was now critical. The natives had been lining up at the banks for three days, demanding their money as the war was lost. After work I went straight to the British military hospital, where I was getting my information from, as there were always lads coming back from the front, wounded. My regiment was fighting at the front, and I know if I met one of them they would keep me informed.

Yes, the Japs were still advancing. Simpson sent for me the following day. He was now a changed man. He had a cold and was hoarse. He said my information was correct. I advised him that my regiment were at the front and I was naturally interested. He then told me that we must be prepared to leave India at a few hours notice. We would be going to South Africa where a factory was being prepared. We now had a new foreman, an Englishman, who had married a Japanese woman. He had been living in Japan but managed to escape into Burma and he left his two children at school in Japan. I became friendly with him and he invited me to his house to meet his wife, who was employed at the bankers[6] office. I found her a charming person.

At this time I got to know a Burmese officer. He was a captain called Jim. The whole Burmese army was now disbanded. But those who desired to transfer to the Indian army were welcome. Jim was a jovial kind of man, very friendly, and always in a good mood, until one night he said his wife (who was known to me) had deserted him and was going out with another man. Jim had been drinking heavily and he lost his revolver belt and holster. I promised to try and replace them for him. I got him a belt and made him a holster in the factory but was unable to get him a revolver. But I said I could borrow one from the fort. It would be in my name and I should want it back every month to go to the bank for the factory wages. He said he would remember that, and was now quite happy. If he could not get a revolver elsewhere, he would let me know. I seen him again a few nights later and he told me what the Japs done in Singapore. How they killed the patients in their beds, raped the nurses and then murdered them.

One day I was called to the office and asked to engage six men for semi-skilled work in the cutting shop as the chargeman, Reggie

Manklew, was absent. He usually employed all daily paid staff. I was shocked and surprised when each man offered me *ten Rupees*. As the men were Bengalis I had to send for an interpreter who told me that it was the practice to pay the first month's salary to the kind gentleman who employed them. This was news to me and I went to see the deputy controller who was too busy to talk to me. So I asked to talk to the controller. The controller was away on business. I met the security officer, who was an Indian, and he asked me to come to his office. He was an ex-major from the Indian army. He was a very polite and kindly man with a well kept beard. He told me it was the custom throughout India and indeed the whole of Asia for the employee or the person who engaged them. But he added it is considered a serious offence in the army or any government department. However if I wished to put the matter on paper he would see that my complaint was forwarded to the competent authority.

Needless to say I heard no more about it. Lieutenant Payne, who was in charge of the inspection department, was being transferred to another factory. He threw a big party before leaving. Payne got drunk and made a speech and boasted of having made 75,000 Rupees in bribes in two years. Shortly after this the controller Major Holt was transferred because of a deficiency of 200,000 yards of material from the factory stores. Major Holt was a good and honest officer. He was a highly educated and efficient man, but was let down by his staff.

During the early part of 1942 I am invited to a party at Firpos Hotel and am introduced to a very beautiful young lady who invites me to her home to meet her mother. Her name is Angela Dennison. Her mother is English and her father French. She lives in the Connani Estates near the big graveyard. We meet almost daily. Her parents are separated. After three months we talk about getting married. We go to an air conditioned cinema once a week where there is a big bar and we have drinks at the interval. I am a member of the Hawaiian Night Club where she sometimes works as a hostess. There is a good bond and she teaches me to dance.

I am most happy in her company. It is just heavenly to be near her. We talk and laugh and make plans for the future. I take her to a Chinese shoemaker. She has her shoes made to measure. We go and have iced drinks at the winter gardens of the grand hotel. With each drink we get free of charge roasted peanuts and tiny sausages. When we finish work I go straight to her house. Her mother told me to. But when I leave her I suffer from the most awful depression. I feel that I am not good enough for her. I think I should leave her, and write telling her. But I am at her house next morning to meet the postman, and I destroy the letter.

In India all favours are paid for. Bribery and corruption although sometimes difficult to detect, exist in almost all works of life. There was little or no corruption in the British forces before the war, and the Regular Army officer although underpaid would never stoop to anything underhand.

1942 is the year of the Bengal famine, due to the shortage of rice. Hundreds of bodies have been picked up. They just littered the streets. The reason for this was not due to any real shortage, but to the hoarding of rice and other food stuffs by the traders and shop keepers. The price of rice has soared and is very many times more expensive than a year ago. I have heard it said more than once that rice is being thrown into the River Hugli in order to keep the price up. The American Flyers are said to be making huge fortunes by buying gold in Calcutta and flying in to China where it is possible to get anything from twenty to fifty times the original price.

Life has changed in this city. We could get a taxi a few years ago for 12 annas, and a rickshaw for 4 annas. But now the drivers don't even stop for us as they know the Yanks will pay them a lot more. They will pay a taxi driver 10 rupees for half an hour, which was a British soldier's pay for the whole week at the start of the war. Beer is rationed to one bottle a month. But we can buy it in the Hawaiian Club at 5 rupees or four times the price of a year ago.

During this time I am finding it extremely difficult to keep my fire fighting crews as many run away whenever there is an air raid. So far we have been lucky as there have been no fires worth talking about. As I said before, my three engines (pumps) are not self propelled but have to be manhandled, two of them, a 'Dodge' and 'Morris' are made up of bits and pieces. They have been redeemed from the scrap heap at the local garage. But the third a Chrysler is new and a powerful machine.

I have been watching carefully the unloading of American war material, and every day can see huge convoys moving north. With all this stuff at the front the Japs must lose the war. But when this material was parked in the area of the docks thousands of trucks, often loaded with ammunition and oil, with tanks and guns, just one bomb in the correct place would have destroyed the lot, because all the vehicles were almost touching each other. The Japs were trying hard, and only missing with their bombs by sometimes only 200 yards.

Last week the warship Ajax a cruiser was in the docks and I met many of her crew, including the Surgeon Commander. I was invited onboard the following evening. But when I reached the docks the ship had already sailed. Imagine my horror the next day when I heard she had been sunk in the Bay of Bengal. There were no survivors.

Am still seeing Angela every day and the time has come when I must make up my mind one way or the other. This is a most terrible ordeal. I love this girl most passionately. There are signs that she is getting impatient. Her mother accused me the other day of wasting the girl's time, and just playing about. Last evening we had a date. But when I got to her house she was just being driven away in a taxi with a young German chap. I had not met the fellow but heard about him. At first I felt somewhat relieved. At last the problem is solved for me. She has another chap and now I shall keep away and forget about everything. But two hours after, I was going about frantic. The thought of her being with another fellow was driving me out of my mind. I went to the Grand and began drinking and from then I went to Firpos. Whilst I was there there was a brawl between the sailors and the police called and asked everyone for their papers. I was charged for wearing plain clothes and having no means of identification. I was allowed to go home, but was too worried to go to work next day. So I went to town and later to the girl's place. She laughed the whole thing off and thought it was all so very funny. We were friends again. I got away with the charges and all was well for a few weeks. She asked me straight out one day if I intended to marry her or not. I said 'yes most definitely' but not at present. She demanded to know the reason why and I told her that only just over two years ago I was a private soldier. My present rank was only temporary for the work I was doing but when the job finished I may have to revert to private, as I was not qualified to hold a similar rank in my own regiment. She then said it did not matter. She would marry me if I was a private soldier tomorrow. But I fully realised that that was only part of the story. I was not well, and I would have to face this awful fact. I was being driven in opposite directions by an equally powerful force. I wanted to marry her more than anything in the world but was afraid that I would not be good enough, or that I would let her down. This was my mental conflict.

A few days later I attend a Hindu wedding. One of my supervisors, a lad of 18 years, has married a girl of 12 years. The ceremony was over when I arrived and now it's just a great feast, which will last for several days. I was there only a few hours during which time we had seven courses of fish, with small dishes of sweets in between. Afterwards I go to the factory. I am in charge of the night shift as the foreman is on holiday. During the night one supervisor has made a great mistake, and has wasted 4000 yards of material. We were cutting uniforms for the Chinese army out of a very thin khaki material, about the same weight as shirting. The cloth was laid out straight for 40 yards a 100 pieces thick that is 100 pieces were placed on top of each other, on a rubber covered floor. The top piece was marked by placing a pattern on it, and marking it by chalk. It was then cut by an electric machine. But my Indian supervisor used the wrong pattern. It was really my own fault as I should have watched him. But as soon as I seen the mistake I hit him two or three times across the back with a yard stick. Just as I did this I realized that it was the first time I had ever hit anyone and I had beaten him in the same manner as I had been beaten so often more than ten years before. I now felt sick and ashamed. I wanted to go and say I was sorry but he would just jabber away in Bengali to humiliate me. He always talked to me in Bengali even though he could speak perfect English. I couldn't do any more work that night but walked up and down outside. I don't know how long I was there, but Pretam Singh a Sikh supervisor came out to tell me he just returned from the Punjab where he had been to get married. He said he could not get married as his brother who was stationed overseas could not get home. I think he said according to his religion all the family must be present or the wedding cannot go on. He thanked me for the wedding present I had given him. But I asked what present. He laughed and said the 20 rupees you gave me going away. I answered him saying 'I did not know he was getting married'. 'I understand', said he, 'you have been drinking', 'always you make very good joke when you drink too much'. I assured him I had nothing stronger than warm water stained with a tea leaf. He then invited me inside and I suddenly remembered about his wedding. 'I have brought you very nice drink from my home'. He went to his pocket and fetched a half pint of 'Rosa' rum and poured me out a whole cupful. Just then I noticed he was drunk. I drank the rum quickly and he gave me another stiff drink. It was very good rum, a lot better than we could buy. I felt better now. He was singing an Indian song. He had his arm on my shoulder. He usually kept his beard nicely combed, but when drinking it seemed to stand straight out. I finished my rum, and I laughed and he laughed. He then said, 'I am not care about marriage. Every day I am drink too much "Rosa" rum,' 'Please you come to Punjab next time I am get married, and every day together we drink too much. After you come to my house for Punjabi food, and you speak with my father he wants to know too much about your country and your wonderful schools'.

The following week I was on day shift and as I was leaving the factory I met Capt. Simpson, who said, 'you have not collected your whiskey ration', which was a bottle every two months. I called at his office and signed for the bottle. It was Canadian rye which I brought along to Angela's house. She said she was going out somewhere. So I just sat and finished the whiskey. Later on I wandered out and had more to drink. I did not go to work the following day and was placed on a charge for absence. Capt. Simpson advised me to go sick, which I did. Several days later he came to see me and said he had seen the doctor who told him there wasn't much wrong with me and I could leave the hospital in a day or two. But when I returned to the factory I felt no better. The work no longer interested me. Angela had finished with me. I suffered from severe headaches and indigestion. Sleep was impossible except when drunk, which made me nervous next day.

There was an air raid and the factory was hit but only slight damage was done. One day the controller sent for me and said 'Your orders have come through. You must report to your regiment. You know what that means'. I answered, 'Yes sir, I will revert to the rank of private'. I was a little shocked but relieved the change would do me good. I really expected to hear this when I left hospital two months before. I had by now completely forgotten about the charge of being absent.

The following day I got posted and travelled north to join my regiment in Burma. I was to travel to Chittagong by train and go to the front with the next draft. But when I got there I discovered that Chittagong was just a camp between two hills and a wood on the south side. We slept in tents and there were a number of fires while I was there due to people throwing lighted matches or cigarette ends. The fire would travel very quickly along through the grass, and often burn down tents before being brought under control.

There was a cinema a mile away and a bazaar and village a little further. I was back where I had started, a private soldier once again. But I wasn't very worried because I had learned something. I wasn't so much afraid of people, and I could speak to an officer without stammering. During the time I was at Calcutta I met a private soldier who had been a chaplain in the medical corps. He was reduced to the ranks for striking an officer. I became very interested in this man and met him regularly. He taught me how to cure stammering by controlled breathing. It was then I discovered the cause of this complaint was incorrect or erratic breathing, a nervous complaint brought about by fear in my case. I now practised deep breathing regularly, and found out that my headaches weren't as bad and I could sleep better. I was now wondering if many other so-called diseases were not caused by incorrect breathing.

Another very good remedy I found out was to sniff handfuls of saline water through the nose. This not only cleaned the nose but also exercised the lazy eye muscles. In my case the left side was nearly always stopped and it was over the left eye I got the pain.

I did not see Captain Jim from the Burmese army before I left. I heard he had gone to the front. The Japs are now being driven back. They did actually get within a mile or two of the Indian border. A small number of prisoners have now reached our camp, and they are surprised because they are allowed to live. They want to know how and when they are going to be killed. They are disappointed because it's such a crime in their eyes to be prisoners. They could never return home. It is not difficult to get information from the Japs. They just sit down and write for hours, and tell everything from the first day they join the army. The interrogation officer said it's because they are afraid of being tortured. This makes me think in this case they must torture the prisoners themselves.

The story I heard about Singapore must be true. I remember when I was in 47 B.M.H. a few months ago, a Burmese soldier was brought in, who was said to have escaped from the Japs. He was a lad about nineteen and had gone completely mad. He kept shouting for his sister and it took four men to hold him. He was then given powerful injections to try to quieten him. But they were ineffective. He must have had a terrible experience.

There were all kinds of lads at Chittagong. There was one lad who used to go to the front once a month to collect his mail from home. After which he would go sick. His mail always went direct to his Regiment. There was another lad called Young. He had deserted from the front and got a year in prison. He was a rogue and a professional pick pocket, but the best hearted fellow I have ever met. When he robbed anyone he would take all his pals out and treat them. He never refused anyone anything. I had a fountain pen which I didn't want to lose so I gave it to him to keep for me until we would get on the boat. By doing this, I knew he wouldn't steal it. We now travel south by train to Dath Dam aerodrome to await orders to go to Bombay to catch a boat. But there is bad news. Two communication ships have blown up in the harbour and Queen Victoria docks have been destroyed. The fires rage for many days and we have to wait for two weeks.

We eventually sail in a twenty ship convoy with an escort of four destroyers. The journey home is without incident, except for one man who threw himself overboard. He left a note saying he had no wish to return home as his wife had left him. We arrived in Liverpool in October 1943 and travelled to Edinburgh. We got two weeks holiday which I took in Leeds.

I am posted to the 52nd mountain division and after a spell of duty at Dreghorn Camp near Edinburgh, we spend the winter up the hills in Scotland. Our camp is at Braemor, a mile from the castle. We have been issued with complete mountain warfare equipment, even to snow glasses. We carry a large rucksack, with sleeping bag, special boots and socks, windproof suit, leather jerkin, 200 rounds of ammunition, 3 grenades, primas stove etc. Altogether we carry as much as our Indian mules. This is really intensive training. This is what I imagined the army to be like before I joined. It's very cold but I like it better than the tropics. Out in the east I found the air too dry because very often it did not rain for almost a year.

After three months of this I am able to do 20 miles with full kit. We are supposed to invade Norway in the spring of '44. But nothing happens. Next we do special training for an airborne landing. Our kit is packed away in aircraft at Woodhall Spa, the bomber base, and for a whole week we are confined to camp. We can only go to the canteen. Finally we are briefed. It's Arnheim, and the paratroopers have already taken off. We are supposed to fly on the second day but the weather is too bad. Several times we are paraded to go aboard the planes. We are fully dressed now and sleep in our clothes for the next three nights. But the weather has let every one down. The paratroopers are now in a desperate position. They are being mowed down and burned to death with flamethrowers. At last the battle is over and a few come back. It's August '44 and still we have not gone into action. We are now stationed at Chalfont St. Giles 20 miles from London. The flying bombs are coming over our... [7]

...Shelling which was spasmodic. We move to a barracks at Hertogenbosch for three weeks. This barracks was recently occupied by the Germans. We are preparing for the invasion of the island of Walcheren, a Dutch island. It is the most heavily fortified island in the world. The Germans are in what we call pill boxes. They are dome shaped, and are just a solid mass of concrete reinforced. The walls being 15 feet thick, shells have no effect on them. The island has been shelled for four days by 600 guns. The Canadian artillery is helping us. The commandos attack at about 4.30 am and the fighting continues all day. We are in the town of Breskins on the coast, only a few miles away. We are due to take off in our little invasion craft at mid-day. There are about 26 men to each small boat. The town of

Breskins is just a pile of rubble. I have not seen a single house with a roof complete. There is not a building intact. We are going on board. They shell us from the island, and we take cover. The shelling is now only light and we make a dash for the boats. Our C.O. tells us we must make it this time as the commandos have now run out of ammo. And they must be relieved before the Germans counter-attack. We have to withdraw again. They have only a small number of guns left but they are accurate. The third time we make the boats and are out at sea. We are still under fire but feel safe. It was when the shells hit the building at the back of us they were dangerous. We are now half way across and the shelling has stopped. But the machine guns have opened up and we can hear the bullets whistling over our heads. We reach the shore and there are no casualties on our boat. We jump overboard into three feet of water and run for the beach. But there are barred wire entanglements under the water. My feet are caught in the wire which I can't see. Like a flash I can see the danger I am in. The machine guns have stopped firing. I keep telling myself to keep calm. I am feeling terribly weak. So far I have not used my hands to try and free myself and I am afraid I may loose my balance and fall over. I am trying to go forward but it's impossible. So I relax and take a few deep breaths, and I now move backwards and manage to free one foot. I am now able to bend down and release the other one without much trouble. I can now feel for the wire and climb over it. The firing has now died down for a while. The island is flooded as the dykes have been blown up. We are now in Flushing. Our platoon takes cover in a big building and we fire the bren gun at a pill box. But we are now under heavy fire from a field gun and trench mortar and two machine guns. There is a bridge between us and the Germans and they are shelling the bridge. This is bad because we have planned to cross the bridge at daybreak and attack the three pill boxes. We now get rocket firing planes to knock out the gun which is shelling the bridge. The gun is silenced in ten minutes and now the rocket planes are attacking the first pill box. Three planes drive one by one and send rockets hurling towards the pill box.

About twenty Germans came out waving the white flag and run over the bridge towards us. They are now lined up on the roadway with their hands on top of their heads. I am detailed to search them for guns or grenades and arms. Most of them are big men and some only look like schoolboys. Most look ill, their faces are green. They must have had a bad time. They have been bombed and shelled now for four days. They immediately ask for work and are helping to carry the dead and wounded on to the boats. After four hours work they are given a meal and a few cigarettes each. One of our officers comes up and demands to know why the prisoners are allowed to remain on the island. He is told there are no boats available.

It's now dark and the firing has died down. We are allowed to rest for a few hours with the exception of those on guard. But it's much too cold to lie down. We have no blankets or overcoats because the boat carrying them was sunk. So we spend the night when not on guard duties making tea. We make our own individually. We each have a tin of white solid fuel. It is in round pieces a quarter of an inch in thickness and one piece will boil a pint of water. There is corn beef and tins of sardines and jam. We are out long before dawn, and cross over the bridge which has many shell holes. We are now under fire from two machine guns one on our right front, and one on the left. These guns have a terrific rate of fire, about 1200 rounds a minute. One round in five is a tracer which lights up and seems to be coming straight for you. We are just over the bridge and the bullets are closer, and many of the lads lie down at the roadside in the soft mud. We come to a big shed full of holes and look around it very quickly. There is no one there. We advance towards a pill box three hundred yards away on the right. There is still machine gun fire. But they are not firing in our direction. At least I can't hear the whistling of the bullets. We have now reached the pill box and take up firing positions, as our platoon commander fires several shots into the entrance, and shouts on the troops to come out. But there is no move. He then fires another shot and shouts 'come out you bloody swine', and another 20 surrender. It's about 7 a.m. as we reach the second box, but there are only two inside, and they are in naval uniform. Outside the pill box there are two dead.

One of our lads goes through the dead men's pockets and is warned by the officer that he is on a charge. The lad answered that he is not looking for personal property, but a Luger pistol. I learned afterwards that the Yanks are paying 5,000 Belgian francs for a Luger. It is very popular because it fires 9 m.m. ammo, which is the calibre of our Sten gun, and the magazine fits neatly into the butt.

We advance along the railway which is built about six feet above sea level, on each side is flooded with the sea water. About three miles further on we came to a village where there are plenty of buildings still standing. There is little firing now, and several thousand prisoners are taken. Some food has arrived – tins of stew, vegetables, beans and sausages. There is a meal prepared and after half an hour we go along the railway towards another pill box. We have been warned by the natives that this ground is mined. But our officer takes no notice. We get within a hundred yards but nothing happens. There is no firing. We walk along a narrow path each side of the railway. The path is only about nine inches in width with grass each side. A native boy of about sixteen explained to us how we should walk along the path, and he demonstrated by walking, one foot immediately in front of the other. We are about 80 yards from the box and still no firing. Scoop Anderson who is 5 yards in front of me said a few minutes ago, 'we are on our way to our death'. Anderson walked off the path, and as he did so turned round and said something to me, what he probably did say was 'get down' as he thought he seen something. As he spoke he got down on one knee behind a small bush. As his knee touched the ground there was an explosion. As I looked to see what happened there was just a cloud of smoke and dust. I shut my eyes for several seconds. As I looked again I seen he had lost both legs. I climbed over the railway. As I was between the railway lines there was a second explosion. I shouted to the officer Lt. Malcolm Stewart. As I did so I realised that the officer had stood on the second mine but was not so seriously injured. He had lost a foot. It was now clear that the Germans had set the mines and abandoned the pill box. I dressed the officer's leg, and helped to carry him back several hundred yards, while the others looked after Anderson. Anderson was the platoon corporal. He died after four hours.

Many thousands of prisoners were now taken. It was now late in the evening and after bringing back the wounded (several of our men had been hit by machine gunfire) and burying the German dead, we had a rest for the night. The following morning mine detectors were brought forward, and used to clear the ground of mines. But the men operating the detectors were also killed or wounded. They now found out that the mines were made from material other than metal, and therefore could not be detected. We remained on the island about a week before returning to the Maas in Belgium. There was very little fighting in Belgium. Our work for the next month was mostly fighting individual snipers in buildings and woods.

We now moved to Holland. The fighting was now in the open country in woods and forests. The ground was mined everywhere and we kept to the roads as far as possible, and when going through fields, we were carried in Kangaroo vehicles, which were not normally used as fighting vehicles but for the transport of troops. In front of our Kangaroos there were flail tanks with an attachment in front with a number of long chains which rotated. The chains beat the ground and exploded the mines before the tanks reached them.

This was a simple yet wonderful invention. It was invaluable when crossing open country.

This is a new kind of warfare. Infantry and tanks working together. One is no good without the other. The Germans work the same way. Their tanks are far superior to ours. Their Tiger tank with its 88 m.m. gun is the last word in precision and perfection. But we are very fortunate because they have not very many tanks. Our losses in tanks are very heavy, but as one tank commander told me, when I asked him how soon he would get a new tank: 'I will get a new tank before I can get a new razor'. 'You know' he said, 'they gave them the wrong name, they ought to be called steel coffins, because very few ever come out alive, once they have been hit'.[8] My battalion is well dug in, in the Reichvelt forest. It's bitterly cold, and I wear so much clothing that I can hardly walk. We have been here a week. We do a fair amount of reconnaissance patrols at night. We have a young officer. He is a Norwegian and he seems to like night patrols and often goes well behind enemy lines. This is my night off. I only have to do my guard on the gun, and go back for water and a box of arms which we need badly as some of the lads are down to twenty rounds. It's about 10.30 p.m. and I go back through the forest with another six lads. We have to walk about a good mile. But it's easy to get lost. The path is shiny and very slippy as its freezing. But there are other paths. I left my overcoat as I have a heavy load to carry back a box of rifle ammo, and a jerry can of water. These cans were captured from the Germans in the desert. So far everything has gone on fairly well – I have never lost my nerve and I am always on my guard. One night when unloading my rifle I fired a round accidentally because my mind was on Scoop Anderson, who was blown up by the mine.

The Germans don't use much artillery. But they have plenty of mortars which are equally effective. We have now collected the water and ammo. And the other lads move off in front. I am usually last at everything. I am last now because the load is heavy and my wrists are weak. I have never done a lot of carrying. I have the box of ammo on my shoulder and the water in my right hand. But have to stop every 50 yards to change over. There is now a fresh wind blowing. I have never been so cold before in my hands and ears. The other lads are now well in front, and I think of a way to warm my hands. I fire my rifle into the ground and warm my hands on the muzzle. I am not so sure that I am on the correct path. But a few minutes later a machine gun opens up. It's a German. I can tell by the rapid fire and it's on my left, which would be correct. The bullets are coming towards me and are very close. I can tell by the loud whistle. I try to judge the distance they are away (the Jerries). I make it between four and six hundred yards, but can't be sure in a forest with a wind blowing. I am trying to calculate the time between the whistle of the bullets over my head and sound of the gun. But now the shelling has started, and something quite new is happening. The shells are hitting the trees and there is the overhead burst. This I have never thought about before. I am unprepared for this. I have never been taught any method of defence or any kind of cover against the overhead burst. I am running with the box on my shoulder. I am confused as I can't be sure whether it's mortars or shells. But the firing continues and I am alone. I have never been alone before under heavy fire. As I run along I slip on the path and the sharp edge of the tin which covers the box cuts my face. It's not painful but I know it's bleeding. I can feel the warm tickling feeling going down my neck. I am now on the ground. I have managed to get to my knees but am weak. The shelling continues, and one has hit the trees right up over my head. I feel that I want to dig into the frozen ground with my bare hands. Oh if only I had a pick and shovel I could dig myself into the earth. There is such a desire to be in a trench or dug-out that one feels that it is one's natural abode. I am now crawling on my hands and knees and am pulling the box of ammo and the water along the icy path. I can't stand up as my legs are too weak. Back at school I learned to keep my balance when my legs were giving way by holding my arms slightly outstretched. I feel that I could do that now if there was nothing to carry. Am I going the correct way? I am not too sure. The firing has stopped. There is not a sound except my own breathing which is irregular. I now stop as I reach a tree and stand up. My hands are like lumps of lead. There are footsteps getting closer. I hide behind the tree and look. My ammo is in the middle of the path. I must hide that in case it's a German patrol. If they see that it will make them suspicious, and they may look around. They are now about thirty yards off and I get a grenade ready, as it's too dark to shoot straight. Besides I would give my position away. I ease the pin slightly out and begin to think what if I should lose my nerve and drop the grenade at my feet? So I put the grenade away. I feel such a fool and a coward. I tell myself I will have some grenade practice at the first opportunity. That is what I ought to do. I should tackle all my fears and grapple with them one by one. That is the only solution to my problem. When I first joined the army I was afraid of officers. But when in the Indian army ordnance I would go out of my way to meet officers, and when I went to Malta I was afraid to swim in the sea. It took a lot of courage to tell my pal Bob Birchall about my fear.

So the following day we both went to the Hay wharf, and after a lot of persuasion I went past my depth, and was soon able to swim a hundred yards. The joy and pleasure when one beats or overcomes a fear is something which one must experience to really understand.

It's a patrol and one of our own. I let them come right up to me before I shout, as there have been accidents lately of patrols being fired on coming back to our own lines. It's Spud Thomson and Hanger and the new N.C.O. from the 51st division. They help me to carry the ammo and we reach our trenches in fifteen minutes. We all have a good drop of rum. There have been a number of lads wounded lately, and we are still getting their rations. We make strong sweet tea and put the remainder of the rum in it. Orders are issued to 'stand to', an attack is expected along the whole front. On such an occasion there is no relaxation. An American patrol wanders into our sector and is fired on. This is a common occurrence and luckily there are no casualties. They wear the same type of steel helmet as the Germans. There have been a lot of accidents lately and we lose more men that way than in actual combat. We are relieved by a battalion of the guards.

It's the first week in December '44 and we march back about fifteen miles. We go to a disused coal mine where we are given a bath and a change of clothing. We are living with the Dutch people about six to each house. In our village there is a British nine inch gun, which breaks windows in the houses as it fires. The natives complain and the gun is moved away another 100 yards. After two days rest we are back up at the front again near the Dutch German border. We are well dug in. During the day we move back to a small village about 200 yards away. It's fairly quiet during day time. But at night as we move forward to the trenches they open up with machine guns and heavy mortar. We send out a strong fighting patrol which meets opposition. They do not return.

The enemy are a thousand yards north in a place called Gilenkerchen.[9] We are relieved a few days before Christmas. We return to the coal mine to get washed and changed and are just beginning to settle down in a native house when we are ordered back to the front. We have not had more than a few hours sleep in weeks. The Germans have broken through the American lines on a wide front. They have advanced to a depth of twenty kilometres, and ten thousand prisoners are taken. Enormous quantities of materiel are also taken. The enemy have been short of petrol for their tanks. They claim that they have captured enough supplies to reach the coast and split our armies. They are still advancing. A number of British divisions are rushed forward and after bitter fighting, have managed to close the gaps.

It's Christmas Eve '44 and my battalion is back in the old position near Gilenkerchen on the border. I was L.O.B. 'left out of battle'. I am twenty miles behind the line. My landlady is preparing for Christmas dinner. Next day there are three young children, two girls, eight and six, and a boy, three. I have given them plenty of chocolate and sweets, and cigarettes and soap to their parents. There is a girl from next door aged 20. She talks about her boyfriend. They are to be married when he comes home. I asked her where he is, and she answered, he was taken prison by the Japs in the Dutch East Indies. On hearing this I shouted, 'O God'. I'm glad she didn't understand what I meant. Just at that moment a truck stopped at the front door and two military police came in, and asked me to show my papers. On looking at my pay book they told me to go quickly and warn all men available to report to them immediately. I managed to find four men. We were then told that our unit was under heavy fire and there were a number of casualties. We would be driven to the front. We were left four hunded yards from the front as it was too dangerous to drive further. We ran two hundred yards, which wasn't too bad. There was still another two hundred yards across open country. The French mortars were as usual accurate, and there were two machine guns firing at us from three hundred yards. The ground was like glass, and was very slippy. The lad in front of me fell right on his face and as I stopped to help him a bullet went through the small pack of my back. He was not injured. The firing died down after about four hours. We were in the trenches all during Xmas. But it was rather quiet. Several nights later the Germans were busy with patrol dogs. This went on for three nights and then they opened fire with everything they had for about eight hours. They attacked in company strength of about 120. We killed fifteen and 90 prisoners were taken. When we went out next morning to collect the dead it was discovered that several of them were in their bare feet. The local inhabitants must have taken their boots.

There was better news from the Ardennes Sector. The Germans were being driven back. Reports have reached us that twenty thousand American prisoners were taken, but no official news has yet been received. Our fourth battalion have lost a large number of men. They are holding a position about a mile and a half away on our left front. An evening shell hit a dump of 'Y5' grenades. This is a flat grenade which is very powerful and is used to blow down a tree or a wall. There were 2,500 in the dump. More than 50 bodies have already been picked up.

A tank driver told me of how there was a serious accident recently. A 75 m.m. gun was fired accidentally from a tank which had another parked in front, blowing up the tank and killing an officer. I am now on the Bren gun and have seen something moving about 60 yards in front of me, which I report to my platoon sergeant. I suggest to him that I ought to go forward and investigate. This is the chance I have been waiting for. I told him I may throw a grenade which he agrees to. He has already warned all our men on each side what is about to happen and they must not fire. There had previously been good light from the moon but a cloud had covered it, and it was much darker. I crawled forward about 30 yards, and waited and listened. But couldn't see nor hear anything. But I must throw the grenade. I now stood up and withdrew the pin, and threw the grenade about twenty five yards to almost the exact position where I thought I had seen a moving object, and immediately flying myself down flat on my stomach. After a few seconds there was a great explosion, greater than is normally made by a grenade. Several officers came up to see what was wrong and now an amazing discovery was made. I had thrown my grenade into a minefield (German). At least one mine was exploded, possibly more. We are relieved after two weeks and after a clean up and a rest we are allowed forty eight hours leave in Brussels. This city is not very much the worse for the war, except that there are few men to be seen. We spend our time either in a cinema or wandering about the cafés where a very mild beer is sold. A few places sell a German spirit called Schnapps. There is also a drink called cognac,[10] or some similar name. We stay at a private house and dine at the St. Michael's café. I find the people here very friendly and they often stop us in the street to have a chat, and we are often invited to their homes. The cafés are very homely and music is always provided.

There is a lot of money changing going on which I know nothing about. A man stopped us in the street yesterday and asked my pal Jack and I to change a lot of Dutch Guilders into Belgian francs. We said we didn't have so much money but he informed us that we could go to the bank the following morning and change a certain amount. We did go and met him after and were surprised when he paid us well for our trouble.

We are now back in the line again near the village of ...?[11] about 5 miles south of Waldefeucht. We have dug ourselves in near a wood. There is a lot of straw in a field and we get bundles of it, which we make beds from as it's very cold. I get the job of bringing back a dozen prisoners to our battalion H.Q. and later have to bury several

147

dead. The ground is so hard it's like concrete and I have already broken one pick. I have only managed to get down two feet. So the sergeant tells me to cover the bodies with snow and we can bury them properly tomorrow. So after marking the graves with a rifle and bayonet stuck into the ground and a steel helmet on top, I lie down to rest in the straw. After half an hour we get orders to move forward. We fall in and march along the road for three miles. We now advance in line. Our orders are to attack the village of Waldefeucht, and during the next two days we shall move forward to our next objective which is the River Ruhr.

We are now about a mile from the village as the German machine guns open up a percentage of the bullets are tracer and each one appears to be coming straight for us. There is a nerve breaking scream as a man on my left is hit. He is wounded in the stomach and is rolling about in the snow. Our orders are to keep on moving. There are two men in the rear to look after the wounded. The guns are still firing but not in my direction. We have reached the village and I climb over a number of dead, mostly German. There is now confusion. Most Germans have withdrawn but a few stay behind and they are shouting in English 'over here A company', 'over here B' and so on and as the company reaches the position directed, hand grenades are thrown amongst them.

My section of a corporal and four men take up the most forward position. We are in a very big house over an arch. The corporal then said in a low voice as if to himself, 'if only I had a torch I could go through this house and search every room'. Like a fool I said there is one in my pack. As he went to my pack I realized I had made a mistake. We went through every room, but found nothing. What we were looking for was booby-traps, which the Jerries were clever at making. You pick a rifle up, or open a door, or lift a dead body to bury it and a bomb goes off.

An hour afterwards the firing started with shell fire and mortars. The firing lasted three hours. The building in which we were in was hit several times but it was strongly built of stone. On one occasion I was thrown across the room on to a pile of broken glass, and the smell of cordite from the bursting shell made me sick.

The Germans counter-attacked the following morning, with Tiger tanks. Most of our troops withdrew a mile. We left the building, but remained in the village. We lost heavily in tanks. The two Tigers knocked out nineteen out of our twenty in little over an hour. My section kept the German infantry busy, so busy that one of their tanks had to withdraw to give them a hand. It was Sunday 21st January

1945. I was wounded in both legs and the right arm and taken prisoner. My wounds were superficial and I was therefore able to walk. I was taken by two Germans to the main road and made to face the wall. One soldier went back into the yard where we had been fighting. He called back to the one who was guarding me. I was touched lightly on the right shoulder with a bayonet which was fixed on to the end of a rifle. As I looked over my shoulder the soldier signalled for me to go back into the yard. As I walked along slowly I could hear the cries of Private Hanger. As I entered the shed where he was lying, it was obvious that he was badly wounded. He had a very deep wound in the side of his head, which he was holding with both hands. The blood was streaming down his hands. His legs appeared to be broken and twisted. He was now half sitting, one of his shoulders was rested against the wall. The Germans signalled for me to carry him but I pointed to my right arm, which was just dead. I was then taken back about 400 yards to a house on the right-side of the main road where there were about 50 other prisoners. There was an interrogation officer there who was talking quite freely to a British office about the progress of the battle, and was commenting on the conduct of our troops and our tanks and weapons in general, just as though he was discussing a ball game. The lads dressed my arm which was now rather painful. We remained there about two hours. Those who were well enough were marched away north, the wounded were assisted on to tanks and taken back to a hospital in Hindsburg. In this hospital was a very long passage and we sat on forms and awaited our turn for the operating table, which was at the end of the passage. As I sat on the form there was a German soldier each side of me. They were also wounded. What struck me immediately about this hospital was that each man took his turn as he entered. The Germans lined up as we did, they were not given preference. I watched about fifteen operations before it came my turn. The surgeon was a fine big fellow about 6 foot 4 inches. His blond hair was cut short, too short to comb. He was about thirty eight. Each patient was undressed completely by a male nurse.

As the table was high and difficult to climb the surgeon lifted the patient by placing his hands under the arms, and lifting them up to a sitting position on the table. The male orderly then assisted the surgeon in examining the patient and locating the wounds. A nursing sister then appeared and administered the anaesthetic by placing a swab of lint or other material over the mouth and nose and asked the patient to count twenty. I did not count more than six because I did not like the smell of the stuff, and hoped the swab would be removed when I stopped counting. The surgeon worked with great speed and efficiency.

It was about 2.30 p.m. when I got on the operating table and about 3.30 a.m. when I awoke next morning. I was lying in a clean bed with snow white sheets. I had not seen sheets for more than six months. There was an orderly standing by my bed with a plate of stew, which I could not even look at. So he laughed and walked away. He returned with a cigarette and a box of matches which I accepted. Some time later the Sister came to apologise, saying 'Your friend, I am sorry, he die'. I did not know who she meant.

Next came the interrogation officer, whose job it is to get information. But this poor man did not bother me about the war, he looked very pale and ill. He knew like every other German the war was lost. He talked about home, his home and mine, his wife and children. He had a notebook and pencil, but put them back in his pocket without writing a word. He left me saying 'I hope you will be well soon and back home in your own country'. I must have gone back to sleep again, and awoke in the middle of an air raid. I have been in air raids before but nothing like this. It was just a continuous earthquake. As it was night time it probably was British bombers. It lasted about half an hour. I can remember the sister running through the ward screaming and covering the patients' heads with sheets as glass came flying from the windows. I don't think the hospital got a direct hit, but the bombs must have dropped all round it.

The orderly came running down the ward and ordered all those who could walk to get up quickly. We got up and dressed, and walked back through the snow to ambulances, buses and trucks which were waiting three hundred yards further back. They dare not venture nearer the hospital because the British artillery was expected to open up any moment. After many stops we eventually reached Cologne, where we were well received. But this hospital was terribly overcrowded. There were hundreds lying on the floor, on straw covered by sheets or blankets. We were about six inches apart. Our wounds were dressed each day. For breakfast we got a pint of coffee in a tall aluminium vessel or jug, which was wide at the top and narrow at the bottom with plenty of bread and butter and honey. Shortly after breakfast three cigars were issued as no cigarettes were available. At eleven o'clock we had 'skilly' which was a thick soup or stew or with meat potatoes and other vegetables. There was a meal at 4 p.m. of coffee, bread and butter, and cheese or sausage. There was a light meal about 7 p.m. of coffee with bread and jam.

It was here I lost my boots, which on any part of the continent are more precious than gold. It is almost impossible to replace boots, which means that most people sleep with their clothes and boots on (trousers are also valuable). After a week here we go by train to Düsseldorf, which is a prison hospital. It is called the 'French Prison Hospital' because the doctors and male nurses are almost all French. Here life is really tough. The food ration is small. Two thin slices of bread a day with a few potatoes (two or three). There is black coffee first thing in the morning with 'skilly' at 11 a.m. and black coffee at 4 p.m. We are dependent on Red Cross parcels but only get one a week between four men. These are British, American and Canadian parcels which are about equal in size and weight. But the American parcel has very much greater trading value. The coffee is really delicious but unfortunately it is too valuable to drink. It is a very tiny tin but we can get five loaves of German black bread for one tin. But I am told it was worth only three loaves a few months ago because American parcels came in greater quantities. The American cigarettes are very popular. There are two packages to each parcel. Most of the lads have stopped smoking and exchange their cigarettes for bread or potatoes. We do most of our trading with the German guards who trade with civilians outside the camp. We also trade with the Russian prisoners who supply potatoes and small pieces of wood for making fires for cooking. The Russians are almost all big men, over six foot. They wear a very long overcoat and soft hat, and they have a beard as few of them shave. Every day two men come to our room. One carries wood in very deep pockets and his companion carries potatoes. Trading with the Russians is difficult, due to the language problem. So we engage a middleman who acts as interpreter. He is an American with one leg. He speaks a little Polish which the Russians understand. The Yank is a clever salesman, and can get better value than we can. His fee is half a cigarette or the equivalent in bread. But he is not a hard man and will often help and advise us free of charge. He keeps us up to date in current market values of the various commodities and will inform us of any change. For example, we now pay eight American cigarettes for a loaf, a week ago it was nine. To pay more than the price laid down would be a most unfriendly act towards our fellow prisoners. Any bartering with jewellery or clothing is left to the Yank. This man cried when he told my pals about the time he sold a diamond ring which his father had given him for fifty cigarettes and six loaves of bread. The Canadian parcels, like the British, contain great food value, but are not as good for trading purposes as American. I like the Canadian ground coffee, which has to be boiled for about fifteen minutes. The Canadian biscuits we soak in water for several hours and fry in butter fat. Chocolate is worth four loaves a pound. British parcels do not contain cigarettes which... [12]

We have a big coal stove and are quite warm. I am sitting next to an American and a British officer and a young American soldier who has lost both hands and is totally blind. This unfortunate boy is terribly depressed and cries all the time. The officers have been prisoners longer than me so I am able to give them information concerning the recent developments at the front. The Yank is terribly upset about the breakthrough at the Ardennes sector. The British officer who is Welsh turns on the Yank and says 'There you are. The British had to give you a hand to fight in your own sector. You said only the other day there were no British troops on the continent'. The Yank answered saying, 'the trouble with you is you can't take a joke'. We were held up several times due to the bombing. We have four German guards who stand around the stove singing in harmony. Prisoners are forbidden to sing. But they sing just the same.

The guards are now eating their food and I can see they have exactly the same rations as us. They are talking amongst themselves and the officers who understand German keep us informed of the subject of their conversation. They talk about the possibility of losing the war, their enormous losses on the eastern front, the dreadful quality of clothing, the inadequate supplies of material to the front, the superiority of Allied aircraft. One guard said the British have more aircraft than the Germans have potatoes. We are allowed off the train for exercise and are given coffee. The guards now take turns to get washed and shaved. They say we should reach Fallingbostel in two hours if there are no more air raids.

14

'I am a Prisoner of War'

As we arrived at the station 'Fallingbostel' about thirty kilometres from Hanover, we were received by two British prisoners and two German guards and four Russians who pushed a hand cart. The cart was to carry those who were unable to walk. Canadian Albemarle cigarettes were handed round by a British prisoner from the camp. The men from the Stalag were light hearted and cheerful, which was a good sign. The distance to the camp was less than a mile, and we walked very slowly as some of the men had no boots but ill-fitting wooden clogs.

As we arrived in camp we were interviewed by a young medical officer from the paratroopers, who was taken prisoner at Arnheim. We were then searched by two Germans, and all personal property was taken from us, which was returned later. We were shown to our rooms, which was not unlike the wooden bungalow type buildings at the prison hospital. It was obvious that those buildings were erected in a hurry and not meant to last a lifetime. They were simple one storey huts with a door at each end and about twelve windows. There were two rows of three tier beds made of wood. The bed was built up each side by a single piece of wood and at each end to give it a box like appearance. I found this box bed rather cosy. The box structure was about six inches high and not only kept out draughts but kept the sleeper from falling out during air raids. Those who were wounded slept in the bottom beds, to save them climbing.

In confinement the prisoner soon learns to develop a remarkable sense of values. Everybody carries a box or bag of some kind where he keeps his food and personal belongings. But most of the Russians carry their belongings in very deep pockets of their overcoats. I carried a square tin box which was given to me by a French male nurse for helping him in the hospital. This box I valued and hoped one day to be able to make a handle for it. I carried my food in the box, but never kept any overnight because I was afraid of being robbed. When I was travelling on the train from Düsseldorf I had a piece of bread and cheese leftover after the first day so I thought it would be wonderful to eat first thing in the morning when I awoke. But I could not sleep or rest that night for fear of losing my valuable hoard. In the end I had to eat it. I could never understand the other lads how they could save food for days. In my tin box I carried my aluminium mug which I had brought from Cologne, a can for boiling water and two small flat stones to rest the can on and a few pieces of wood and a few old paper bandages which I used to make a fire with to make tea or coffee. I had nails given to me by the Russian carpenter, several buttons, a piece of string, a boot polish tin where I kept a needle and thread and a razor blade. I had a small cigarette case that held only five, which I found in Holland and a note book (I still have) and a piece of broken glass. Everything in camp has some value. Everything is saved: bits of paper for rolling dried tea leaves, which some of the lads smoke, even matchsticks are saved. Many of the older prisoners who were taken at Dunkirk spend most of their time walking around the compound looking to see what they can find. There are West African prisoners as well as Indians from the Punjab, Poles, Dutch, and Serbs. We have one American Negro. Many Italians have now arrived, as they are at war with Germany. On the first evening of our arrival we are given a mug of sweet cocoa and a thin slice of bread and butter. The cocoa is from Red Cross supplies. The bread and butter is given by the Germans. The following day we are moved into another hut which is terribly over-crowded. All the English speaking prisoners are now together, British, Americans, Canadians and a few Australians and I think there is one New Zealander.

At sick parade the first morning there are about 2000 in line and only one doctor, the British Capt. Ramsey.[13] After this sick parade the doctor has to go to the hospital where there are several thousand bed patients. The death rate is about three or four a day. An old prisoner told me how I would know the number of deaths. He said there are a number of coffins stacked up outside the mortuary each morning about 9 a.m. The number is usually half a dozen, or as many as the carpenters are able to make and you can tell by the number left at night. So the following morning I went to the mortuary just after roll call and right enough there were six very plain coffins. They were just unpainted wooden boxes. At six in the evening there were two left. The death rate amongst the Russians is much higher than others. They mostly die from typhus. They get no Red Cross supplies and I am told have refused our Red Cross parcels. The Russians are in a different compound and do not mix much with the other national-ities, except the Russian from cities who are usually tradesmen and work in any part of the camp. They are mostly smaller and better educated than the others, who I am told are peasants from the

Ukraine. The Russians are said to get a smaller ration than other peoples because as the Germans put it, the Russians ill-treat the German prisoners.

Many of our lads go out to work daily to cut wood in the forest, for which they get two cigarettes and an extra bowl of 'skilly'. But such work is voluntary. I am told they are asked to sign papers to the effect that they will not try to escape whilst out of camp. Before I arrived here prisoners often went to Hanover and other towns to assist the injured and clean up generally after air raids. But there were so many escapees, and so many prisoners injured that such work was discontinued.

It is March and many more Americans and British have arrived, and we are more over-crowded. Several hundred have no beds but sleep on the floor, with just a thin blanket. Nobody undresses and consequently many prisoners are verminous. There are two people to each bed. The bread ration has been cut down and there are less parcels arriving. We get a bath each week and our clothing is fumigated in a room next to the bathroom. All clothing is placed on a wire hanger with our number on it, and is collected after the bath. In spite of all these precautions and efforts at cleanliness, many of the prisoners are simply walking with lice, which reminds me of my school days at Letterfrack. This camp has much in common with the industrial school. The unhealthy colour of the face, prominent cheek bones, sunken eyes and round shoulders. But unlike Letterfrack there is no ill-treatment. I have not seen or even heard of anyone being beaten.

The guards are always apologising for the small rations, and the poor living conditions. But they can't help it. There isn't any food in the country and they have many millions of prisoners and displaced persons. When I was taken prisoner at the front the German soldiers asked me for food. Several thousand American prisoners arrived but had to leave again due to lack of accommodation. During this time there were tens of thousands on the road simply because there was no room for them. Such prisoners and displaced persons were not always well received by the civilian population in the towns and villages, especially after heavy air raids. I have heard reports, first hand, of how in one small town the people refused to give the prisoners a drink of water and the guards had a terrific job to defend the prisoners from being beaten up. The air raids were now almost continuous and our food was often delayed for more than an hour, as we were not allowed outside the huts during raids. We had to go to the next compound to draw the 'skilly' which now was always sauerkraut[14], which played havoc with the bowels and many men ran to the toilet between 20 and 40 times daily. For such a complaint there was no cure except good solid food.

To reach the cook house we had to go through a small hospital compound, where there were a large number of seriously wounded Russians. Many had lost legs and arms. Some were trying to get about without the use of a crutch or stick. It was here I seen the Russians go mad as they attacked a French cook as he was emptying a basin of bones and potato peelings. They just fought like wolves over the bones. I saw a man lying face downwards grasping a large bone and being savaged by other hungry men. One man was *biting his ear*. The man on the ground never let go the bone.

There was enormous supplies of Red Cross parcels and clothing held up at Luebeck which was the H.Q. for Red Cross and it could not be moved due to shortage of petrol and drivers. So one day we heard that the Red Cross were supplying petrol. A large number of British and allied drivers volunteered to go to Luebeck and bring back the food and clothing. I can't remember if they ever left, they certainly never returned if they did leave. Our water supplies were bombed and we had to go outside the camp to a pump about a mile away. When I was on the way to the pump one day I see many thousands of displaced persons hobbling along the road with a German escort. Many of these people had no proper clothing but rags and straw tied around them.

There was a bit of trouble between the British and American prisoners. The Yanks liked to take their boots off going to bed, and sometimes they were stolen. So one night they took turns at staying awake and eventually caught two Glasgow lads stealing a pair of boots. There was a fight next morning and the Yanks got the worst of it because the Scots used their heads. The Americans refused to share the same room with the British so we had to move and find other accommodation. The Germans didn't mind us fighting and would often stand around looking on and clapping their hands. There was a football in our compound, and the British as always loved to play or watch a game. So one morning as a game was in progress there was loud cheering when a goal was scored. So the Germans all rushed out brandishing guns thinking there was a mass break out. It took a long time to explain what happened. There is a very small two page paper published monthly called *The Camp*. It was in this paper about two months ago there appeared the names of 50 R.A.F. officers who were executed for a mass escape. I feel sure I knew one of the officers. His name is Christiansen and was a Flying

Officer in Calcutta, but has since been promoted to Flight Lieutenant. He was a New Zealander.[15]

My left leg has completely healed but my right has become worse, due to the fact that I can't keep it covered. My right arm has healed but still hurts when I drink anything warm. British prisoners have arrived from Poland who worked in the salt mines and on farms and they tell us amazing stories about conditions in other camps. One chap tells me about a camp where prisoners used to distil their own spirits until a number of lads were poisoned. The punishment for being found with such liquor was two years. In another camp the prisoners lived so well that they were taken to the pictures and to meet their girlfriends. This privilege had to be paid for of course in cigarettes and chocolate or coffee. They got a parcel every two days. Prisoners have been known to buy their way out of a prison camp, and they left with a gun, a map and compass. This may cost from two to three thousand cigarettes. We have been warned that there are only two weeks supply of rations at the present level and no chance of replacements.

The bread ration is two thin slices a day, two potatoes, a portion of sausage meat, a table spoonful of sugar, and on alternate days we get a portion of honey or jam. There is now no salt. We get black coffee twice daily and the sauerkraut which the doctor has advised us against eating. The bread ration is half what we got at Letterfrack. The potato ration is about the same. The sugar is slightly more in prison than at Letterfrack. The butter or margarine is about the same. At Letterfrack we got fish or rice or rhubarb on Friday, which we don't get in prison. Here in prison there is a cheese ration once a week or sometimes twice. So taking the food ration all round we were slightly better off at school in Ireland. But there is more variety in prison. But older prisoners from different camps say that it is the smallest ration they have seen. Don't forget we are living in a country which has been fighting a bitter war for six years. She has been fighting three of the most powerful nations on earth. Life here in Stalag 11B Fallingbostel during the last months of the war is hard and unpleasant. Yet it is a Heaven on earth in comparison to my life at school. In Ireland, where children were brutally beaten and tortured, for no other reason than the lustful pleasure of the Christian Brothers.

The fighting is now less than 20 kilometres away and we can hear the guns at night. There are aircraft overhead. But they are spotter planes for the artillery. There is little or no German opposition. They are just falling back because they are sick and tired and hungry. Our camp is left with only a few guards. The supplies are almost finished. Everything has been distributed. It is now almost the end of April 1945, it is warm in the sunshine, and the tanks of the 7th British armoured division are advancing in line and are within sight. There is a mad roar as the tanks just drive through the barbed wire entanglements

Many of the British prisoners had been in captivity since Dunkirk. One airman was taken prisoner on the first or second day of the war, when his plane crash-landed in Germany. Within an hour of freedom ambulances, Red Cross units and Salvation Army mobile units as well as Church Army units were now distributing food, cigarettes and clothing with the result that many simply made themselves ill eating. We remained in camp for three days until all the bed patients who were well enough could be removed to hospital in Britain. The Americans were first to go. They travelled south in long convoys of trucks.

We left on the third day and travelled about seventy miles south by road to a camp already prepared. We lived in tents. Next to the camp was a big airfield. The following day we flew to Brussels in Dakota aircraft, where we stayed for three days. From here we flew to Horsham in England in Sterling bombers. It was the journey in the Dakota twin engine plane that interested me most. It was my first time in a plane and I enjoyed it thoroughly. It was not unlike being in a bus on a rather bumpy road. The plane lost height over woods because, I learned, of air pockets. It was a beautiful sunny day and we got a grandstand view of the south of Germany and Holland, which had been a gigantic battlefield. The roads and fields were littered with burned out tanks, trucks, motor vehicles and planes of all descriptions. Just north of the river Rhine was the worst. There I seen dozens of gliders. I remember the stories we used to hear about the Rhine Crossing. There were many attempts made but all had failed. A German guard once told me that a crossing had been made successfully. But after several days severe fighting we had been driven back. That was the worst news of all. The Prison Hospital at Düsseldorf was terrible for rumours or stories. We heard the war was over several times. We heard Churchill had arrived in Germany to talk peace. We heard New York had been bombed and all women and children had been evacuated. But the only reliable information came from the new prisoners coming in straight from the front. This was the information the German guards relied on. One day at 11B a guard, knowing I was new in the camp, asked through an interpreter where I had been taken prisoner. But I misunderstood and told him where I had just come from, which was Düsseldorf. I gave him to understand that we had crossed the Rhine. The guard run away shouting excitedly and it was a long time before I was able to grasp the situation.

I did not like the way some of our men behaved towards the German guards when it became clear the war was almost over. It happened in only a few cases. I am happy to say a very small number of prisoners insulted and laughed at the guards and jeered at them and made life intolerable for them. This was an awful pity because I found the German soldier to be a good and clean fighter, at the front, in hospitals and prisons. The doctors and nurses were good and kind, friendly and helpful. The officers and guards respected the prisoners, and gave them what little they had. I was hopping mad when I heard that some prisoners made serious complaints against the staff of Stalag 11 B. I even heard that some officers were sent to prison for alleged ill-treatment of prisoners. But by the time the news reached me it was too late to do anything. I did, however, make a report to the competent authority of my own personal experience.

I spent my three months holiday in Leeds because it was convenient to attend the hospital for treatment. My right leg was completely healed in a month. It took several months before I was able to regain the full use of my right hand. I was stationed in Edinburgh for the last six months of my service, and it was here I met an officer, Lt. Malcolm Stewart who I had helped to carry from the minefield on Walchem Island, and he told me he could dance quite well with his artificial leg (he lost his leg from below the knee). I was demobbed in December 1945 and discharged about six months later.

15
I Return to Civilian Life

I was employed on inspection work for the Ministry of Supplies in the north of England and travelled to various factories where government uniforms were being made. I worked mainly in Leeds, Middlesbrough, Newcastle, Dewsbury and Bradford. It was my job to examine and pass or reject the finished garments. I found this work very easy, but interesting, as I liked the travelling about to various factories in different towns. I had never worked in English factories before, where suits are mass produced, and are manufactured almost completely by machine. It is so much different to the old handicraft method.

The man I served my time with at home after leaving school often talked about mass-produced or modern methods, where a garment was handled by 50 or more people, which cut down the cost of production, resulting in a cheaper suit, which was more in keeping with present day requirements, after all people of to-day didn't want a suit to last ten years, like their fathers. They wanted something cheap to be cast off after a year or two. This new divisional system, as it's often called, is said to have been started by a group of Russian Jewish tailors who began to work their way westwards during the last 100 years, due to economic and political conditions at home. The new methods of manufacture require far less skill, as each person is only responsible for one operation, for example pockets, linings, collars, sleeves, etc. The main reason for this new system was cheap labour. Children could be taught a single operation in a matter of weeks. Tailoring was once a trade for men, but now there are about three women to every man, probably because they seem to be more efficient in mass production methods, and also due to the shortage of men from 1914 until 1918, when this divisional system really got a grip in this country.

This job lasted almost two years and I must say I was beginning to really enjoy life. I had learned to mix and enjoy people's company instead of being the odd man out. I was no longer afraid of people. I had learned to cast aside that terrible inferiority complex. I didn't blush or tremble when I met superiors. I didn't jump out of my skin when my name was called. Yet I was not afraid to fly in an aircraft, and thought it strange when I seen a fine big healthy looking chap having to be assisted on board the Dakota. He was ill all the journey. I found out at the front, that other people had fears as well, and the different way in which they were affected. One officer we had whenever he went on night reconnaissance patrol, lost his voice and had all the symptoms of a severe cold, but was well again next day. One chap who was terrified of mines after seeing several people blown up when they walked on to mines, always got pains in his feet and legs when walking through fields where there was likely to be mines. Yet when walking along the road he was in perfect health. We had another chap called Spud Thompson. He was in charge of the bren gun, which was always out of action at night. The gun was out of order so it wouldn't fire. I feel sure that this gun was deliberately put out of action so that he would *not* give his position away by firing. For a whole week I tried to get a chance to strip down the gun because I think there was a faulty part, which was put there on purpose. On my last night at the front when we were attacking *Waldefeuct* we were depending on the bren gun for support. I said to Thompson on the way to the village, I hope your gun is OK. He answered, it's no good, it won't fire. I made up my mind there and then to have the gun examined the following day. This same chap didn't like doing guard duties at night. It was the practice for the sentry to hand over a pocket watch to the next man, but when the morning came the watch was always an hour or two fast. Instead of doing an hour on sentry, Thompson would do half an hour, and put the watch on half an hour. It took us a whole month to find out who the culprit was. I caught him by borrowing a second watch and checking the time when he was being relieved. He actually put the watch on half an hour on two occasions the same night. This man was a proper show-off and a bully behind the line.

Yes I had beaten most of my fears. I learned to cycle, I learned to drive a car, but failed in the test, which didn't worry me because I feel I could pass another time. I learned to swim, and done a lot of mountaineering whilst in the Himalayas. So there was a good deal to be thankful for. I was afraid of going in the boxing ring, not so much of being hurt as being laughed at. I did eventually put my name down and entered the ring at the depot in Berwick on Tweed. But my opponent had such long arms I couldn't get near him.

I was made redundant from the Ministry of Supplies with forty others for economy reasons. After working a year in Leeds and Halifax in factories I decided to take a holiday in Dublin with a view to settling down there eventually. It was during the winter of 1948-

49 I caught the train to Liverpool and the night boat to the North Wall. It was many years since I had been to Ireland and the last few years had made me almost forget my school days which by now was just a bad dream. I had just been unlucky in going to a bad school at a bad time. It was all so long ago and nothing like that could possibly happen to-day. What really made me forget was the fact that during the last twelve years I had only met a handful of Irish people. But now I was getting ready to disembark in a country where there was a lot of my own people. It was about 7 a.m. when I put my bag in the left luggage office at Amiens Street Railway Station, before having a walk round for an hour or two, before looking for accommodation. My first impression of Dublin was good. Previously I had only passed through it and didn't take much notice. But there seemed to be a lot of business as the people rushed here and there on foot or on bicycles. I was quite pleased with what I saw. I bought a paper and had breakfast and moved into a small hotel near the city centre. About eleven I wandered out again. There was less activity now but I didn't think much about it. I wandered into a public house where I imagined they got first hand information, economically. I made conversation with the boss or landlord by asking him to have a drink. He refused by saying 'I don't drink that stuff, I only sell it'. He appeared to have a load on his mind but wasn't unfriendly. We had a chat. 'What are you doing in Dublin' he asked. 'Oh, just came over for a holiday from Yorkshire' I answered, 'and to look for a job'. 'What are you talking about man? A job in this city? Sure, there's a stampede every night for the boat to get away from it.' But I said 'the city appeared to be busy enough this morning'. 'What's wrong with you man, sure it's only mass they were going to.' 'If they spent only half as much time working as they spend praying we should be a happier people. Dublin is the most religious capital city in the world. Yet we have the greatest percentage of rogues and bloody liars. My house has been broken into three times in the last year, and the last time I was robbed they even took away my tea and sugar'.

I spent the next few days going around the clothing factories but they were sacking people because of lack or orders. I did however hear of a small factory near Guinness' Brewery, where there may be a chance of a job. It was late in the evening when I got there and found everyone kneeling down saying the rosary. I was told they always spent the last quarter hour praying.

I decided against going home just yet, and promised myself that I would probably do so next summer, so I returned to Leeds,

Yorkshire. On my first evening in Leeds I met Christy Joyce, a tailor I used to work with. He said he was on his way to the Fenton Hotel and 'would I care to come along'. As we were standing in the passage having a beer we could see into the public bar, and Christy recognised a chap he knew, and said 'let's go into the public bar, I want you to meet a tailor called *Tom Thornton*, a chap with one leg'. As we were being introduced, Thornton recognised me immediately, and before I had a chance to speak 'O Yes, I know Peter, we met in Ballinrobe' said Thornton, and as he did so gave me a wink. There was no mention of Letterfrack (I have never been to Ballinrobe). When Thornton and I were alone for a few seconds, he said very quickly 'Don't say anything about Letterfrack, if ever you want to speak about the school, always call it the *SHIP*.' It is the most awful disgrace in the world to be identified as a boy from the Christian Brothers. I had forgotten about this and I had actually told several lads about Letterfrack including Christy Joyce.

I arranged to meet Thornton the following night. This is the news I received the following evening. Mr Griffin was dead. Brother Dooley became manager after I left. Brother Vale had entered a mental home and had since died there. Big McLaughlin (or Kangaroo) was in a mental home. Joe Baker, who had been severely beaten by Brother Fahy and left bleeding from the mouth and nose, had died shortly after leaving school.

I went to London where I heard wages were much higher than in the Midlands, and found great changes since 1935. In spite of the bombing, and the great shortage of houses, the population had increased by several millions. I spent a day in the east end, and found that whole streets had disappeared. Later I went to north London to find digs but was shocked and amazed to learn that the Irish were most unpopular. Most landladies simply shut the door in my face when they learned I was Irish. They usually asked what nationality you were. This was a new experience to me. One landlady was more friendly and advised me to go to the Irish quarter. I said I didn't know that there was such a place. 'Oh, yes', she answered, 'Camden town is where most Irish people live. There they can get drunk and fight as much as they *like*. We always had Irish lads here until they started going about with bombs in their pockets, just before the war'. 'I am sorry', she added, 'I don't wish to offend you, but your lads are too big a risk'. Every word cut into me like a knife. I didn't look for digs any more that day, but wandered about the streets, I couldn't think clearly any more.

I stayed in an expensive hotel that night, but never slept. The following morning I was thinking of returning to the Midlands but changed my mind. This would only be running away. I must stay at least long enough to see for myself whether or not this is true, and try to find out the cause of such behaviour and the best way to find out would be to move into Camden town. I wasn't worried about a job just yet. Besides, I understood there was plenty of work in my trade.

I tried a number of boarding houses in Camden town, and was offered digs in three different houses. It just meant moving another single bed into a room where there were already six or seven people sleeping. There was no such thing as a chair or table or even a wardrobe. Such furniture was only in the way and took up valuable space. I tried another house but would have to share a double bed, which I refused, explaining that I was a poor sleeper. I was told to come back later in the evening as there may be a vacant single bed in the room upstairs which was an attic. There had been a boy there for a week, but he had not been seen for several days, and she wasn't sure whether he was coming back or not. His money was overdue. His bed had not been slept in for two nights. But there was an old suit case under his bed. This meant nothing as lots of chaps often left their old clothes behind. I returned later that night and was given the single bed. I shall probably never find out what happened to Paddy Rooney the lad who slept there before me. At least that was the name I seen on an envelope I found under the bed. The landlady informed me that 'it was the normal routine for the lads to leave without saying anything. It would be a good thing if people were compelled to give a week's notice'. She told me about a chap called Pat Tracey who stayed there for several months, and left owing two weeks rent. She would not have known where he was, only for her husband happened to drop into the barbers down the street. Pat had told the barber he was going back to Ireland but didn't think of telling the people he stayed with.

The lads in my room were nice enough. Three used to go out to work early and come straight home for their tea except when they decided to go straight into the pub from work. This often happened on Friday night, and would arrive home any old time between 11 p.m. and 1 a.m. They always brought back a few bottles of beer, and fish and chips, and of course they had to wake me up for a drop of beer and a few chips. Martin Joyce from Ballina had been a P.O.W. in Italy for two years. He was taken prisoner in North Africa. He was an awful man for talking and would often sit on my bed until three in the morning, telling stories about his captivity. I often went to the post office with Martin on Saturday to write a letter for him to his brother at home. The writing was never done in the digs in case anyone should find out that Martin was illiterate. Martin thought it a terrible disgrace not to be able to read or write. I told him I had two brothers who could neither read nor write on leaving school. But one has since learned and is now quite good. I told Martin that he could learn very quickly because he was very intelligent and he had a good memory which was true. I did start to teach him and he was progressing favourably but got tired after a week. He just would not persevere. Once he said 'I can't learn because I am too stupid'.

Once in the room one of the other lads passed a newspaper to Martin to let him read an interesting article. Martin glanced at the paper for a few minutes pretending to read it. Instead of saying, 'Please read it for me, as I am illiterate', he gave to understand that he had read the paper, which was all so foolish and unforgivable. Why be ashamed or afraid to admit something which is a fact? It seems to me that Martin is going to go through life telling a lie, a lie which is all so silly and can never do him any good. On the other hand, it could be the basis of an inferiority complex, which may be injurious to his own health.

Every Saturday night was like the New Year in Scotland. There were people coming in at all times. I heard a clock strike four as the front door banged for the last time. There was talking and singing and the wireless was full on downstairs. There was one or two arguments outside in the street which sometimes finished up in a fight. But there was no fighting in the house during the time I was there. I never realized how many were in that house until Sunday morning. I heard people moving about just after 8 o'clock. But the rush hour was really between 10 and 11. Over twenty chaps had to get washed and shaved and have their breakfast before eleven o'clock mass. There were three sitting for breakfast in a rather small kitchen, but the last sitting was always late for mass which didn't seem to worry anyone. It was a very quiet house after eleven. Everyone went to mass, or at least gave to understand they were going. But I know that many didn't go because I used to see them standing piously outside the pub at 11.45 a.m., with both hands in the trousers' pockets of their blue suit, and giving an occasional glance down at their brown shoes.

The Paddy is a lonely man wherever he goes, and it seems to me he can only find solace in the public house. The pubs in Camden town do a roaring trade all the year round, simple because it's a town of bachelors who have no responsibility except to pay for their lodgings, after which most of the money is spent on drink. The young

Irish lads go dancing at weekends and only patronize their own dance halls. They usually have a fair amount to drink which gives them courage to get on to the dance floor, and after each dance they get dry again and must go out for a thirst quencher. But they give up dancing at an early age and from the time they reach the thirty mark it's just a constant pub crawl. Only about one in every three ever get married, and those who do marry, often wait until they are in the late middle age. The men generally speaking may be said to be poor husbands and fathers. The criminal neglect of children in Catholic Ireland is a disgrace to any so called civilized society. Hence the large number of young children in industrial schools and convents. The number of children admitted to such places as a result of neglect is more than the one in every eight of the population. These places are most unsuitable for any child because the people who run them are not qualified to look after children, owing to the fact that they never had children of their own. The nuns and Christian Brothers live a most unhealthy and unnatural life. They become lonely and frustrated as a result of their interpretation of the religious laws.

The care of children is the most important work in any society, and those whose responsibility it is to train and educate children ought to be chosen by a team of doctors. There is a mental hospital for nuns just outside Dublin, with several hundred patients. Surely this speaks for itself. If those unfortunate women were permitted to live a normal and natural life, I feel sure such a home would be unnecessary. Convents and industrial schools are places where children are destroyed mentally and sometimes physically.

My vocabulary is too limited to explain to my reader the degree of destruction which takes place to the child in the Catholic school in Ireland. In order to give you some idea of what I mean I will make a rather crude comparison between a most beautiful and perfect human machine, namely the child, and the most beautiful and perfect machine made by the hands of man, a watch costing £2000. I have actually seen a watch in a shop window in Regent Street, London, on sale for this figure. As I looked at this watch I thought of the man who made it. I imagined I could see the master craftsman sitting down, measuring, cutting, making and polishing each minute component part to a thousand of an inch, and spending perhaps years making this precision machine from the most precious materials in the world. Now just imagine the watch falling into the hands of a madman, who places it on an anvil, and strikes it many times with a fourteen pound hammer. The degree of destruction caused to the child in the Catholic school is much worse because the watch can be repaired very much easier than the mind of the child who has been in the hands of some foul and wretched religious fanatic whose only purpose in life is to cause pain and suffering to an innocent and defenceless creature, knowing full well the child cannot hit back.

It is a most dreadful state of affairs that this is going on in almost every Catholic school in Ireland to-day. Not only is this savage ill-treatment permitted by the Catholic authorities, but a powerful section of our society is fighting to preserve it. It was bad enough having witnessed and suffered cruel and sadistic beatings myself for many years of agony. But now I must listen to the stories of others. It's only six months since I sat in a small café near Kings Cross Station, London, and listened to a young girl of sixteen tell her sad story of how she was beaten every day by a Catholic nun in a convent in the town of Lanark in Scotland. I asked her to come with me to the police, and make a report, but she begged me to say nothing, and asked me to promise faithfully to do nothing about it because she had two small brothers in this convent only three weeks ago. I met a woman called Anne Bethell who lives at 2 Royal College Street, London NW1 who was an inmate of St Vincent's convent Berrington Street, Hereford, England until 1943. She complains of being beaten with a scrubbing brush in the bathroom daily, by Sisters M and P[16] (they are Sisters of Charity). Both the Sisters were about 27 years old in 1943. Not far from where I live there is a man called Mr Corrie who left a Christian Brothers school in Ireland twelve years ago. He complains of being beaten with a wet towel in the bathroom, and being beaten around the yard with a stick. (He says he has given up the Catholic religion).

The Irish dance halls in London, Birmingham, Leeds and Liverpool are often the subject of serious reports by the police, who complain of drunken brawls, and rowdyism after the dances. I have seen many times hand to hand fighting on the main streets of Leeds and London during which time traffic has been held up. This usually happens after the public houses are closed. A famous Irish dance hall, called the 'Blarney Club' in Tottenham Court Road, London, is a special headache for the local police. A number of police with police dogs may be seen on duty at the main entrance during the last hour of the dance. The large number of Irish prostitutes in Hyde Park London was the subject of a front page article in an English newspaper two years ago.

I have now started work in Goswell Road near the city. It's a small tailor's shop. The manager who gave me the job has not asked what nationality I was, but in the course of the day mentioned casually that he did not like Irish workmen because they only come to work when they are broke and they often make trouble with the other men. 'They are bad tempered and narrow minded. They think if you are not a Catholic there is something wrong with you'. I asked him if he realized that I was Irish, he looked surprised, and said 'no'. 'But', he added 'there are exceptions. I have met some nice Irish lads'. I wanted to leave the job that first day, but decided to remain for a week. But I stayed three months.

Back in my lodgings I went out occasionally with three of the lads on the building, the other two in the room with us kept to themselves. One lad had a girlfriend he saw two or three times a week. The other boy was young and rather shy and didn't bother with anyone. My three companions hardly ever went any place except the pub. We usually went to the Holny Arms at the end of Chatform Road, just under the bridge. This is where a large number of the lads congregate on Sunday morning and can be seen at 11.45 a.m. in the digs. It's taken for granted that everyone is a Catholic and actually they all go to mass. It would be a terrible thing if anyone thought you did not go to mass. We are in the pub and my pals are all drinking pints of draught Guinness. I only drink half pints, and I always carry the fountain pen and pencil. 'What do you carry the pen and pencil for?' asked one of the lads. I answered saying 'I had a poor education and was learning how to write'. They looked puzzled. These lads are terrible drinkers, ten pints each opening session is about their capacity and they always carry out a few bottles. They talk about very little else. They judge a man by the enormous amount he can consume. If a man treats them to a drink he is a good fellow – one of the best. If you are a slow drinker or drink only half pints you are looked on as mean, you are out of place in the public bar and should be in the lounge with the gentlemen. A non-drinker is a most extraordinary individual. A chap who goes with a girl is looked on as a cissy, he is soft, or unmanly. My pals sometimes go the 'Blarney' dance for the last hour. They don't dance but only go there for the crack, that is to meet other lads they know, and make conversation. The dance night is usually on a Saturday. They therefore go to the pub a lot earlier so that a full quota of drink is ensured.

I have changed my job many times, and am living in a furnished apartment in Highbury North London. It's better now as I can have a meal out or cook a light meal in my apartment. I am working in Regiment Street for Hector Power and I get on fairly well until it's discovered that I am Irish. Three of the men don't speak to me except to remind me of the shortcomings of my people. I am kept fully informed of any fresh shooting incident in Northern Ireland. I am now fed up with everyone and I walk out of my job at 10 a.m. one Monday morning and wander about the streets for several hours. I called to the post office. Why I couldn't be sure. I now made up my mind to write home, and inform my mother I would be going to see her shortly, after which I should go abroad. Where, was unimportant. I gave a Leeds address, and travelled north that night. I started work two days later, and had completely forgotten about my letter home. When I received a card with a Dublin postmark from my brother telling me that my mother was dead and he had sold the small farm.

As I had little or nothing to do with my family for many years I felt no great sorrow. On the contrary, I was relieved. My mother had been ill for as long as I can remember. She had lost the use of her hands several years ago due to rheumatism. During the few years I spent at home after leaving school I used to wonder how long my mother would have to go on living. She was suffering terribly and would cry most of the night. It was then I began to look upon death as a companion and true friend. The first time I thought seriously about death was when I saw John Kelly dead, the boy who was run over by the coal lorry. He looked so relaxed and peaceful. He looked as though about to smile, very much different to the frightened and terrified look on his face when he was being beaten. My father had died during the first year of the war.

I changed my mind about going abroad. Instead I would try to find out why my people were so disliked. Was their behaviour very much different to that of other nationalities? If so, why? I knew four different families of Irish people living in Leeds, that is chaps who came over to this country (England) and married Irish girls. In some cases the children have already grown up. I study those children for about a year almost daily. I drop in to their houses. I see them playing football or playing in the street. I fail to see any difference in behaviour to that of any other English boys or girls. There are two brothers I know very well aged 17 and 19. One was born in Ireland and came to this country as a baby. The youngest was born here. They are about the same age as Irish lads usually are when they emigrate. The behaviour of the two brothers who have been educated in England is far better than boys of the same age coming from Ireland. As well as observing the boys myself I get reports from their parents. They are honest, truthful, and moderate in their habits. The younger children are more intelligent. They are healthier and happier than most children at home in Ireland. I am talking about the children who go to the day schools and come home in the evening (not those in convents and industrial schools). I am now convinced that it is not the true character of the Irish to be of bad behaviour, but is the result of a bad home life, and a bad system of education at home.

Before leaving London I made a habit of visiting the Irish public houses in the East End (Whitechapel) where almost all the customers are Irish, and I must confess that the behaviour of many of the men was a disgrace to any community. I was severely beaten up for telling them what I thought. I told them we were known abroad as irresponsible liars and drunkards. That the Catholic religion had kept us the unhappy and the most backward race in Europe. Evidence of our ignorance and backwardness lies in the fact that only a fraction of our people can earn a living at home, and also due to the fact that there were hundreds going about with guns in their pockets. We were a nation of gangsters. I told them there were thousands of overfed priests living on the backs of the people. These parasites must be made to do some useful work. The priest is Ireland's greatest enemy. He is doing untold harm. The Catholic religion based on fear and myth is the main cause of the high degree of mental illness.

We must have a new religion founded on love, friendship and understanding. Ireland ought to be for the people. The priest has made life intolerable for us at home, hence the stampede to emigrate. We want home rule, NOT *ROME RULE.*

Notes

1   There is a variation in Tyrrell's spelling of this name: Discum/Diskan
2   Spelt 'putcheen' in the Mss
3   This word is illegible in original text.
4   Tyrrell inserted in parenthesis: 'This is in late 1942 and early 1943'
5   'This was in 1943 early'
6   Originally spelt 'Bencors'
7   At least one page is missing from the original manuscript.
8   Tyrrell inserted: 'It's Nov. 1944'.
9   This section begins with the heading 'We landed at Antwerp'.
10   Spelt 'Coneyack'
11   Tyrrell could not remember the name and intentionally left it blank.
12   page missing from original manuscript.
13   Spelt '*RamC*' by Tyrrell.
14   Spelt 'sour crab'
15   There was a New Zealander named Christiansen [Tyrrell's manuscript spells his name 'Christianson'] who was murdered in response to what has subsequently been popularised as *The Great Escape* by the Steve MacQueen film. His details are: Army No. 413380 Flight Lietenant Arnold G Christiansen, a New Zealander, 26 Sqdn, born 8-Apr-21, PoW 20-Aug-42, recaptured at Flensburg, murdered 29-Mar-44 by *Sturmbannfuhrer* Johannes Post of Kiel Gestapo.
16   I have removed these names as I cannot prove their presence in this institution at that time.

Appendix

Address to Aug 30th: La Michounette,Route de Berck
FORT-MAHON (Somme)
France

Mr Peter Tyrrell
'o Mr C.Joyce
2, Warrick Terrace
LEEDS 2.

SEANAD ÉIREANN

BAILE ÁTHA CLIATH
(Dublin)

18th Aug 1958

Dear Mr Tyrrell,

Thank you for your letter of 12th August and enclosures which reached me here, forwarded from Dublin, yesterday. I read your letter and statement with interest and emotion. I am convinced that all you say is true. Not that I am in the habit of believing evrything I am told by every correspondent, but your story has the ring of truth,unadorned. That such conditions should exist for young unprotected children is a scandal,and a disgrace to our so-called civilisation.

As you may know I have for some time been trying to stop the stupid beatings that go on in our National Schools for the most trivial offences. I am opposed to beatings of any kind for any offence, but even if the Department Regulations were applied(they lay it down that"under no circumstances"must a child be beaten for "mere failure at lessons"), it would not be so bad, though still stupid. The Rules, however, are widely flouted, partly because of seriously over-crowded classes(not the fault of the children!), partly owing to stupid and inadequate teachers, and partly owing to the frustrations of the religious life, as it is interpreted by thw religious orders, which lead both priests and nuns to work off their pent-up feelings on defenceless children, while persuading themselves that they are doing God's work. The snag when one comes to try and combat all this beating, is that one at once finds that most of it is done by Christian Brothers, Sisters of Mercy, and Presentation Bros., or else by lay teachers responsible under our system only to the P.P. This being the case, anyone who ventures even to suggest that the Regulations ought to be applied is branded as an attacker of the Church; as indeed he is, in a sense, for the Church instead of being on the side of decency in the matter is all on the side of the wielders of the stick. There are decent individual exceptions; I am sure you know some; there may even have been one or two whom you canremember at Letterfrack; but that they are the exceptions is shown by the failure of the Church effectively to combat this evil, which could be stopped to-morrow if it cared to say the word.

I am sure that all this will be known to you, but I mention it to show what thoughts go through my mind when I come to consider what I can do about the facts you reveal.

In the first place, my interest, and probably yours, would be mainly concerned to prevent such uncontrolled savagery from continuing now against other children, rather than to exact vengeance upon some foul and wretched Christian Brother, even if he is still alive. In a lecture which my mother gave throughout the States on the murder of my father in 1916, she made it clear that she regarded as even worse than the murder itself, the way in which the authorities consistently "covered up" their criminal inferiors. So too at Letterfrack.

Now, what can now be done? X Suppose I write to the Bishop of Galway? Useless. He is an arrogant and unscrupulous bully, whose only interest in such a matter would be to warn any evil-doers, so that their tracks could be covered. Write to the Minister for Justice? I should be more hopeful there, though of course all these political figures are a bit afraid of a row with anything that looks like a clerical collar. I know what he would tell that the matter was being looked into, that it was all a long time ago, and that suitable action would be taken if required, but that it was not the practice to divulge what action, if any, had been taken. It so happens that I received to-day a letter from a friend telling me about an action taken against a teacher, and also giving me an "Evening Mail" cutting in which the Editor has some pretty strong things to say about the way Ministers evade their responsibilities in such matters. Please return both cuttings to me when you have time. I may add that the father in the action won his cases and got £100 with costs.

However, to return to your own experiences, although I shall try on my return to Ireland to find out more about the present running of this Letterfrack school (for all I know it may no longer be used a an industrial school), my present feeling is that the best way in which attention could be focussed on the place and on the whole question of how such schools are in fact run, would by having a factual account of your own experiences there written. I don't know how well you would be able to tackle this yourself, or whether you have a friend who would give you a hand, but what I am thinking of is a simple account of how you went to the place, what your first impressions were, what the various people in charge were like, how the years passed, what your final impressions were, and how you feel now about what it did to you, and the others there with you. This might take from 5,000 to 10,000 words. In the days of the "Bell" they would have been interested in such an article, I am sure. They ran an excellent series, later published as a book, under the title "I did penal servitude". I know the man who wrote it, and I know that he did a lot of good for prisoners in general by writing it. I don't know, but I think the then Editor, Sean O'Faolain, gave him a hand in putting it together.

Now, if you think that such an idea for you would be at all feasible, and if you think I could be of any assistance to you I should be very happy to help in any way I could. One would have to be very careful about libel and all that, of course, and the names would have to be changed, but the picture could be a devastating one, and not only would evryone know that it was an Irish school, but many chaps from other such schools would recognise it as being very like theirs. I believe that if you could face the task of getting it onto paper, this would be the way that would hurt the bullies and their protectors most, and I am fairly confident that I could get it publication somewhere. Mind you it would not in any sense rake in the shekels! I take that that aspect

SEANAD ÉIREANN

BAILE ÁTHA CLIATH
(Dublin)

would not be a prime one for you. You never know, of course, but as a rule the type of paper or magazine which has the courage to print such material is not a financial success!

I don't know if you are ever in Dublin. My address there is: the Cottage, Hazelbrook House, 69, Terenure Road West, Dublin. I shall be back there by Sept 7th next. If you were ever over, a personal chat might help to see what could be done.

I am glad that you enclosed the "News of the World" reply, because of course that would be the stock reply from most people to-day, unless they were interested in seeing that such horrible maltreatment of young children was no longer possible anywhere.

I should be glad to have your opinion on the above. I shall be here in Fort-Mahon(a little sea-side place near Boulogne) till the 30th, and after that at 98., Rue Louis Thuillier, Amiens, France, until the 6th Sept.

All good wishes to you. I hope that it may be possible to find some way of taking useful action on the facts you relate.

Yours sincerely,

Owen Sheehy Skeffington.

Index

Please note that PT stands for Peter Tyrrell